Albert M. Phillips.

PHILLIPS GENEALOGIES

Including the Family of George Phillips, First Minister of Watertown, Massachusetts, through Most of the Traceable Branches from 1630 to the Present Generation; Also the Families of Ebenezer Phillips, of Southboro, Massachusetts, Thomas Phillips, of Duxbury, Massachusetts, Thomas Phillips, of Marshfield, Massachusetts, John Phillips, of Easton, Massachusetts, James Phillips, of Ipswich, Massachusetts—*with Brief Genealogies of Walter Phillips, of Damariscotta, Maine, Andrew Phillips, of Kittery, Maine, Michael, Richard, Jeremy, and Jeremiah Phillips of Rhode Island; and Fragmentary Records, of Early American Families of This Name*

Compiled by

Albert M. Phillips

HERITAGE BOOKS
2010

HERITAGE BOOKS

AN IMPRINT OF HERITAGE BOOKS, INC.

Books, CDs, and more—Worldwide

For our listing of thousands of titles see our website
at
www.HeritageBooks.com

A Facsimile Reprint
Published 2010 by
HERITAGE BOOKS, INC.
Publishing Division
100 Railroad Ave. #104
Westminster, Maryland 21157

Originally published

Auburn, Massachsuetts
Compiled by
Albert M. Phillips
1885

International Standard Book Numbers
Paperbound: 978-0-7884-1638-5
Clothbound: 978-0-7884-8515-2

INTRODUCTION.

A popular historian has said that the study of history "sets before us striking examples of virtue, enterprise, courage, generosity, patriotism; and, by a natural principle of emulation, incites us to copy such noble examples." We, of the present generation, know but little of the trials, fatigues, hardships, fears and anxieties, which our fathers and mothers of early New England days experienced and willingly endured, that they might establish a government and found a nation, where the privileges of civil and religious liberty, and the benefits of general education, should be the blessed inheritance of their posterity for all time.

Having been accustomed to the even temperature and mild winters of the British Isles, the abrupt change of location, with unavoidable exposure to the harsher climate and rigorous winters of New England, caused many of the delicate ones among the first settlers to waste rapidly away with consumption or other unlooked-for diseases, while even the most vigorous of the first one or two generations after immigration, being subjected to the unceasing toil and the perils incident to early settlements, rarely attained the age of three-score and ten. But they looked beyond the present with the affairs that concerned themselves only and comprehended the possibilities of the far-distant future, and with laudable self-sacrifice and persistent efforts amidst harassing discouragements, made such provision for the well-being of their descendants as their opportunities afforded. It was evidently a chief desire and great aim with them so to establish in the lives of those committed to their care, principles of piety, morality and virtue, and habits of industry, mental culture and economy, that they in their turn, and each succeeding generation, should, in the words of the

Psalmist, "make them known to their children; that the generation to come might know them, even the children which should be born, who should arise and declare them to their children."

When it seemed certain that they were securing the germs of the blessings they had so fondly sought, they were sorely embarrassed by having their precious liberties curtailed, and were suddenly deprived of the privilege of having rulers of their own election, and obliged to submit to the arbitrary dictation of governors appointed from beyond the sea. Their best men were often demanded as soldiers, and required to take long and perilous marches through the unknown wilds of the forest, and were exposed to the dangers of camp and battle-field in distant parts of the land, in order to carry on wars for the crown of England; and then, as if this were not enough, they were burdened with taxes to defray the expenses of those wars. They were often in terror of midnight attacks, when their homes were liable to be reduced to ashes, and they or their families slaughtered by a foe more wily and treacherous in his nature, more cruel and unrelenting in his hate, than any previously known in history. They were obliged to work early and late with but little diversion, in order to wrest from a stern and unyielding soil, the products necessary for the comfortable maintenance of their several households; the numbers of whose members as compared with the size of some of the families of modern civilization, could our hardy ancestors be permitted to see the startling change, might well cause them to blush for their posterity and feel alarm for the future existence of their race. They would have spurned the practices followed by modern voluptuaries in the pursuit of ease and pleasure. Constant bearing of life's heavy burdens, experience of trying hardships and the practice of sturdy virtues, enabled them to build the foundations of a race whose characteristics of energy, perseverance and general progress, have excited the admiration of the world. Although occasional personal misdemeanors and a few public acts, which might be cited, show that we must not extravagantly claim for all of

them unexceptionable purity and integrity, or that as a body
they always acted wisely and justly; yet, considering the state
of society in England prior to their emigration, and the injustice and abuse to which they and their ancestors had in some
cases been subjected, we can but be surprised that high moral
principles were so generally exemplified in their lives, and that
their public decrees toward those whom they regarded as
propagators of error were so seldom characterized by vindic-
tiveness. As well do the deeds of piety, patriotism and benevolence which they actually performed, as the rigid self-denials
which they practised and the crushing hardships which they
patiently endured, entitle them to our admiration. In seasons
of danger to the body politic they voluntarily and promptly
offered their time and services to relieve the community from
the threatened perils. And taking a later and less general
view, subsequent to the first century of settlement, after persistent industry united with manly energy and judicious management had won the smile of Providence in the accumulation
of ample fortunes, we see, in several instances, a large proportion of those fortunes yielded up and benevolently and piously
contributed for the promotion of education, morality and
religion. It is a sacred duty that we, especially as their
descendants, owe to such noble men and women as these, to
preserve carefully the memory of their lives, that their posterity
to the remotest generation, being incited by the " natural
principle of emulation," may be led " to copy such noble
examples."

" PHILLIPS," a name spelled in a variety of forms, is of
ancient and classical origin, being derived from the Greek,
Philos-hippos, or horse lover. In Wales and other parts of
Great Britain its use as a surname has continued for a long
period, evidently for five hundred years, and perhaps much
longer. It is said that " Phillipse " is Welsh and that
" Philips " is from Worcestershire. It is stated by good
authority that the Watertown family of this name were of the
" Philips " of Worcestershire. Some are positive that all the

English families of this name had their origin from Wales and subsequently spread over Great Britain. Several different ways have been employed in spelling, as Phillips, Philips, Phillipse, Philipps and others, some of them so peculiar as hardly to be recognized as having a common origin.

Families and individuals of this name began to emigrate from the Old World at a very early date in the history of this country, as early as 1630, and some a little earlier, and locate at different points near the sea-coast, but more especially in New England. From that time to the present they have continued to multiply and spread, by natural causes and by emigration, until now they are to be found in every State from Maine to California; and those in this country who spell their name by the more common form of Phillips, are numbered by thousands.

It is now exceedingly difficult to establish the relation which existed between many of these earlier Phillipses or to trace out satisfactorily the several lines of their descendants. Of the family of Rev. George Phillips of Watertown, Mass., there have been at least ten generations. There may be some now of the eleventh, but if so, no notice of them has come to the writer. None of the first five generations are now living. The last one, probably, of the fifth generation died in 1865 at the great age of nearly 105 years. There are five divisions of this family so marked by long continued residence in particular localities that they might well be designated as distinctive branches. These are the ANDOVER BRANCH, from Rev. Samuel Phillips who located in that town in 1711; the BOSTON BRANCH, from Hon. John Phillips who went there to live about 1718; the BROOKHAVEN BRANCH, from Rev. Geo. Phillips who located in Brookhaven, Long Island, 1697; the MARBLEHEAD AND SALEM BRANCH, from Jonathan Phillips who removed from Watertown to Marblehead about 1719; the OXFORD BRANCH, from Joseph Phillips who went there from Watertown not far from 1725. It will perhaps be noticed that the Christian name Samuel occurs in nearly every generation of the Andover branch; while in the Oxford branch there is an almost entire absence of either of the names Samuel, Sarah or William. Some members of each of these branches might have been found living in or near the several towns from which the respective branches take their names, at any time during the last one hundred and fifty to two hundred years.

Some of the earliest progenitors of the New England families of this name of which the line of descent has not been fully traced appear to have been the following :

Nicholas Phillips (Deacon) of Weymouth, 1640, seems to have had a large family, and a large number of the name at the present day are doubtless his descendants. The recurrence of such names as Joshua, Richard, Benjamin, Caleb and Experience, goes to show that one branch of his family removed to the vicinity of Dighton, Mass., at an early day. Some who have given the subject attention are of the opinion that part of those of the name in the early history of Rhode Island were his descendants.

John Phillips was of Duxbury and Marshfield, 1638 to 1677 or later and probably had a large number of descendants ; but the statement on page 123 that his family appears to include those given under Nos. 70 to 89 is found to be incorrect so far as it relates to Capt. John Phillips of Easton, page 135, who came probably from Weymouth prior to the year 1700, and whose apparent age would place his birth not far from the year 1670, giving so much ground for believing that he may have been the son, born June 21, 1669, of Nicholas Phillips of Weymouth, page 192.

John Phillips (Col.) of Charlestown, about 1655, had a large family and numerous descendants.

William Phillips of Boston, 1640, had descendants living about one hundred years later.

Henry Phillips of Boston, 1640, afterwards of Dedham, had descendants in the vicinity of Boston more than one hundred years later and appears to have had a numerous progeny.

James Phillips of Taunton, son, probably, of William, 1643, of same place, had children born from 1661 to 1675.

Andrew Phillips of, or near, Charlestown, married prior to 1659, had descendants living more than sixty years later. A recurrence of several names would lead to the conclusion that he was the ancestor of Ebenezer Phillips of Southboro, page 97, whose origin is involved in mystery, but nothing as yet found goes to prove the connection.

At the time of commencing this work, in 1877, it was the purpose of the compiler to include only the descendants of Joseph Phillips of Oxford, Mass., a grandson of Rev. George Phillips of Watertown; and it was only a few weeks before going to press that it was decided to include all that is embraced in these pages. But in the collection of material for completing the original design, considerable amount of records and interesting items of history of other families or branches of this name came into the possession of the compiler, and he was led to take in historical matter of families of the name apparently not connected with the Watertown family. Had it been known at the beginning how much was to be included, a still more extended research would have been made in some directions, and the arrangement might have been somewhat different.

That the genealogies given in this work are all correct can hardly be expected. Different individuals, in giving their recitals of the same event, sometimes make statements at variance with each other; sometimes they give different dates for the same event, and frequently the town records differ from those kept in families. These differences have at times made it a difficult matter for the compiler to decide which was to be received and which rejected; but in cases of doubt he has taken particular pains to arrive at what appeared to be strict truth. In some cases of a disagreement in dates, both dates are given. The transcriptions have all been carefully reviewed, and it is believed that each name and date, except a few in which errors were apparent, is given exactly as furnished to the compiler. Some of the incidents related are from oral statements by elderly but well-informed persons, some of whom long since passed away. Many have manifested a deep interest in the work, and kindly furnished whatever, in their possession, was likely to aid in its preparation. On the other hand, large numbers showed no interest at all ; and of the many hundreds to whom inquiries were sent out, soliciting records and other historical information, not one half ever gave a response. This will account in some measure for the want of completeness in portions of the genealogies.

The writer takes pleasure in extending his sincere thanks to all who have kindly contributed genealogical matter for these pages. The number is so great that want of space forbids the mention of each by name. In the necessary correspondence a sort of letter acquaintance has been created, which, to say the least, will leave pleasant memories, and in some cases it is trusted has ripened into permanent friendship. Some have rendered special assistance in various ways and it would hardly be proper to close without giving them more than a general notice.

Early and liberal subscriptions from Daniel Phillips of Hartford, Conn., and Walter P. Phillips of New York City, without which this book could not have appeared in its present attractive form, entitle them to grateful acknowledgments. For some of the principal sketches acknowledgments are due to Mrs. E. W. Clark, Westboro, Mass., Mrs. J. H. Westgate, Malden, Mass., Mrs. Geo. B. Eaton, Jersey City, N. J., Israel Phillips, Greenfield, Mass., Dea. Charles C. Phillips, Greenfield, Abner S. Phillips, Bondville, Vt., Joseph Christie, Philadelphia, Penn., Geo. Bassett, Ashfield, Mass., Nelson Phillips, Black River, N. Y., Nathan P. Dodge, Council Bluffs, Ia., and Miss E. M. Phillips, late of Medway, Mass. ; also to the authors and publishers of numerous publications from which miscellaneous extracts have been frequently taken. Perhaps the greatest amount of material drawn from any

B

one work is from Dr. Henry Bond's Genealogies and History of Watertown, a work of great value, in which a large number of New England families may trace their pedigree. The descendants of Rev. Samuel Phillips of Rowley, 1651, are given in the following pages mainly as found in that work. It will be seen that the New England Historical and Genealogical Register, a work which no writer of genealogies should be without, has contributed a great number of items, some of them quite essential in making out the proper connections. Obligations are gladly acknowledged to the few who have generously agreed to insert portraits of themselves or friends at their own expense. Grateful acknowledgments are due to Mr. E. M. Barton, the cordial and communicative librarian of the American Antiquarian Society, for his helpful suggestions and oft-repeated permission to examine the books of the library. The printing has been executed at the press of Charles Hamilton, and the neat and symmetrical arrangement of the typographical work is due to the watchful oversight of Mr. Benjamin J. Dodge, a printer of long experience, the present results of which well meet our anticipations. The lithotype portraits are from the works of the Lithotype Printing Co., Gardner, Mass., and many thanks are due to their faithful and affable agent, Mr. Frank Lawrence of Worcester, for his repeated and patient efforts under all circumstances, sometimes perplexing, to secure unexceptionally satisfactory work. For the steel engraving of Hon. Samuel Phillips thanks are due to Mr. Geo. P. Smith of Boston, agent of the Congregational Publishing Society, for permission to use the plate in their possession. The autographs are printed from the neatly and faithfully executed work of Messrs. Kyes & Woodbury of Worcester.

The following arrangement is by families and sub-families rather than by generations, though the number of the generation is shown by the Roman letters at the left. Each special family is numbered at the head, and for convenience in reference, these numbers are continuous through the book. The name of each family head is printed in bold type, and when the children of any married daughters are included, their surnames are given in Italics. The fragmentary records at the close of the book are given in the hope that they may assist some in retracing their family line, and enable them to make the proper connection with other branches. The abbreviations most used are, b. for born, bap. baptized, d. died, m. married, dau. daughter, ch. child or children, res. residence.

The number of names in the following genealogies is upwards of three thousand.

Whatever the defects of this work, and the compiler is aware of many, he trusts that he has preserved a few interesting, and perhaps not altogether unimportant, historical items, as well as some links in the chain of genealogical succession which might otherwise have been lost. There is still a wide field for genealogical research among the families of this name. To aid and encourage any who may be willing to correct errors or supply omissions which come to their notice, and to the end that correct and more complete genealogies of the several families of this name may be produced at some future time, a copy of this work with a large number of blank pages interleaved will be deposited in the rooms of the New England Historic Genealogical Society, Boston, Mass., and letters of correction forwarded to that address will receive proper attention. It is hoped that all who can will avail themselves of this opportunity to assist in producing, as nearly as it can be done, perfectly correct and complete genealogies.

The compiler cannot expect to regain pecuniary remuneration for his labors, his experience being somewhat similar to that of other genealogists who have asserted at the close, that had they known the amount of labor involved they never would have attempted the task; but if what is here given shall only cause those of the name into whose hands it may come to preserve carefully all items of family history and lead some one in each of the main branches of the name, parts of which are to be found in this book, to work out a complete genealogy of his own branch, one great object of its production will have been accomplished ; and the labor will not have been lost if any are led to emulate the benevolence, the devotion to duty, the patriotism or the piety of the worthy examples found recorded on the following pages.

ALBERT M. PHILLIPS.

Auburn, Worcester Co., Mass.,
Sept. 22, 1885.

CONTENTS.

PORTRAITS.

CORRECTIONS FOR PHILLIPS GENEALOGIES.

Page 68, 25th line, " Juno " should read Junia.
Page 78, at top, " No. 37 " should read No. 36.
Page 88, at top, " No. 25 " should read No. 43.
Page 92, 24th line, " Farms " should read Farm.
Page 98, foot note, 18th line from bottom, " 1685 " should read 1683.
Page 152, at top, " No. 96 " should read No. 95.

GENEALOGY OF THE FAMILY

OF

REV. GEORGE PHILLIPS,

OF WATERTOWN, MASS., 1630.

" A Phillips crossed the water with John Winthrop, and from him descended a long line of ministers, judges, governors, and councillors—a sterling race, temperate, just, and high-minded."—*Writer in Harper's.*

No. 1.

(I.) **Rev. George Phillips,** the first minister of Watertown, Mass., son of Christopher Phillips of Rainham, was born about 1593, at Rainham, St. Martins, near Rougham, in the hundred or district of Gallow, County of Norfolk, England.* He graduated as B. A. from Gonville and Caius College, Cambridge, 1613, and received the degree of M. A., 1617. "He gave early indications of deep piety, uncommon talents, and love of learning, and at the University distinguished himself by his remarkable progress in learning, especially in theological studies for which he manifested an early partiality." He was settled for a time in the ministry in Suffolk Co., but suffering from the storm of persecution which then threatened the non-conformists of England, he determined to leave the mother country and take his lot with the Puritans.

He embarked for America, April 12th, 1630, in the *Arbella,* with his wife and two children, as fellow-passengers with Gov.

---

* The parish of Rainham was visited in May, 1875, by Henry A. Phillips, now of Boston, who found that none of this name were living in that place, but ascertained that some were living in an adjacent town.

Winthrop* and Sir Richard Saltonstall, and arrived at Salem, June 12th.   Here his wife soon died and was buried by the side of Lady Arbella Johnson, both, evidently, being unable to endure the hardship and exposure incident to a tedious ocean voyage. †

He soon located in Watertown, and without delay was settled over the church in that place which was called together in July.

At the Court of Assistants, Aug. 23, 1630, it was "ordered that Mr. Phillips shall have allowed him 3 hogsheads of meale, 1 hogsh of malte, 4 bushells of Indean corn, 1 bushell of oat-meale, halfe an hundred of salte fish."   Another statement from the same source says, "Mr. Phillips hath 30 ac of land graunted him vpp Charles Ryver on the South side." ‡   His first residence was burnt before the close of the year.   There is a tradition that his later residence is still standing "opposite the ancient burial ground, back from the road." §

He continued to be the pastor of this church, greatly respected and beloved, till his death fourteen years after his arrival.   He died at the age of about fifty-one years, July 1, and was buried July 2, 1644.   "He was the earliest advocate of the Congregational order and discipline.   His views were for a time regarded as novel, suspicious and extreme, and he, with his ruling elder, Mr. Richard Brown, stood almost unaided and alone, until the arrival of Mr. John Cotton, in family maintaining what was and

---

* Before the final embarkation which had been considerably delayed, Gov. Winthrop says, in a letter to his son, John Winthrop:

"From aboard the Arbella, riding before Yarmouth, April 5, 1630.

Yesterday we kept a fast aboard our ship and in the *Talbot*.   Mr. Phillips exercised with us the whole day, and gave very good content to all the company, as he doth in all his exercises, so as we have much cause to bless God for him."

† It cannot be thought egotistical for one who does not trace his origin to *this* Mrs. Phillips, to say that there is now little or nothing from which to form an opinion of her except the lives and characters of her noble descendants; and judging from these, it is reasonable to conclude that she was a woman of high social standing, lofty moral virtue and strong intellect.

‡ *Mass. Records*, Vol. 1, pp. 102, 730.

§ This old house whose solid oaken frame is said to have been brought over by Sir R. Saltonstall, has a projecting second story, partly concealed by a modern piazza, and stands well back from the street.   Externally there is nothing to indicate great age, but its interior retains many marks of antiquity.   It formerly had three porticos, which have been removed from its front, and a steep roof which has given place to one of much less altitude.—*Hist. of Middlesex County*, p. 450.   *S. A. Drake.*

still is, the Congregationalism of New England. It is not now easy to estimate the extent and importance of the influence of Mr. Phillips in giving form and character to the civil and ecclesiastical institutions of New England." His name appears in the list of those who were admitted freemen, May 18, 1631, which is the earliest date of any such admission.

His inventory amounted to £550 2s. 9d., a sum, allowing for the difference in commercial value between that time and the present, equivalent, at least, to seven or eight thousand dollars. His library was valued at £71 9s. 9d.

He married (1st) a daughter of Richard Sargent. He married (2d) **Elizabeth** ——, probably a widow of Capt. Robert Welden. She died in Watertown, June 27, 1681. In speaking of his descendants, the writer quoted at the beginning of this record says:

"In Brechin Hall at Andover, the library of the theological school, in the great halls of the academies at Andover and Exeter, and in Memorial Hall at Harvard College, one may see hanging upon the walls portraits of one and another man and woman of this family, which belongs among the untitled nobility of New England, representing the best element of life there— not that which always dwells in the brightest glare of publicity, but that which directs and shapes the current of public opinion."

Children (by first marriage):

1. SAMUEL, b. 1625; of Rowley. (No. 2.)
2. ELIZABETH, b. in England; m. previous to May 17, 1651, JOB BISHOP. of Ipswich.

(By second marriage):

3. ZEROBABEL, b. April 6, 1632; went to Long Island, and settled at South Hampton as early as 1663; was living in April, 1682. He m. ANN WHITE.
4. JONATHAN, b. Nov. 16, 1633. (No. 15.)
5. THEOPHILUS, b. May 28, 1636. (No. 19.)
6. ANNABEL, b. Dec., 1637; d. April, 1638.
7. EPHRAIM, b. June, 1640 or 1641; d. soon.
8. OBADIAH; d. very young.
9. ABIGAIL; m. Oct. 8, 1666, JAMES BARNARD; d. in Sudbury, Sept., 1672. No ch.

No. 2.

(II.) **Rev. Samuel Phillips** (son of George, of Water-town : No. 1,) was born in England, 1625, probably at Boxstead, in the County of Suffolk ; grad. at Harv. Coll., 1650 ; settled in Rowley in 1651, as colleague of Rev. Ezekiel Rogers. "He was highly esteemed for his piety and talents, which were of no common order, and he was eminently useful, both at home and abroad." He married in Oct., 1651, **Sarah Appleton**, born in Reydon, Eng., 1629, dau. of Samuel Appleton.* He died Apr., 22, 1696, "greatly beloved and lamented," and his widow died July 15, 1714. Her funeral sermon was preached by her grandson, Rev. Samuel Phillips of South Andover, in which he says, "She was an early seeker of God, and spent much of her time daily in reading the word and in prayer. . . . . She took care of her children's souls. . . . . She was always humble and penitent, and as she lived, so she died, depending on Christ for righteousness and salvation." Their remains repose in the ancient burying-ground at Rowley. Some of their descendants have been among the most distinguished of New England people for their intellectual talents, piety, benevolence and public services. There have been seven Samuels in this line in direct succession, with the exception of a John between the fifth and sixth, and all since the first two were residents or natives of Andover. The seventh and last was recently cashier of the Maverick Nat. Bank, Boston.

Children :

1. SAMUEL, b. Mar., 1654 ; d. young.
2. SARAH, b. Feb. 7, 1656 ; m. STEPHEN MIGHILL, b. 1651, son of Thomas and Ellen Mighill of Rowley. Ch. :
   1 and 2 ; daus.

---

* A carefully arranged ancestral table of Jonas Phillips Phœnix of New York, gives the following: William Appleton, of Little Waldingfield, Co. Suffolk, Eng., descended from John Appleton, of same place, who d. 1436. He m. Rose Sexton, dau. of Robert and Agnes (Jermyn) Sexton, of Lavenham, Co. Suffolk, Eng. Thomas Appleton, of Little Waldingfield, son of Wm. and Rose, emigrated to New England, 1635. His son, Samuel Appleton of Ipswich, Mass., b. in Eng., 1586, came to New Eng. with wife and ch., 1635, rep. in Gen. Court, d. at Rowley. June, 1670, in the house of his dau. Sarah Phillips. He mar. at Preston, Eng., Jan. 24, 1616, Judith Everard, b. in Eng. His dau. Sarah m. Rev. Samuel Phillips, above.

    3. Nathaniel *Mighill*, b. 1684; m. Priscilla Pearson. Ch. :

        1. Stephen *Mighill*, b. 1707.
        2. Ezekiel *Mighill*, b. 1710.
        3. Nathaniel *Mighill*, b. 1715.
        4. Thomas *Mighill*, b. 1722.
        5. Jeremiah *Mighill*, b. 1724. And 5 daus.

3. SAMUEL, b. Mar. 23, 1657–8 ; of Salem. (No. 3.)

4. GEORGE, b. Nov. 23, 1659 ; d. Jan. 18, 1662.

5. ELIZABETH, b. Nov. 16, 1661 ; d. June, 1662.

6. EZEKIEL, b. Feb., 1662 ; d. Mar. 1, 1662–3.

7. GEORGE, b. June 3, 1664, of Brookhaven, L. I. (No.14.)

8. ELIZABETH, b. Aug. 2, 1665 ; m. Nov. 7, 1683, Rev. EDWARD PAYSON, b. June 20, 1657, son of Edward and Mary (Elliot) Payson of Roxbury; grad. Harv. Coll., 1677; of Rowley; settled as colleague of Mr. Phillips, Oct. 25, 1682. She d. 1724. He d. Aug. 22, 1732. Ch. : twenty, of whom ten survived him and three, not named, d. in infancy :

      1. Elizabeth *Payson*, b. 1684.
      2. Sarah *Payson*, b. 1686.
      3. Mary *Payson*, b. 1687; m. Joseph Jewett, jr.
      4. Eliphalet *Payson*, b. 1689.
      5. Mehitabel *Payson*, b. 1691; m. Humphrey Hobson.
      6. Samuel *Payson*, b. 1693; grad. Harv. Coll. 1716; d. 1768.
      7. Edward *Payson*, b. 1694.
      8. Elizabeth *Payson*, b 1697; m. Ezekiel Northend.
      9. Hannah *Payson*, b. 1698.
    10. Elliot *Payson*, b. 1700; m. Mary Todd; 5 sons and 2 daus.
    11. Stephen *Payson*, b. 1701.
    12. Sarah *Payson*, b. 1702.
    13. Jonathan *Payson*, b. 1703.
    14. David *Payson*, b. 1705.
    15. Phillips *Payson*, b. 1707; d. same year.
    16. Sarah *Payson*, b. 1709.
    17. Susannah *Payson*, b. 1712; m. James Hibbert.

9. DORCAS, b. 1667 ; d. young.

10. MARY, b. Feb., 1667–8 ; d. young.

11. JOHN, b. Oct. 23, 1670 ; d. Nov. 23, same year.

No. 3.

(III.) **Samuel Phillips** (son of Samuel and Sarah : No. 2,) was born March 23, 1657–8, and removed to Salem, where he followed the occupation of goldsmith, and died Oct. 13, 1722, aged 65. He married (1st) May 26, 1687, **Mary**

Emerson, dau. of Rev. John and Ruth (Symonds) Emerson of Gloucester, and gr. dau. of Dep. Gov. Samuel Symonds of Ipswich. She died Oct. 4, 1703, aged 42. He married (2d) 1704, **Mrs. Sarah (Pickman) Mayfield.** Children, all by first marriage except the 8th :

1. PATIENCE ; d. very young.
2. SAMUEL, b. Feb. 17, 1689–90 ; of Andover. (No. 4.)
3. SARAH, b. Jan. 28, 1691–2 ; m. WILLIAM WHITE of Haverhill.
4. MARY, b. Aug. 5, 1694 ; d. Oct. 5, 1785, aged 91 ; m. Capt. GEORGE ABBOT of Andover.
5. RUTH, b. Sept. 4, 1696 ; m. SAMUEL WHITE of Haverhill.
6. ELIZABETH, b. Mar. 5, 1698–9 ; d. Aug. 7, 1700.
7. JOHN, b. June 22, 1701 ; of Boston. (No. 11.)
8. PATIENCE, b. Aug. 8, 1706 ; m. Rev. DAVID JEWETT.

No. 4.

(IV.) **Rev. Samuel Phillips** (son of Samuel and Mary : No. 3,) born Feb. 17, 1689–90 ; grad. Harv. Coll., 1708. He was the minister of the church at the South Parish, the present "Old South Church," Andover, for sixty years, where he commenced to preach in 1710, and was ordained Oct. 17, 1711, the same day the church was organized. Here he continued till his death, June 5, 1771. "In his individuality, simplicity, decision, energy, strength, and pristine hardiness of character, he abated nothing from the spirit of his worthy ancestors. He was, like them, also a model of industry, and frugality, and resolute self-restraint, and order in all that he did. His portrait * bespeaks a man of authority, born to command, and knowing his birthright ; and such was he in an eminent degree, a conscious and acknowledged leader wherever he was known." † He m. Jan. 17, 1711–12, **Hannah White,** dau. of John White, Esq., of Haverhill, deacon of the church, and captain of the company in that town. It was her practice to accompany her husband on his parishional calls, at which time he rode on

---

* His portrait may be seen in Bond's Genealogies of Watertown.

† Memoir of Judge Phillips, p. 7.

horseback, with his wife seated on a pillion behind him.   She d. Jan. 7, 1773.

Children :

1. MARY, b. Nov. 30, 1712 ; m. Oct. 12, 1736, SAMUEL APPLETON of Haverhill.
2. SAMUEL, b. Feb. 13, 1715.   (No. 5.)
3. LYDIA, b. June 10, 1717 ; m. May 18, 1742, Dr. PARKER CLARK of Newbury (or Andover).   She d. Nov. 4, 1749.   Ch. :
    1. Hannah *Clark*, b. April 2, 1743; m. July 23, 1767, Dr. Edward Russell of North Yarmouth, Me., and had one child.
    2. Lydia *Clark*, b. Aug. 16, 1744.
    3. Elizabeth *Clark*, b. Aug. 18, 1746.
    4. Parker *Clark*, b. Apr. 3, 1748.
4. JOHN, b. Dec. 27, 1719 ; of Exeter, N. H.   (No. 6.)
5. WILLIAM, b. July 6, 1722 ; of Boston.   (No. 9.)

No. 5.

(V.) **Hon. Samuel Phillips** (son of Samuel and Hannah : No. 4,) was born Feb. 13, 1715 ; grad. Harv. Coll., 1734 ; was engaged for some time in teaching a grammar school, but he had a natural taste and rare fitness for mercantile and other business pursuits, into which he soon entered with zeal and a determination to succeed.   His natural sagacity and deep foresight, strengthened by a long and varied experience in different departments of business life, gave him confidence and insured the success which enabled him in after life to perform the acts that have caused his name to be associated with works of usefulness and beneficence.   He was extensively engaged in the manufacture of gunpowder at the time of the Revolution, and for this he erected an expensive mill, which in 1778 was destroyed by an explosion in which there was a loss of life of three persons.   "In 1788, he built a paper-mill, which was carried on by Phillips and Houghton.   He was often the representative of Andover, and member of the Executive Council before the Revolution, and in the Revolution was a staunch whig ; was many years a civil magistrate, discharging the duties thereof with the most exemplary fidelity.   Such were the sternness and precision of his manners, always frowning on vice and disorder,

that they did not contribute to his popularity. Early habits of exactness and economy enabled him to accumulate a large estate, much of which he appropriated to the public good."*
The crowning act of his life, that which more than anything else causes his memory to be held in grateful and perpetual remembrance, that which makes hundreds of professional, and other learned men his beneficiaries, was the part he performed as founder of the Academy at Andover. In this, however, he acted in connection with his brother, Hon. John Phillips of Exeter, N. H., afterwards sole founder of Phillips Exeter Academy, to whom is perhaps due an equal share of the honor, and at the suggestion of his son Samuel, known as Judge Phillips, to whom is to be accredited the further honor, that he conceived the original design, worked out the plan, and drew up the constitution. The School was established April 1, 1778, the two brothers having given for the purpose one hundred and forty-one acres of land in Andover, two hundred acres in Jaffrey, N. H., and five thousand dollars in money. "The lands they directed to be let out on proper terms, the money to be put on interest on good security, and the profits to be forever appropriated and expended for the support of a public free school or academy, in the South Parish of Andover."† The school was opened with twenty scholars, on the 28th of April, 1778, in a joiner's shop, purchased from the funds subscribed; and thus, Phillips Academy, known at first as Phillips School, had a practical beginning. In speaking of the relations of these three men to the two academies, a writer before quoted says : ‡

"The three men—and the older ones especially were men of sound judgment, who moved cautiously, and were not led away by any blind enthusiasm—together planned the enterprise, determined the locality, and took the necessary steps to bring the school into active existence. The combined gifts of these and other members of the Phillips family for the endowment of the academy amounted, in round numbers, to one hundred thousand

---

* Genealogies of Watertown.
† *Lawrence American*, June 7, 1878.
‡ *Harper's Magazine*, Vol. 55, p. 564.

dollars, and for half a century it was under the fostering care of some member of the family. Phillips Academy at Andover, was incorporated by an act of the Legislature in 1780, being the first academy so incorporated in America. Six months later, Dr. John Phillips, of Exeter, secured the incorporation of Phillips Exeter Academy. . . . . . Thus these three men were founders of the two schools; and though the sums bestowed, when measured by the standard of more modern gifts, do not cause astonishment, when compared with what others were doing at that time, both in America and in England, they are simply magnificent. . . . . It was an act of faith, of strong will and high purpose, and the spirit which underlay the design is embodied in the elaborate constitution which serves for both schools. . . . . The present school building replaces one that was destroyed by fire. It stands near the top of a hill which is crowned by the buildings occupied by the theological seminary of the Congregationalists, established in 1808. We mention it here because it has an organic connection with the academy, the two institutions being under the same board of trustees, the younger having sprung from the loins of the elder, partly as the consummation of a purpose originally formed by the founders of the academy, partly as the solution of a difficulty which had arisen when the incorporation of the theological seminary had been sought. It is plain, too, that the academy is influenced in many ways by the presence of the seminary. . . . . Friendships spring up between the older and younger men, and the two institutions help to correct each other. The fact of the theological school as organically connected with the academy has served in many ways to deepen the religious character of the academy and to identify it more closely with the religious denomination with which it is affiliated."

He married July 11, 1738, **Elizabeth Barnard,** daughter of Theodore Barnard of Andover, and gr. dau. of Rev. Thomas Barnard of North Andover, who died 1718. By this marriage with an only child, the real estate at North Andover, formerly owned by the Barnard family, became the homestead which has been retained in the Phillips family for so many succeeding generations. The store carried on by Mr. Phillips in that place was opened in a part of the same house occupied by the family. He died Aug. 21, 1790, aged 75. She died Nov. 29, 1789, aged 71. "Her letters are very interesting, and show her to have been a woman of great piety and strong religious views." Their epitaph contains the following words: "This pair were friends to order in the Family, Church and Commonwealth; Examples of Industry and Economy, and patrons of learning and religion." Children; of whom it will be seen that only one out of the seven survived them:

1. THEODORE, b. May 2, 1739; d. Jan. 25, 1740.
2. HANNAH, b. Jan. 20, 1742; d. June 15, 1764.
3. SAMUEL, b. Nov. 6, 1743; d. Dec. 24, 1744.
4. THEODORE, b. Sept. 6, 1745; d. Dec. 1, 1758.
5. ELIZABETH, b. Oct. 31, 1747; d. June 24, 1748.
6. SAMUEL, b. Feb. 7, 1750. (No. 7.)
7. ELIZABETH, b. Oct. 18, 1755; d. Apr. 19, 1757.

No. 6.

(V.) **Hon. John Phillips** (son of Samuel and Hannah: No. 4,) was born Dec. 27, 1719; grad. Harv. Coll., 1735. He taught in public schools in Andover, Exeter and other places, after which he had a private Latin School in Exeter. He fitted himself for the ministry, and received a call from the church in Exeter, but for some reason relinquished all plans for preaching and entered extensively into mercantile life. He was a justice of the peace, a trustee of Dartmouth College for twenty years, from which he received the degree of LL.D. in 1777, "and founded and endowed in that College, the Phillips Professorship of Theology." He "was authorized to be, in some singular cases, one of the Judges of the Superior Court." In his business he was eminently successful, and accumulated a large fortune, all of which he devoted to benevolent objects. He gave liberally with his brother for the founding of Phillips Academy, Andover, in 1778, and in 1789, gave it the further sum of twenty thousand dollars, "for the virtuous and pious education of youths of genius and serious disposition." He bequeathed, by his last will, one-third of all the estate of which he died possessed, "for the benefit more especially of charity scholars, such as may be of excelling genius and good moral character, preferring the hopefully pious, and for the assistance of youths liberally educated, designed for the ministry, while studying Divinity under the direction of some eminent Calvinistic Minister of the Gospel, until a professor of Divinity, able, pious, and Orthodox, should be supported in this Academy, or at Exeter, in New Hampshire, or in both." It was this purpose of the founders, of securing, permanently, instruction in Theology, which led, about thirty years later to the founding of the Andover Theological Seminary.

He was the founder of the Academy in Exeter. In 1781, he "secured the incorporation of Phillips Exeter Academy from the New Hampshire Legislature, giving to the school in life and by bequest property amounting at the time to about sixty-five thousand dollars, but now, under admirable management, greatly enhanced in value." In speaking of his acts in connection with this institution, a writer before quoted says : "Phillips Exeter Academy has its own history and characteristics quite independent of Andover. It is almost wholly the child of Dr. John Phillips. . . . Dr. Phillips was one of the trustees at Andover from its first organization till his death, and for the last five years of his life president of the board. His endowment of Exeter thus was an act in generous emulation of his own beneficence. The wise provision which he made for the support of the school, and the care exercised by those in charge of the endowment, have given to the Academy a wholesome independence, so that it occupies to-day a position of self-reliance and integrity, having funds sufficient for its support irrespective of its receipts from tuition fees. During the century which has nearly closed since its incorporation it has had, until recently, but three principals in succession. . . . . Dr. Benjamin Abbot, the former of these, graduated at Harvard in 1788, and immediately went to Exeter as principal. The choice of this man hints at one distinction between Andover and Exeter. Dr. John Phillips, like his brother and nephew, was a firm adherent to the old school of

New England orthodoxy: He was also a man of deep humility and large-mindedness. He saw in Benjamin Abbot, an Exeter youth, the qualities which constituted a wise teacher, and he chose him to the place, although their theological preferences were at variance,—Abbot belonging to the new school which in process of time became organized Unitarianism. To measure Dr. Phillips's liberality, one must needs place himself among his contemporaries, and not among his descendants. Not only did Mr. Phillips make this appointment, but two of the trustees originally chosen by himself, and three others chosen during his lifetime, held theological opinions opposite to his own. . . . . The connection with Harvard University has always been a close one, and no other school in the country, save the Boston Latin School, has sent so large a number of students to Cambridge, while the standard of scholarship has been of the highest. The largest proportion of boys at Exeter has Harvard in view, and the reputation for scholarship which Exeter enjoys at Harvard has been unbroken for nearly a century."

He married (1st) **Mrs. Sarah (Emery) Gilman,** dau. of Rev. Mr. Emery, and widow of Nathaniel Gilman. He m. (2d) **Mrs. Elizabeth (Dennet) Hale,** dau. of Hon. E. Dennet of Portsmouth, N. H., and widow of Dr. Hale. He died Apr. 21, 1795, aged 75. No children.

No. 7.

(VI.) **Hon. Samuel Phillips** (son of Samuel and Elizabeth: No. 5,) commonly known as Judge Phillips, was born Feb. 7, 1750; grad. Harv. Coll., 1771; a member of the Provincial Congress at Watertown, 1775; Lieut.-Governor. He was the only heir to a large estate; but with a spirit of heroic self-sacrifice, he prevailed on his father to divert the property, which would legally fall to him, to the founding of the Academy at Andover. And it is to this self-sacrificing spirit, his benevolent heart, his desire to promote the education and good morals of the youth in his community, and check the growth of vice which he saw spreading with the advance of

Samuel Phillips

civilization, by the establishment, in his native town, of a permanent school worthy of the Commonwealth in which he lived, that the institution owes its existence.   A long distance in advance of the people of his day, his deep and far-seeing mind conceived the original design, and he cautiously, deliberately and wisely drafted the constitution, now in service for both this and the Exeter Academy.   "This instrument, with its multitudinous emendations, erasures, and additions, bears witness to the minute care with which the founders sought to formulate the principles of the schools. . . . . No one can read this paper without perceiving its weight and perspicuity.   It was formerly, and perhaps now is, read yearly at the meetings of the board of trustees, and drew from one member, who had sat on the board for forty years, the remark that its language seemed to him more like inspiration than any thing else except the Bible. . . . . . The constitution, while defining the courses of study and discipline, the duties of trustees and masters—not omitting to caution the trustees against extravagant entertainment at their yearly dinner— lays great emphasis on the conduct of the students, and the means to be taken for education in morality and religion, declaring that 'above all, it is expected that the master's attention to the disposition of the minds and morals of the youth under his charge will exceed every other care; well considering that though goodness without knowledge (as it respects others) is weak and feeble, yet knowledge without goodness is dangerous, and that both united form the noblest character, and lay the surest foundation of usefulness to mankind.' " *

"Samuel Phillips was an extraordinary man; but it is difficult to give, at this day, a just expression of his character.   The religious and moral element in it were mixed so intimately, and yet so unaffectedly, with the business of the world and the habits of active life, that he seemed to be a perfect embodiment of the Christian statesman, scholar, and philanthropist. . . . . I have never met, through my whole life, with an individual in whom the spirit of christianity and of good-will to mankind were so naturally blended with an indomitable energy and enterprise in

---

* *Harper's Magazine*, Vol. 55, p. 564.

active life. He was a leader in the church, a leader in the State; the young loved and listened to him, the old consulted and deferred to his advice. . . . . . In his capacity for business, there was, as it were, an universality or ubiquity. In the town, in the Senate, in the courts of justice, in committees of the legislature, as a referee in cases of great importance, in all other associations or affairs of business, his influence was, as far as was possible in respect of any one man, paramount. For twenty years he was a member, and for fifteen years president, of the Senate of the State, at a period when Statesmen were not made out of every sort of wood. He was judge of the Essex Court of Common Pleas, a member of every important committee, on like occasions a referee, and, at the same time, owned and took a general superintendence of two stores, one at Andover, another at Methuen, of a saw-mill, a grist-mill, a paper-mill, and a powder-mill on the Shawshine, giving to each a sufficient and appropriate share of his oversight; with a spirit subdued by the predominancy of the religious sentiment, he was as earnest, active and indefatigable in this multitude of his engagements, as though this world was everything." *

" He was religious in study, in trade, in neighborly kindness, in domestic life, in politics, in every civil office, and in his zeal to promote learning, as well as in public worship or public charities. It was emphatically a religious institution which he was intent upon establishing; a religious vitality which he sought to breathe into all education within its atmosphere. . . . . Thus *he was intensely methodical and careful.* Any one of his hundreds of manuscripts now extant, taken up at random, would be an illustration of this trait. He erased, he interlined, he changed the collocation of words or paragraphs, he put in after-thoughts and side-thoughts, in a common family letter, with as much painstaking as in the draft of a State paper. In writing the most familiar communications to his son or his wife, he would copy, or give an apology for not copying, as if he would not consent to do anything which he was not anxious to do well; and the

---

* Extract from a letter written by Josiah Quincy to Rev. John L. Taylor, dated Boston, Dec. 13, 1855, in Memoir of Judge Phillips.

same scrupulous exactness was shown by him through the whole circuit of his labors, not more as a habit than as a purpose. . . . So, too, *he was a prodigy of activity:* not of haste and bustle, but of rapid, effective labor, in a quiet, unruffled spirit. His equilibrium was one secret of his momentum. Serene and sunny in temperament, he sang with the morning and evening birds. Men everywhere said, 'he is too busy,' 'he will soon be spent,' but he heard them not; work had a charm for him—any work, all work, if so be it were only good. . . . . . . He cherished a special fondness for the young. . . . . Companion of Statesmen as he was, and a proverb for his gravity, he was never more in his element than when conversing with a little child, or dropping his goodly maxims, like the gentle dew, into the heart of some listening youth." *

His business very often took him to Boston; and it was his habit after the close of the fatiguing labors of the day in that place, to mount his horse and ride to Andover, arriving at home about midnight. His friends remonstrated against this imprudence, but he gave them little heed, feeling that all available time should be devoted to useful labor. This exposure of his health, which was never very firm, with constant and incessant application to the extensive round of his business duties, doubtless laid the foundation, as is almost invariably the case under like circumstances, for the physical troubles which terminated his days of great usefulness, when not much past what is usually considered middle life. He left by will, four thousand dollars to be added to the fund for maintaining instruction in divinity in connection with the Andover Academy. Although his father, Hon. Samuel Phillips the elder, in connection with the brother, Dr. John Phillips, of Exeter, is regarded, and not improperly, as founder of Phillips Academy on account of his magnificent life-gifts and bequests; yet, to style Hon. Samuel Phillips the younger, as *the* founder of that institution, while doing no injustice to his worthy parent or liberal-minded uncle, is but yielding to him the honor to which he is justly entitled. In the connection of the two Samuels, father and son, with the establishment

* *Memoir of Judge Phillips,* pp. 266, 303, 304, 310, 311. *By Rev. John L. Taylor.*

of Phillips Academy it is difficult to separate them.   They were considerably associated with each other in the pursuits of life, and in the accomplishment of their grand design they acted in harmony.   Two more useful and noble men, or more worthy, upright and high minded citizens, from one family, never honored, or were honored by, the Commonwealth in which they lived.   He died Feb. 10, 1802, aged 52.   He married, July 6, 1773, **Phebe Foxcroft**, born Aug. 12, 1743, dau. of Hon. Francis Foxcroft, of Cambridge.   She died Oct. 7, 1812, aged 69.   Children :

1. JOHN, b. Oct. 18, 1776.   (No. 8.)
2. SAMUEL ; d. 1796.

No. 8.

(VII.)   **Col. John Phillips** (son of Samuel and Phebe : No. 7,) born Oct. 18, 1776.   "Assistant in Phillips Academy. . . . . When Andover Theological Seminary was about to be founded in 1807, he with his noble-minded, pious and benevolent mother, engaged to build a large edifice for the accommodation of students.   He was commander of an independent company, aid of Gov. Strong, and State Senator."   He married Dec. 22, 1798, **Lydia Gorham,** dau. of Hon. Nathaniel Gorham, of Charlestown.   He died Sept. 10, 1820, aged 44.   His widow survived him about forty years.   Children :

1. PHEBE, b. Dec. 1, 1799 ; m. May 27, 1824, Rev. JONATHAN CLEMENT ; she d. Dec., 1874, aged 75.   He was b. in Danville, Vt., June 20, 1797 ; grad. Middlebury Coll., 1818 ; studied Theology at Andover; teacher in Phillips Acad., 1820–30 ; ordained Oct. 13, 1830 ; settled over the following churches : Chester, N. H., 1830–45, Topsham, Me., 1845–52, Woodstock, Vt., 1852–67 ; preached in Quechee. Vt., 1869–74 ; removed in 1867 to Norwich, Vt., living there 1880 ; D. D.
2. SAMUEL, b. May * 8, 1801 ;   grad. Harv. Coll., 1819 ;   Law School, 1825 ; d. Jan. 21, 1877.   He m. Oct. 23, 1827, SALLY SWETT, of Boxford.   Ch. :
    1. Samuel, b. in Andover, Sept. 30, 1828 ; cashier for several years of the Maverick Nat. Bank, Boston.   Ch. :
        1.   Caroline S——, b. in Malden, Mass., Aug. 17, 1852.

* One says March 8.

2. Sarah Allen White, b. in Salem, Oct. 27, 1857.

2. Sarah Webb, b. Feb. 22, 1830; m. Oct 31, 1859, Henry A. DeFrance of Davenport; d.

3. Anne Woodbury, b. Dec. 25, 1832; unm., 1878.

4. Helen, b. June 5, 1834; m. 1864, Hamilton Willis.

3. REBECCA GORHAM, b. Aug. 19, 1802 ; d. Feb. 6, 1870, unm.

4. LYDIA, b. Apr. 12, 1804 ; lived in Boston ; d. in Andover, Apr. 23, 1874 ; m. Oct. 15, 1850, Dr. JOHN CALL DALTON of Lowell, grad. Harv. Coll., 1814, M. D., 1817; d. 1864. No ch.

5. JOHN (twin), b. Apr. 12, 1804 ; d. Oct. 22, 1863 ; m. (1st) Nov. 26, 1829, SARAH ANN DORR of Roxbury ; m. (2d) Mar. 22, 1851, CAROLINE LITTLE of Newburyport ; m. (3d) ANN JANE GARDNER of Dorchester.

6. ELIZABETH BARNARD, b. Dec. 17, 1805 ; m. June 30, 1839, Judge WILLIAM STEVENS of Andover.

7. SARAH WHITWORTH, b. Feb. 18, 1807.

8. MARY ANN, b. March 17, 1808 ; m. Sept. 9, 1833, WILLIAM GRAY BROOKS, a merchant of Boston, son of Cotton Brown and Jane (Williams) Brooks* ; resided for some time preceding his death in the old Phillips mansion at North Andover, where he d. Jan. 6, 1879, aged 73. Ch. :

1. William Gray *Brooks*, b. July 2, 1834.

2. Phillips *Brooks*, b. Dec. 13, 1835; grad. Harv. Coll., 1855; distinguished clergyman of the Episcopalian denomination, and popular lecturer, of Boston. He is the present owner of the Phillips homestead at North Andover.

3. George *Brooks*, b. Dec. 18, 1838.

4. Frederick *Brooks*, b. Aug. 5, 1842.

5. Arthur *Brooks*, b. June 11, 1845; grad. Harv. Coll., 1867; Episcopalian clergyman; ordained June 25, 1870; of Williamsport, Pa., Chicago, Ill., and New York, N. Y.

6. John Cotton *Brooks*, b. Aug. 29, 1849; grad. Harv. Coll., 1872; Episcopalian clergyman; ord. 1876; of Bristol, Pa., Providence, R. I., and Springfield, Mass.

9. SUSAN LOWELL, b. Mar. 5, 1809.

10. CAROLINE, b. Aug. 3, 1810.

11. JULIA, b. Feb. 9, 1813 ; m. ISAAC THOMPKINS of Manchester ; d. Mar. 6, 1867.

12. AMELIA (twin), b. Feb. 9, 1813 ; d. Sept. 15, 1865.

13. NATHANIEL GORHAM, b. June 24, 1816.

---

* Capt. Thomas Brooks,[1] and wife Grace, were of Watertown, 1636; Caleb,[2] and Hannah Brooks of Medford; Capt. Samuel,[3] m. Sarah Boylston; Samuel,[4] m. Mary Boutwell; Rev. Edward,[5] m. Abigail Brown; and Cotton Brown,[6] m. Jane Williams, as above.

3

No. 9.

(V.) **Hon. William Phillips** (son of Samuel and Hannah : No. 4,) was born July 6, 1722. The following brief sketch, given in *Bond's Watertown*, shows something of his life and character : "At the age of fifteen years he went to Boston, and became an apprentice to Edward Bromfield, Esq., a highly respectable merchant of that town, son of Hon. Edward Bromfield, for many years one of his Majesty's Council in the Province of Massachusetts Bay, and a great grandson of Rev. John Wilson, the first minister of Boston. At the termination of his apprenticeship he married, June 13, 1744, o. s., **Abigail Bromfield**, eldest daughter of his late master, and engaged in mercantile pursuits, in which he was very successful. By this marriage a grt.-gr. son of the first minister of Watertown was united with a grt.-gr. dau. of the first minister of Boston. He was for many years a deacon of the Old South Church, and was repeatedly elected representative and State senator. 'He took a decided and active part in the proceedings which preceded and attended the Revolution; was on many of the committees appointed by the town of Boston in those trying times, and often contributed liberally of his estate to promote the measures which issued in the establishment of our independence.' He was one of the committee sent to demand of Gov. Hutchinson that the tea should be sent back to England; was rejected as a Councillor by Gov. Gage; was a member of the Convention for framing the Constitution of the Commonwealth, and that of adopting the Constitution of the United States. Upon the outbreak of the Revolution, he moved his family to Norwich, Conn., where they remained while the British had possession of Boston, occupying the Arnold mansion, the same house in which the traitor, Benedict Arnold, was born." He gave by his last will five thousand dollars to Phillips Academy, Andover. He died Jan. 15, 1804, aged 81. Children :

1. ABIGAIL, b. Apr. 14, 1745 ; d. March 25, 1798 ; m. JOSIAH QUINCY, Jr., of Revolutionary fame.
2. WILLIAM ; d. young.
3. WILLIAM, b. Mar. 30, 1750. (No. 10.)

4. SARAH; d. young.
5. HANNAH; d. young.
6. HANNAH, b. Nov. 29, 1756; m. SAMUEL SHAW. No ch.
7. SARAH (twin), b. Nov. 29, 1756; m. EDWARD DOWSE of Dedham. She d. 1839. No. ch.
8. MARY; d. young.

No. 10.

(VI.) Lieut. Gov. William Phillips (son of William and Abigail: No. 9,) was born March 30, 1750; of Boston; deacon of the Old South Church, representative, and, from 1812 to 1823, Lieut.-Governor; from 1804 until his death in 1827, president of the Massachusetts Bank; presidential elector at large in 1820 when the vote of the State was cast for Mr. Monroe. To the already very liberal endowments of Phillips Academy, Andover, he added the sum of fifteen thousand dollars, and gave ten thousand dollars to Andover Theological Seminary. His generous gifts, distributed among about a dozen worthy objects, amounted to sixty-two thousand dollars.

"He came into possession of an ample fortune, to the management of which, and to the duties of his family and of friendship, to the service of the public, and to deeds of benevolence, he was thenceforth chiefly devoted. He was eminently a domestic man, fond of retirement, and of the society of his family and intimate friends. Yet he was not averse to the calls of public duty." The Rev. Dr. Wisner in preaching his funeral sermon said: "Scarcely a measure has been adopted or an association formed in this city and vicinity for the improvement of the physical, the intellectual, the moral or the spiritual condition of men, which has not received his co-operation and liberal support."

He married Sept. 13, 1774, **Miriam Mason**, born June 16, 1754, 3d dau. of Hon. Jonathan Mason of Boston. She died May 7, 1823, "greatly lamented." He died Saturday evening, May 26, 1827. Children:

1. WILLIAM WILSON, b. in Norwich, Dec. 10, 1775; d. Jan. 1, 1784.
2. JONATHAN, b. May 2, 1777; d. Oct. 27, following.

3. JONATHAN, b. Apr. 24, 1778; of Boston; Hon. A. M., Harv. Coll., 1818. About 1853, not long before his death, he gave to the city of Boston, ten thousand dollars for the public library. He m. (1st) Sept. 30, 1805, REBECCA SALISBURY, b. Aug. 16, 1776; d. March 13, 1828, dau. of Samuel Salisbury of Boston. He m. (2d) Aug. 27, 1839, MARY MAGEE, b. Mar. 19, 1791, dau. of James and Margaret Magee. She d. June 23, 1849. Ch. :

  1. Martha Salisbury, b. Dec 28, 1806; d. Mar. 24, 1839.
  2. Jonathan Mason, b. Apr. 24, 1810; d. Oct. 21, 1811.
  3. Miriam, b. July 2, 1811; d. Dec. 19, 1816.
  4. Rebecca Salisbury, b. Oct. 19, 1816.
  5. William, b. Jan. 11, 1819.

4. MIRIAM, b. June 9, 1779; m. Jan. 4, 1803, SAMUEL HALL WALLEY, b. Apr. 12, 1778. He d. July 25, 1850. She d. Mar. 26, 1827. Ch. :

  1. Samuel H——— Walley, b. Aug. 31, 1805; grad. Harv. Coll., 1826; counsellor-at-law; speaker of the Mass. House of Representatives. He m. Oct. 14, 1829, Mehitabel Sumner Bates, b. June, 1810, dau. of Hon. Isaac C. Bates of North-ampton. Ch. :

    1. Martha Henshaw Walley, b. Dec. 17, 1832; d. Feb. 15, 1833.
    2. Miriam Phillips Walley, b. Aug. 28, 1834.
    3. Samuel Walley, b. Sept. 3, 1836; d. Sept. 13, 1837.
    4. Henshaw Bates Walley, b. Sept. 14, 1838.
    5. Theresa Maria Walley, b. Oct. 26, 1840; d. Aug. 9, 1843.
    6. William Phillips Walley, b. Apr. 11, 1843.
    7. Abigail Bromfield Phillips Walley, b. Sept. 4, 1845.
    8. Hetty Sumner Bates Walley, b. Feb. 15, 1848.
    9. Isaac Chapman Bates Walley, b. Jan. 15, 1850.
    10. Edward Walley, b. June 6, 1852.
  2. Sarah Hurd Walley, b. Jan. 18, 1816; m. William K. Brown.
  3. Abigail Bromfield Phillips Walley, b. May 25, 1818.

5. EDWARD, b. June 24, 1782; of Boston; deacon of the Old South Church. He m. (1st) 1807, MARY SALISBURY, b. May 18, 1787; d. Apr. 28, 1815. He m. (2d) Nov. 3, 1820, THERESA HENSHAW of Northampton. He d. Nov. 4, 1826. Ch. (by first marriage) :

  1. William, b. Aug. 8, 1808; d. Jan. 13, 1829.
  2. Edward, b. July 6, 1810; d. Feb. 15, 1812.
  3. Abigail, b. Nov. 3, 1814; m. Apr. 27, 1836, Edward Elbridge Salisbury. He grad. Yale Coll., 1832, and was afterwards professor there. She d. in New Haven, Dec. 13, 1869.

(By second marriage) :

4.　Miriam M——, b. Aug. 5, 1821; d. Feb. 22, 1824.
5.　Edward B——, b. Oct. 5, 1824; grad. Harv. Coll., 1845; d. June 21, 1848.　He gave by bequest to Harv. Coll. one hundred thousand dollars for the Observatory.
6.　Theresa Henshaw, b. Aug. 22, 1826.

6.　ABIGAIL BROMFIELD, b. Feb. 5, 1790 : m. Rev. EBENEZER BURGESS, a graduate of Brown Univ. ; of Dedham.　Ch. :

　　1.　Miriam Mason *Burgess.*
　　2.　Ebenezer Prince *Burgess.*
　　3.　Edward Phillips *Burgess.*
　　4.　Martha Crowell *Burgess.*

7.　WILLIAM, b. Oct. 13, 1791.

This concludes the list of those whose ancestors were of Andover.

No. 11.

(IV.)　**Hon. John Phillips** (son of Samuel and Mary : No. 3,) born June 22, 1701 ; a stationer, and afterwards a merchant, of Boston.　He possessed much of that rare adaptability to mercantile and general business life which has been so frequently displayed by the descendants of Samuel and Mary Phillips of Salem, and in his business was eminently successful. He was deacon of the Brattle Street Church, justice of the peace and of the quorum, Colonel of the Boston Regiment, and several times represented the town in the General Court.　He married (1st) Nov. 21, 1723, **Mary Buttolph,** born May 8, 1703, dau. of Nicholas Buttolph of Boston.　She died Aug. 15, 1742, and he m. (2d) **Abigail Webb,** dau. of Rev. Mr. Webb of Fairfield, Conn.　He died Apr. 19, 1768, "and was buried with military honors."　Children (by first marriage) :

1.　JOHN, b. Nov. 29, 1726 ; m. ELIZABETH GREEN.　Ch. :
　　1.　——; m. Mr. —— Thurston.
2.　SAMUEL, b. Mar. 15, 1729 ; m. ELIZABETH FAYERWEATHER. Ch. :
　　1.　——; m. Mr. —— Clarke.
　　2.　——; m. Henry Prentice.
3.　ABIGAIL, b. Feb. 14, 1733 ; m. Mar. 19, 1778, Col. ELISHA PORTER of Hadley.

4. SARAH, b. Apr. 7, 1735 ; m. NATHANIEL TAYLOR, a merchant, of
    Boston, son of Rev. Mr. Taylor of Milton.
5. WILLIAM, b. Aug. 29, 1737.   (No. 12.)
6. MARY ANN, b. July 25, 1741 ; m. Dr. NATHANIEL NOYES.   She
    d. Apr. 20, 1791.
    (By second marriage) :
7. JOSEPH.

No. 12.

(V.) **William Phillips** (son of John and Mary: No.
11,) born Aug. 29, 1737 ; married June 12, 1761, **Margaret
Wendell,** b. Aug. 20, 1739, 11th and youngest child of Hon.
Jacob Wendell.*   He died June 4, 1772, aged 34 yrs., 9 mos.
She died Feb. 27, 1823.   Children :

1. MARGARET, b. May 26, 1762; d. Feb. 19, 1844; m. Judge
    SAMUEL COOPER.
2. SARAH, b. Apr. 6, 1765 ; m. MARK NEWTON of Andover.
3. JOHN, b. Nov. 26, 1770.   (No. 13.)

No. 13.

(VI.) **Hon. John Phillips** (son of William and Margaret : No. 12,) born Nov. 26, 1770 ; grad. Harv. Coll., 1788 ;
president of the Mass. Senate. and first mayor of Boston.   He
married Dec. 18, 1794, **Sally Walley,** b. Mar. 25, 1772,
dau. of Thomas and Sarah (Hurd) Walley.   He died May 29,
1823.   She died Nov. 4, 1845.   Children :

1. THOMAS WALLEY, b. Jan. 16, 1797; grad. Harv. Coll., 1814;
    Clerk of the Municipal Court, Boston, for many years; d.
    1859. He m. Mar. 18, 1824, ANNA DUNN, dau. of Samuel
    Dunn of Boston. Ch. :
    1. John.
    2. Samuel.

---

* Mr. Wendell was a merchant, Colonel of the Boston Regiment, and one of the
Governor's Council. He m. Aug. 12, 1714, Sarah Oliver, bap. Dec. 20, 1696, dau. of Dr.
James Oliver of Cambridge, who m. Mercy Bradstreet, dau. of Dr. Samuel and Mercy
(Tyng) Bradstreet of Cambridge, and gr. dau. of Gov. Simon Bradstreet, by his first
wife Anne, dau. of Gov. Thomas Dudley.— *Watertown Gen.*

2. SARAH HURD, b. April 24, 1799; m. (1st) April 24, 1823, FRANCIS JENKS, Jr., b. Aug., 1798. He d. 1837, and she m. (2d) 1840, Prof. ALONZO GRAY of Brooklyn, N. Y. Ch. :

    1. Mary Elwell *Jenks*, b. June, 1824; m. Rev. R. S. Storrs of Brooklyn, N. Y.
    2. John Phillips *Jenks*, b. 1826; d. 1828.
    3. Francis Jenks, b. 1828.
    4. Grenville Tudor *Jenks*, b. July 18, 1830.
    5. Ames *Jenks*.
    6. Alice Elizabeth *Gray*.

3. SAMUEL, b. 1801; d. Feb. 20, 1817, while a member of the Soph. Class, Harv. Coll.

4. MARGARET, b. Nov. 29, 1802; m. Dr. EDWARD REYNOLDS of Boston. He grad. Harv. Coll., 1811; M. D. ; living 1880, son of Edward and Deborah (Belcher) Reynolds of Boston, gr. son of John and Dorothy (Weld) Reynolds of Prov., R. I., grt.-gr. son of Benjamin and Susanna (Rawson) * Reynolds of Bristol, R. I. Ch. :

    1. John Phillips *Reynolds*, b. Nov. 20, 1825; grad. Harv. Coll., 1845; physician; living, 1880.
    2. Adeline Margaret *Reynolds*, b. July 4, 1827; d.
    3. Miriam Phillips *Reynolds*, b. May 6, 1829.
    4. Anne Foster *Reynolds*, b. May 2, 1831.
    5. Margaret Elizabeth *Reynolds*, b. May 14, 1833.
    6. Adeline Ellen *Reynolds*, b. July 29, 1835.
    7. Augusta Theresa *Reynolds*, b. Dec. 29, 1837.

5. MIRIAM; m. June 8, 1831, Rev. GEORGE W. BLAGDEN. He was b. Nov., 1802, in Washington, D. C. ; grad. Yale Coll., 1823; at Andover Theolog. Sem., 1826 ; D. D. 1843 ; first pastor of the church in Brighton after its organization in 1827 ; pastor of the Salem Street Church, Boston, 1830-36; of the Old South Church, Boston, from his installation, Sept. 26, 1836, till his resignation, 1872, but continued pastor *emeritus* till his death; overseer of Harv. Coll., 1854-59 ; d. Dec. 17, 1884, in New York City, at the home of his son-in-law, Mr. E. C. Sampson, where he had been spending the last years of his life. Ch. :

    1. Anna *Blagden*, b. July, 1832; d.
    2. John P——— *Blagden*, b. Aug. 6, 1833; d. young.
    3. George *Blagden*, b. Apr., 1835.

---

* Susanna Rawson was eldest dau. of Rev. Grindal and Susanna (Wilson) Rawson, and this Susanna Wilson was a dau. of Rev. John Wilson of Medfield, and gr. dau. of Rev. John Wilson, first minister of Boston.— *Watertown Gen.*

4.　Edward R——— *Blagden*, b. Feb., 1837.
5.　Thomas *Blagden*, b. Oct., 1839.
6.　Samuel P——— *Blagden*, b. Oct., 1841.
7.　Sally P——— *Blagden*, b. Aug., 1843.
8.　Miriam P——— *Blagden*, b. Nov., 1845; d. 1849.

6.　JOHN CHARLES, b. Nov. 15, 1807; grad. Harv. Coll., 1826; Andover Theolog. Sem., 1832; ordained Dec. 18, 1833; pastor of First Church, Weymouth, 1833 to 1837, and pastor in Methuen from 1839 to 1860; afterwards resided in Boston till his death Nov. 5, 1878. He m. Dec. 24, 1833, HARRIET WELCH, dau. of Francis Welch of Boston. Ch.:

1.　Margaret W———, b. July 12, 1835.
2.　John Charles, b. Oct., 1838; grad. Harv. Coll., 1858; living, 1880.
3.　Emily Susan, b. June, 1842.
4.　Harriet W———, b. May, 1845; d. young.
5.　Miriam W———, b. May, 1849.
6.　Anna Dunn, b. Oct., 1850.
7.　Caroline Crowninshield, b. July, 1852.

7.　GEORGE WILLIAM, b. Jan. 3, 1810; grad. Harv. Coll., 1829; counsellor-at-law; of Boston. During the latter part of his life, his home, except during the winter months, was in Saugus, Mass., where he had a fine estate. He took an active interest in the welfare of the town, and was one of the leading citizens, as well as one of the wealthiest. He had been in Boston on the day of his death, but returned to his Saugus home and was at work in his hay-field when he fell and died almost instantly. This was July 30, 1880. He m. (1st) June 1, 1836, EMILY BLAGDEN, b. in Washington, D. C., sister of Rev. George W. Blagden. She d. Apr. 28, 1842, and he m. (2d) June, 1845, MARY ANN BLAGDEN, sister of his first wife. She d. Apr. 22, 1848, leaving no children. Ch. (by first marriage):

1.　Emily B———, b. Apr. 1, 1842; m. Charles A. Welch.

8.　WENDELL, b. Nov. 29, 1811; grad. Harv. Coll., 1831, and at

the Cambridge Law School, 1833; LL. B., 1834. He was gifted with intellectual talents and powers of eloquence which

might have made him the foremost jurist and greatest lawyer of his time, but he gave up all hope of popularity or personal emolument from the practice of law, and made it his exclusive life work to plead, on the public rostrum and at every favorable opportunity, the cause of the oppressed, of every nation, creed and color. Sympathy with the classes whose cause he advocated led him to give freely of his means to the poor and distressed. It is said that no really needy and deserving man or woman ever appealed to him in vain ; yet, his gifts were bestowed "so silently that no records remain on earth save in the hearts who love him." The following extracts give a very brief but clear portrayal of his life and character.

" Especially may the colored men rejoice that it pleased God to raise up in their behalf this inspired advocate of their inalienable rights, this terrible denunciator of their wrongs, this sincere sympathizer with their sufferings, this brave, true, stalwart friend. Their rights vindicated before the world, their wrongs wiped out, their sufferings soothed and healed, their race set free, enfranchised, educated, elevated, long will the colored race remember—how can they ever forget—their debt of gratitude to Wendell Phillips, to whom was due, as much as to any man on earth, this revolution in their lot. . . . . . . Not to the needs of his own country alone could Wendell Phillips limit his sympathy. The whole world had no wrong which did not set his soul on fire, to hate it always and abate it if he could. . . . . The terrible evils of intoxication led no man to be a stronger advocate of prohibition than Wendell Phillips. The rights and interests of the working classes found in him a devoted friend. . . . . His intense earnestness carried conviction home to his hearers, his tenderness touched their hearts with irresistible sympathy, his pathos moved them to tears, his vehemence carried them on with contagious fire, his commanding presence filled them with respect, his simplicity and directness and almost absence of manner left them in doubt whether art were perfect or wholly absent. . . . Gifted by nature with a voice of exquisite smoothness, sweetness, flexibility and grace, and yet of wonderful power when roused in some great cause, the whole man grew instinct with the fire and force of impassioned oratory ; and he swept his audience almost at his will, yet always without apparent effort, through the varying emotions which he sought to stir. . . . . . Strong faith and deep piety marked his walk through life. His fellow-citizens have always respected him for every domestic virtue, and for a grandly stoical simplicity of life. Full of the generous spirit of self-sacrifice, seeking no public honor, devoting his life and his great powers to the cause of the oppressed even to his own great loss, standing firm against any and all injustice like the rugged hills of his native State, volcanic in his outbursts of wrath against oppression, Wendell Phillips stands as the strongest type of the fearless, uncompromising intolerant New England reformer." *

" No one had probably addressed so many audiences or charmed so many ears and fired so many breasts by his wonderful eloquence. . . . His first appearance as an orator was at a meeting in Faneuil Hall in 1837, called to protest against the cruel murder of Elijah P. Lovejoy at Alton, Ill., for publishing an anti-slavery paper. . . . . . James T. Austin, attorney general, made an apologetic speech, condemning Lovejoy and almost justifying the mob for his murder. Then Wendell Phillips fired with a righteous indignation, mounted the platform amidst objections and efforts to suppress him, and poured forth a torrent of burning eloquence. This young lawyer, without experience and without a name in his profession, met and vanquished, routed and annihilated the official chief of the bar of Massachusetts. . . . . His eloquence was not of the grand style, majestic and imposing like that of Webster, with solemn periods and elaborate rhetoric. It was impetuous, swift and scathing, but with the beauty of a noble simplicity, a clear, trumpet-like voice, manner and gesture full of force and grace. Throughout his life his habits and manners were those of a patrician, kindly, neither arrogant nor obtrusively affable, but with a dignified reserve which commanded some measure of deference from all who came into contact with him. . . . . He was the greatest orator and agitator of his time, and as such he did a work so great, and so associated his name with a reform whose influence on the destinies of mankind cannot be overrated, that his failings may well be and doubtless will be forgotten, and his name will live in honor." †

---

* Report, accepted Feb. 6, 1884, of committee appointed by Massachusetts Legislature.

† *Massachusetts Spy*, Feb. 8, 1884.

Some of his most greatly admired lectures, such as "Lost Arts" and "Daniel O'Connell," it is said, were never written. The first of these was repeatedly delivered for thirty years without losing its freshness; and his efforts in preparing the other, which he did not expect would gain a reputation, consisted in getting together "material enough to enable him to talk an hour on the subject he had in hand."

He married, Oct. 12, 1837, ANN TERRY GREENE, dau. of Benjamin Greene of Boston. There is a little story told, on pretty good authority, concerning their marriage. She was to attend a convention in Albany and Mr. Sumner was expected to act as her escort; but he being unable to go, Mr. Phillips accepted the trust "and lost his heart to her before he got back." After several unsuccessful efforts to gain an interview, she being in feeble health, he at last succeeded, having "almost broke his way to her and offered her his hand. She said she would never marry a man unless he would swear eternal enmity to slavery; but it was not necessary for Mr. Phillips to take that oath — he had already sworn it in his heart. So they were married." To his wife, who was always an invalid, he was chivalrously devoted, regulating his entire life by affection and consideration for her, and his best acts he ascribed to her influence. He always resided in Boston with the exception of one year in Florence. He died Saturday evening, Feb. 2, 1884, at fifteen minutes past six, after a short but painful illness. Two days before his death, during a brief interval of rest, after an agony of pain, he said to his physician, "I have no fear of death; I am willing to die to-day as well as any time, but for my poor wife." About an hour before he breathed his last, on reviving from a fainting spell, he said, "I'm dying; I'm dying." He did not rally, but continued to sink slowly and passed away "as quietly as if he was just going to sleep." He left no children.

9.   GRENVILLE TUDOR, b. Aug. 14, 1816; grad. Harv. Coll., 1836; counsellor-at-law; of Boston; d. 1863.

No. 14.

(III.) **Rev. George Phillips** (son of Samuel and Sarah: No. 2,) born June 3, 1664; grad. Harv. Coll., 1686. He was the second permanently settled minister of Brookhaven,* L. I., where he commenced to preach in 1697, though he preached four years previously in Jamaica, L. I., and is said to have been one of the early ministers of Brookfield,† Mass. He continued his ministry in Brookhaven till his death in 1739, at the age of 75. " His character and qualifications were of a high order." "Mr. Phillips was distinguished for a peculiar vein of natural wit. His ordinary discourse was tinctured with this peculiarity and tradition has preserved many of his speeches that exemplify it." He married **Sarah Hallett,** born March 19, 1673, dau. of William and Sarah (Woolsey)‡ Hallett of Newtown, L. I.§ His descendants have been quite numerous, and scattered at an early date about Long Island and to other parts of New York State and to Connecticut and New Jersey. Children :

1. GEORGE, b. Apr. 1, 1698; of Smithtown, L. I.; d. Nov. 21, 1771. He m. Apr. 11, 1726, ELIZABETH MILLS, b. Aug. 16, 1705, d. Apr. 19, 1775. She was dau. of Timothy (b. 1667?), d. 1751, and Sarah Mills of Jamaica and Smithtown, gr. dau. of Jonathan (b. 1636?) and Martha Mills of Jamaica, gt. gr. dau. of George Mills of Jamaica, probably a clergyman, b. in Eng., 1585 and d. in Jamaica, Oct. 17, 1674. Ch. :
    1. Samuel, b. Oct. 26, 1728; d. June 3, 1806. He m. 1754, Sarah Mills. Ch. :
        1. Isaac Mills, b. June 18, 1760; m. Hetty Smith. Ch. :
            1. George S———.
    2. Sarah, b. Feb. 26, 1730.
    3. George, b. Jan. 16, 1732. Ch. :
        1. George.
        2. Michael.
        3. Deborah.

---

* One writer says he was not ordained till 1702, about which time this town voted him 100 acres of land *in fee,* and subsequently 200 acres more on condition of his serving them during his life.—*Hist. of Long Island,* 1845. *N. S. Prime.*

† Hist. and Gen. Register, Vol. 35, p. 339.

‡ Sarah Woolsey, dau. of George and Rebecca (Cornell ?) Woolsey of Jamaica, L. I. He was b. in Yarmouth, Eng., Oct. 27, 1610, embarked, 1623, with Dutch settlers to New Amsterdam, one of the early settlers of Jamaica, where he d. Aug. 17, 1698.—*Ancestral table of Jonas Phillips Phœnix.*

§ Capt William Hallett, who m. Sarah Woolsey, was b. 1647; justice of the peace; d. Aug. 18, 1729. He was son of William Hallett, b. in Dorsetshire, Eng., 1616, early settler in Greenwich, Conn., owned a large estate at Hallett's Cove, L. I., in 1652, removed to Flushing, in 1655, sheriff, 1656, justice of the peace; d. about 1706, at Hallett's Cove.—*Id.*

4. Jonas, b. in Smithtown, Mar. 12, 1735; of Morristown, N. J., where he d. Dec. 25, 1813. He m. 1764, Anna Lewis, b. 1746, d. Oct 25, 1765, dau. of Rev. Thomas* and Joanna (Booth) Lewis, and gr. dau. of David† and Anne (Mills)‡ Booth: Ch.

    1. Anna Lewis, b. in Morristown, Oct. 8, 1765; d. in same place Mar. 13, 1854. She m. Daniel Phœnix of same place, b. in New York, Oct. 14, 1761; d. in Morristown, Dec. 3, 1828. Ch. :

        1. Jonas Phillips *Phœnix*, of New York; m. Mary Whitney.
        2. Lewis *Phœnix*.
        3. John D——— *Phœnix*.
        4. Daniel A——— *Phœnix*.
        5. Elizabeth *Phœnix*. And three others, daus.

5. Elizabeth, b. Mar. 23, 1737.
6. Mary, b. Apr. 15, 1741.
7. Moses, b. Mar. 8, 1742–3; d. Sept. 9, 1818. He m. Jan. 22, 1768, Sarah Wisner; settled in Phillipsburg,·N. Y.§ Ch. :

    1. Gabriel Newton.

* Rev. Thomas Lewis, b. Aug. 6, 1716, grad. Yale Coll., 1741, Congregational clergyman; d. in Mendham, N. J., Aug. 20, 1777. He was son of Dea. Joseph Lewis of Waterbury, Conn., b. Mar. 15, 1677; d. Nov. 29, 1749, a man of large means, many years selectman, m. Apr. 7, 1703, Sarah Andrews, b. Mar. 16, 1684, d. Mar., 1773; gr. s. of Joseph and Elizabeth (Case) Lewis of Windsor and Simsbury, Conn., gt. gr. s. of John Lewis, who was of New London, 1648, and d. Dec. 8, 1676. Elizabeth Case who m. Jos. Lewis, was dau. of John Case, who was of New London, 1656, Windsor, 1657, of Simsbury from 1669 till he d., Feb. 21, 1704. He was representative from S. several years. He m. 1657, Sarah Spencer, b. 1636, d. Nov. 3, 1691, dau. of Wm. Spencer who was of Cambridge, 1631. Wm. Spencer was rep. 1634–8, Lieut. of Militia and one of the founders of the Ancient and Hon. Artil., removed to Hartford, March, 1639, rep. 1639–40; d. 1640.

† David Booth, b. 1698, d. 1773, was son of Joseph and Hannah (Wilcoxson) Booth of Stratford, Conn., and gr. son of Richard Booth, b. 1607, living 1689, who m. Elizabeth Hawley, sister of Joseph Hawley, who was first town clerk of Stratford.

‡ Anne Mills, who m. June, 1727, David Booth, was b. 1702, d. 1793, and was dau. of Peter and Joanna (Porter) Mills of Windsor, Conn., and gr. dau. of Peter Mills of Windsor, "a Hollander, his real name being probably Pieter Wouters Van der Melyn." He d. Apr. 17, 1710.

Joanna Porter, b. Feb. 7, 1671, m. July 21, 1692, Peter Mills, above, was dau. of John Porter of Windsor, b. June 3, 1651, gr. dau. of John Porter of Windsor, b. in England, d. Aug. 2, 1688, gt. gr. dau. of John and Rose Porter of Windsor, 1638, who were m. in England.—*Ancestral table of Jonas Phillips Phœnix.*

§ His gr. son, John Everston Phillips, Esq., b. in Phillipsburg, Mar. 20, 1805, fitted for college at Goshen Academy, Orange Co., grad. Williams Coll., 1825, studied law with Henry Wisner, Esq., of Goshen, was admitted to the bar, and established himself for a short time in his profession in Brookfield, Orange Co. He then returned to Goshen and entered into partnership with Mr. Wisner. He m. Mar. 1, 1832, Elizabeth S. Wisner, dau. of his partner, and d. Dec. 17, 1841, leaving a widow and three daus.—*Annals of Williams Coll.*, pp. 423, 424. *Rev. Calvin Durfee, D. D.*

    2. George.
    3. Henry Wisner.
    4. Moses.
    5. William.
    6. Sarah.
    7. Samuel.
    8. Elizabeth.

2. SAMUEL; d. young.
3. ELIZABETH.
4. DANIEL.
5. WILLIAM; m. SYBIL SMITH; settled in Smithtown, L. I., and d. Jan. 1, 1778. In his will, dated March 1, 1775, proved Jan. 10, 1778, he mentions his law books. She d. Oct. 31, 1767, aged 74.* Ch. :

    1. John, b. Sept. 3, 1737; d. in Milford, Conn., Mar. 12, 1780.
    2. William, b. May 27, 1741; d. in Brookhaven, Mar. 27, 1799. Ch. : 1. William.†
    3. Richard.
    4. Mary.
    5. Zebulon, b. Apr. 14, 1746; d. in Peekskill, N. Y., Jan. 13, 1815.
    6. James, b. Mar. 13, 1751; d. in Coventry, N. Y., Jan. 25, 1841.
    7. Ebenezer, b. July 15, 1753; m. Jan. 17, 1782. Mary Benedict of Norwalk, Conn., where he settled, and where he d. Aug. 5, 1829. Ch. :
        1. Esther, b. Mar. 5, 1787; d. Feb. 5, 1788.
        2. Esther, b. Apr. 17, 1788.
        3. Sally, b. Dec. 11, 1790.
        4. Elizabeth, b. July 9, 1798.
    8. Sarah, b. Oct. 24, 1756; d. in North Salem, N. Y., Feb. 12, 1827.
    9. Philetus, b. Nov. 24, 1759; d. in Greenville, N. Y., May 17, 1818. Ch. :
        1. Ebenezer; minister of East Hampton; d. 1830.
    10. Elizabeth, b. Nov. 9, 1762; d. in Brookhaven, Feb. 4, 1844.

6. JOHN, b. 1715; grad. Harv. Coll., 1735; taught school in several places, fitted for the ministry and preached, though he appears never to have been settled as a pastor; was appointed chaplain to Gen. Winslow's Brigade, and was present at the

---

* This age is evidently wrong, perhaps should be 54.
† There is a record of one William Phillips, who was of Brookhaven many years ago, and seems to have been one of the above, though the evidence is not quite conclusive. He had wife Mary and four sons, William, Josiah, Joseph and Moses, and four daus., Sarah, Mary, Hannah and Elizabeth. Moses m. —— Jessup, lived and d. at Quogue, L. I., had ten ch., Elijah, Benjamin, William, Hendrickson, Moses, Susan, Mary, Abigail, Elizabeth and Stephen. Elijah m. Jerusha Rogers, and had one ch., William R., who m. Betsey A. Rogers, and was living, 1878, at Speonk, L. I.

second siege and capture of Louisburg in 1758.* Gov. Shirley soon after appointed him Chaplain of *Castle William and Mary*, in Boston Harbor, which he held till appointed commander of the castle by Gov. Barnard. "In 1772, amid the difficulties between the colonies and the mother country, Major Phillips was removed from this command by Gov. Hutchinson; but he continued to receive pay until the commencement of hostilities in 1775." He d. Jan. 9, 1787. He m. Oct. 28, 1762, MARY WINTHROP, sister of Prof. John Winthrop, LL. D., F. R. S. of Harv. Coll., and dau. of Col. Adam and Anne Winthrop of Boston. She d. Nov. 15, 1794. Ch.:

   1. Mary. b. Sept. 23, 1763; m. Oct. 21, 1788, Dr. William Spooner of Boston. He d. 1836.

This concludes the list of descendants of Rev. Samuel Phillips of Rowley, 1651.

No. 15.

(II.) **Jonathan Phillips** (son of Rev. George and Elizabeth: No. 1,) born Nov. 16, 1633; a justice of the peace, of Watertown. "He appears to have lived on the homestead with his mother." He married, in his 47th year, Jan. 26, 1680–81, **Sarah Holland.** He died in 1704. Children:

1. SARAH, b. Sept. 14, 1682; d. Nov., 1688.
2. ELIZABETH, b. Nov. 27, 1684; m. Mar. 22, 1704–5, JOHN ORMES.
3. RUTH, b. Mar. 28, 1687; m. Aug. 12, 1717, EBENEZER HASTINGS.
4. SARAH; bap. Aug. 4, 1689; m. JOHN BARNARD.
5. ABIGAIL, b. Apr. 22, 1693; d. young.
6. JONATHAN; bap. June 20, 1697. (No. 16.)
7. HANNAH; bap. Apr. 23, 1699; m. Sept. 7, 1727, NATHANIEL DEWING. Ch.:
      1. Jemima *Dewing*, b. Apr. 18, 1728.
      2. Hannah *Dewing*, b. Oct. 19, 1731.
      3. Nathaniel *Dewing*, b. Dec. 18, 1739; m. 1763, Mary Collar of Needham.
8. GEORGE; bap. Feb. 23, 1700–1: Daniel Harrington of Watertown, guardian.

---

* "Oct. 1, 1755, Mr. Phillips preached all day." Diary of John Thomas, Surgeon, Winslow's Expedition to Acadia.—*Hist. and Gen. Reg.*, Vol. 33, p. 393.

9. NATHANIEL ; bap. May 2, 1703 : John Fiske, guardian.
10. BENJAMIN ; bap. Apr. 8, 1705 ; d. young.

No. 16.

(III.) **Jonathan Phillips** (son of Jonathan and Sarah : No. 15,) a carpenter ; removed from Watertown to Marblehead about 1719, and about 1740 to Newport, R. I., where he died. He married Feb. 27, 1716–17, **Hepzibah Parker,*** dau. of Stephen† and Susanna Parker of Watertown, and gr. dau. of Joseph Parker of Newbury. Children :

1. STEPHEN, b. July 18, 1718. (No. 17.)
2. —— ; m. Mr. —— Devereux of Marblehead, and had children.
3. ——, a dau. who went South.
4. RUTH, b. 1735 ; m. (1st) —— EDWARDS, and m. (2d) NICHOLAS TILLINGHAST.
5, &c. ; [?] Several other children.

No. 17.

(IV.) **Dea. Stephen Phillips** (son of Jonathan and Hepzibah : No. 16,) b. in Watertown, July 18, 1718 ; of Marblehead ; appointed deacon, 1765. " He was for many years a deacon of the Cong. Church, was at the head of the Committee of Safety, and an influential leader in the Revolution." He married **Elizabeth Elkins**. He died March 1, 1801, and she d. Sept. 30, 1803. Children :

1. MARY, b. Aug. 22, 1755 ; m. THOMAS MEEK, who d. in 1812. She d. Aug., 1844. No ch.
2. ELIZABETH, b. Nov. 28, 1757 ; m. JOB GRISTE. She d. 1835. No ch.
3. SARAH, b. Feb. 23, 1760 ; d. 1834 ; unm.
4. STEPHEN, b. Nov. 13, 1761. (No. 18.)
5. LYDIA, b. Jan. 17, 1767 ; d. Sept. 10, 1794 ; unm.

* Hepzibah Phillips was a member of the First Church, Marblehead, 1718.
† Stephen Parker d. in Watertown, May 2, 1718, aged 62 yrs. 2 ms., and his wife Susanna d. there, May 5, 1718, aged 58 yrs. 2 ms.

6. WILLIAM, b. Nov. 15, 1769 ; of Fredericksburg, Va., where he
   d. 1805. He m. 1799, ELIZABETH EMERSON. Ch. :
   1. Mary ; d. 1809.
   2. Elizabeth, b. June 1, 1805; m. (1st) June 1, 1821, Capt. ——
      Paull of Fredericksburg, who d. 1835. She m. (2d) May
      18, 1837, Robert Dickey of Fredericksburg. Ch. :
      1. Mary Ellen *Paull*, b. Dec. 26, 1822; d. May 6, 1830.
      2. Maria Elizabeth *Paull*, b. Aug. 9, 1828; d. March 6,
         1833.
      3. Annie Carter *Paull*, b. May 13, 1831.
      4. Ellison *Dickey*, b. Feb. 26, 1838; d. Dec. 7, 1839.
      5. John *Dickey*, b. Dec. 22, 1839.

No. 18

(V.) **Capt. Stephen Phillips** (son of Stephen and
Elizabeth : No. 17,) born Nov. 13, 1761 ; appears to have been
a sea-captain prior to his removal from Marblehead to Salem in
1800, and after that a merchant. He married (1st) in 1800,
Dorcas Woodbridge, born Apr. 1, 1774, dau. of Dudley
Woodbridge of Salem. She died June 15, 1803, and he married (2d) **Elizabeth Pierce,** born Mar. 1, 1774, dau. of
Nathan Pierce of Salem. He died Oct. 19, 1838, and his
widow survived him about twenty years. Children :

1. STEPHEN CLARENDON, b. in Salem, Nov. 4, 1801 ; grad. Harv.
   Coll., 1819 ; counsellor-at-law ; member of Congress from the
   Southern Essex District, 1834–38 ; second Mayor of Salem,
   1838–42 ; Free Soil Candidate for Governor, 1848 and 1849 ;
   perished in the flames at the burning of the steamer *Montreal*,
   on the St. Lawrence River, June 26, 1857. He m. (1st) JANE
   APPLETON PEELE, who died Dec., 1837; (2d) Sept. 3, 1838,
   MARGARET MASON PEELE, both daus. of Willard Peele, Esq.,
   of Salem. Ch. (by first marriage) :
   1. Stephen Henry, b. Aug. 16, 1823, grad. Harv. Coll., 1842; coun-
      sellor-at-law, the practice of which he commenced in Boston,
      but removed to Salem in 1849 ; editor of the *Law Reporter*,
      district attorney for several years.
   2. Willard Peele, b. Sept. 7, 1825 ; a merchant, res. in Salem ;
      living, 1878 ; m. May 22, 1850, Mary Hodges, dau. of Francis
      Boardman, Esq., of Salem. Ch. :
      1. Jane Appleton, b. Jan. 16, 1852 ; m. Oct. 24, 1877, G.
         H. Mifflin.

4

  2. Lawrence, b. Mar. 31, 1854; d. Feb. 10, 1865.
  3. Mary B——, b. Dec. 11, 1859.
  4. ——, twin brother; d. next day.
  5. Francis B——, b. Dec. 31, 1861; d. Aug. 17, 1864.
 3. George William, b. Nov. 27, 1827; grad. Harv. Coll., 1847; civil
  engineer; removed to Three Rivers, Canada; living, 1878;
  of New York City; unmarried.
 4. Elizabeth Griste, b. Apr. 10, 1831.
 5. Jane Peele, b. Feb. 24, 1833.
 6. Margaret Peele, b. June 30, 1835.
 7. Abbott Lawrence, b. Dec. 7, 1837.
 (By second marriage) :
 8. Walter Mason, b. May 26, 1839.
 9. Charles Appleton, b. Jan. 30, 1841; grad. Harv. Coll., 1860; a
  lawyer; enlisted and served through the war of the Rebellion; commanded the 5th Mass. Battery; d. March, 1877.
10. Edward Woodbridge, b. Aug. 3, 1842; enlisted in the war of
  the Rebellion, was fatally injured at Port Hudson, lingered
  for about three years and d. at home.
11. Catherine, b. July 7, 1844.

No. 19.

(II.) **Theophilus Phillips** (son of George and Elizabeth : No. 1,) born May 28, 1636; res. of Watertown, where
he married (1st) Nov. 3, 1666, **Berthia** ——, with last name,
it is said, difficult to tell on account of the illegibility of the old
hand-writing, but probably might be either Kedal, Bedell,
Kettell or Kendal. She died Mar. 15, 1668–9, and he married
(2d) Nov. 21, 1677, **Mary Bennet.** She, a widow, made
her will in Hopkinton, Dec. 3, 1730. Children (By first
marriage) :

1. BERTHIA, b. Dec. 21, 1668; d. young.
 (By second marriage) :
2. SAMUEL, b. Feb. 20, 1679–80; of Weston, Mass.; d. Nov. 9,
  1752. He m. Feb. 12, 1710–11, DEBORAH DIX. Ch. :
   1. Deborah, b. Dec. 15, 1711; m. May 30, 1737, Daniel Warren.
   2. Samuel, b. Sept. 14, 1713; m. July 25, 1735, Abigail Gale of
    Watertown. She was dismissed to Framingham, Mar. 5,
    1747–8. Ch. :
     1. Abigail, b. Mar. 7, 1736–7.
   3. Mary; bap. Sept. 23, 1716: d. young.

4. Lydia, b. June 27, 1719; m. Mar. 7, 1754, David Sherman of Sudbury.
5. Ebenezer, b. Feb. 19, 1721-2; of Weston; m. Apr., 1749, Mary Warren of Waltham, b. Aug. 11, 1729, dau. of Daniel and Mehitabel (Garfield) Warren. Ch. :
   1. Ruth, b. May 27, 1750.
   2. Mary, b. May 21, 1752; m. Aug. 5, 1773, Samuel Poole of Boston.
   3. Samuel, b. May 15, 1754.
   4. Eunice, b. Mar. 20, 1756.
   5. Ebenezer, b. Feb. 18, 1758.
3. BENJAMIN ; of Waltham ; m. MARY ——, and d. 1740, leaving no ch.
4. MARY, b. Sept. 16, 1684 ; d. June following.
5. MARY, b. Nov. 15, 1685 ; m. —— COOK, and was a widow, 1740.
6. THEOPHILUS, b. June 24, 1688 ; m. May 28, 1723, ALICE COOK, and settled in Hopkinton.*
7. JONATHAN ; bap. July 13, 1690.
8. JOHN, b. Dec. 10, 1692 ; m. Oct. 29, 1719, REBECCA LIVER-MORE. Ch. :
   1. John, b. Jan. 23, 1720-1.
   2. Rebecca, b. Nov. 8, 1722.
   3. Priscilla; bap. Nov. 26, 1724.
   4. Mary ; bap. June 4, 1726. "Soon after this he moved, probably first to Lancaster, where he belonged in 1731, afterwards to Worcester, where he d. July 20, and his widow Rebecca d. Dec. 29, 1780." †
9. ELIZABETH ; m. Nov. 7, 1716, BENJAMIN EDDY.
10. LYDIA, b. June 20, 1695 ; m. 1725, JONATHAN PRATT of Oxford ; d. leaving one ch., Kezia.
11. OBADIAH, b. Feb. 22, 1697-8 ; estate administered by his brother John, Jan. 23, 1726.
12. JOSEPH, b. Dec. 4, 1702 ; of Oxford. (No. 20.)
13. DAVID, b. Dec. 15, 1707 ; never married ; under guardianship of his brother Theophilus ; d. in Hopkinton, Nov., 1740.

---

* Theophilus and Elizabeth Phillips of Hopkinton had sons, Obadiah, b. Mar. 13, 1732, George, b. Aug. 27, 1734, Ebenezer, b. Oct. 16, 1739. It does not appear quite certain whether this Theophilus was the one mentioned above who came from Watertown, but it seems probable that he was.

† John Phillips d. Nov. 23, 1776, aged 56; his ch.: John d. Oct. 29, 1776, aged 5 yrs.; Samuel d. Nov. 2, 1776, aged 3 yrs.; Rebecca d. Oct. 29, 1776, aged 22 months. John Phillips d. Jan. 3, 1763, aged 76. Mrs Lydia Phillips d. May 31, 1760, aged 29. Rebecca Phillips d. Feb. 4, 1775, aged 53. Jotham Phillips d. Feb. 20, 1780, aged 44.—Gravestone inscriptions.—Marvin's History of Lancaster, p. 637.

OXFORD BRANCH OF THE WATERTOWN FAMILY.

No. 20.

(III.) **Joseph Phillips** (son of Theophilus and Mary:
No. 19,) born Dec. 4, 1702. He married **Ruth Towne,** and
settled in Oxford, Mass., locating, as nearly as can be ascertained, in the present limits of Auburn,* on Prospect Hill, an
elevation of beautiful and fertile table land, and one of the
pleasantest rural spots in Worcester County. The hill com-
mands an extensive and charming view of the surrounding
region, including in its range of vision, a pleasant succession of
mountain, hill and valley; also, the now flourishing city of
Worcester, and glimpses of several villages. He owned several
other tracts of land in Oxford and vicinity, but this, doubtless,
is the place on which he settled. The late Col. Edward Phillips
of Sturbridge, a great-grandson, had a fixed impression that
his grandfather, Dea. Jonathan Phillips, the oldest son of
Joseph, was born on Prospect Hill. Col. Phillips also regarded
this place as the old family homestead. After his death, this
farm was owned and occupied by his son, Israel Phillips, and
later, by Simon, son of Israel. At the time of Israel's death
the farm contained, by estimation, eighty acres, but was probably somewhat larger. At the death of Simon the ownership
of the farm passed out of the Phillips name, having been owned
in the family nearly ninety years. The house still standing is
said, by one who once lived there, to have been the same one
occupied by his gr.-son, Simon; and a little to the rear there
was remaining, a few years since, the foundation and cellar of
another building, supposed to be the original home. The house
is about one mile from the station of North Oxford Mills, on a
branch of the Boston and Albany R. R., and, to any of the
hundreds of his descendants who feel a special interest in the old
homestead of one of their early ancestors, a visit to the place on

---

* When Oxford was divided and Auburn set off, the line passed directly through
the farm, but leaving the buildings on the Auburn side.

a pleasant summer day might well repay the effort.   The farm is the same one lately owned and occupied by Wm. D. Dalrymple.

His wife died July 4, 1760.   He married (2d) Dec. 10, 1760, **Mrs. Bathsheba Towne** of Oxford.   He died April 23, 1771, "in the 69th year of his age."

It is impossible, at this day, to give anything like a personal description of him; but, from the fact that he left the vicinity of his father's home when a young man, and sought a home for himself, in what had been so recently an unbroken wilderness, where it required constant toil and hardship to secure the necessaries of life, we must conclude that he was a man of vigor, energy and perseverance; qualities which have been inherited in a large degree by a good number of his descendants.   His place of burial is not known.   In the old Auburn Cemetery, near the church, several of his descendants are known to have been buried, though not a monument has been erected in the yard by friend or relative, to mark the last resting-place of any of them.

The descendants have, in years past, usually been somewhat above the average size, not tending much to corpulence, but of large frame rather than fleshy, and with features rather heavily marked.   Most of them have had " a keen appreciation of wit and humor," and heartily enjoyed a sharp joke.   Not many of them have been graduates of colleges or entered the professions. The greater part have lived in farming communities, and more have followed farming than any other occupation.   A good number rendered efficient aid to their country during the war of the Rebellion; some of whom extended their service from their enlistment in the early days of the war to its close.   It is to be regretted that the materials are not at hand for more extended sketches of many worthy individuals of whom but brief mention is now made.   Many of them have been men of integrity, of exemplary lives, and of firm and honorable principles.   Children, all born in Oxford:

1.   JONATHAN, b. Aug. 12, 1732; of Sturbridge.   (No. 21.)
2.   JOSEPH, b. April 11, 1734; m. Nov. 11, 1756, LYDIA WILLSON of Oxford, b. March 30, 1735, daughter of John and Mary

Willson. Joseph Phillips was one of twenty-three who were enlisted from Oxford in an expedition against Crown Point in 1759. Ch. b. in Oxford:

1. Lydia, b. April 15, 1757; m. May 28, 1776, Thomas Pratt of Oxford.
2. John, b. Aug. 21, 1759; d. Jan. 11, 1767.
3. Joseph, b. Nov. 23, 1761. This brief record includes all that could be ascertained concerning him; and the same is true respecting the two following brothers.
4. Samuel, b. Oct. 4, 1764.
5. Deborah, b. April 25, 1767.
6. Rachel, b. April 8, 1770.
7. John, b. Nov. 15, 1772.

3. ISRAEL, b. Aug. 17, 1737. (No. 30.)

4. DANIEL, b. July 6, 1740; a farmer and blacksmith in Oxford. He appears to have united with the Baptist Church in Charlton, but probably continued his residence in Oxford. He m. 1763, RACHEL NICHOLS of Oxford, b. July 2, 1743, dau. of Alexander and Margaret Nichols. In his will, dated Dec. 1, 1786, he gave to his wife Rachel the use and improvement of one-half his real estate; to his son James, one-half his real estate including his blacksmith shop, all his blacksmith tools, half his farming tools, half his live stock, also gave him his silver watch, reserving the use of the same to his wife as long as she remains his widow. Will presented for Probate May 1, 1787. Inventory £591, 3s. 7d. Child:

1. James, b. in Oxford, April 25, 1764; m. Jan. 22, 1789, Tamma Tucker of Charlton.

5. RUTH, b. Oct. 17, 1744; m. in Charlton, April 28, 1763, EBENEZER LAMSON, b. in Concord, Mass., April 13, 1741, son of Timothy and Mary (Thompson) Lamson of Concord. He afterwards became a clergyman, and was first ordained over the Baptist Church in Ashford, Conn., in 1778, also resided for a time in Sutton, Mass. He d. July 4, 1832, at Mt. Washington, Mass. Children, all born in Charlton except the youngest:

1. Isaac *Lamson*, b. Feb. 17, 1764; m. (1st) 1784, Kasiah Sharpe; m. (2d) 1805, Deborah Brey; m. (3d) 1814, Waitstill Patterson. He went to Mount Washington, Mass., where he d. Jan. 24, 1844. Had fifteen children.

2. Mary *Lamson*, b. Sept. 2, 1765; m. 1780, Thomas Smith; went to Sutton where she d.   Had four children.

3. William *Lamson*, b. Aug. 21, 1767; m. 1793, Hannah Tucker of Charlton; lived in Oxford; d. in Thompson, Conn., July 21, 1824.   Had two children.

4. Ebenezer *Lamson*, b. April 27, 1769; d. June 9, 1769.

5. Ebenezer *Lamson*, b. Aug. 5, 1770; m. (1st) May 5, 1795, Huldah Gould; m. (2d) Aug. 28, 1802, Elizabeth Rich.   Lived in Charlton, where he d. July 20, 1853. Had eleven children.

6. Timothy *Lamson*, b. March 10, 1774; m. March 29, 1798, Betsey Boyce; lived in Thompson, Conn., where he d. March 4, 1814.   Had four children.

7. Ruth *Lamson*, b. Nov. 6, 1775; m. 1797, Samuel Davis, Jr. of Oxford, where she d. the same year.

8. Tirzah *Lamson*, b. March 9, 1778; m. 1797, Jonathan Sibley of Oxford, where she d. Feb. 20, 1869.

9. Horace *Lamson*, b. Aug. 24, 1782; m. Jan. 1, 1810, Anna Mann; lived in Orrington, Maine; d. in Canandaigua, N. Y., Aug. 1, 1821.   Had one child.

No. 21.

(IV.) **Dea. Jonathan Phillips** (son of Joseph and Ruth: No. 20,) was born Aug. 12, 1732; a farmer in Sturbridge, and deacon of the Baptist Church in that town.   He and his brothers, Joseph and Israel, were in a detachment of thirty-four soldiers that marched from Oxford, Aug. 18, 1758, for the relief of Fort William Henry, on the shore of Lake George.   He was the first settler in his immediate neighborhood, and his extensive farm, located at the head of Cedar Pond, two miles north of Sturbridge Centre, was owned and occupied by himself and his descendants for one hundred and twenty years.   Perhaps no place in America has been held as a homestead by any family of this name for a greater length of time unless possibly we except the Andover homestead.   The buildings stand in a very secluded place, nestled away on the westerly side of the valley, at a considerable distance from any traveled road; while a little farther up the valley, toward the north, stood the old saw-mill, where several generations took their turn at rolling in the logs, and patiently watched the "up-and-down" saw as it heavily and tediously jerked its way through. The house in which he lived was still standing when the place was last visited by the writer, in 1865, though not used as a dwelling-house. The family at that time occupied a neat and commodious brick residence, erected close by, by his grandson, Col. Edward Phillips, which, though unfavorably situated for attracting attention and scarcely to be seen from the main road, is well worthy of a commanding situation. He married, Oct. 4, 1753, **Rachel Humphrey**, daughter of Dea. —— Humphrey of Oxford. He died in Sturbridge, June 25, 1798. Children, all born in Sturbridge :

1. MARY, b. May 24, 1754; m. DAVID CURTIS of Sturbridge (now Southbridge), where she d. Oct. 26 1796.* Ch. :

    1. Jonathan *Curtis*. Ch. :
        1. Jonathan Perry *Curtis;* d. in Westboro, Mass.
        2. William *Curtis;* physician; living, 1885, in Westboro.
    2. Daniel *Curtis*.
    3. Sylvanus *Curtis;* physician; settled and d. in Maine.
    4. Hannah *Curtis*.
    5. Theodora *Curtis*.
    6. Barlow *Curtis*.

2. EBENEZER HUMPHREY, b. July 17, 1756; of Charlton. (No. 22.)
3. RACHEL, b. June 25, 1758; m. 1784, ISAAC LARNED; d. Nov. 17, 1795 (one record says 1799.)
4. JOHN, b. June 29, 1760. (No. 24.)
5. JONATHAN, b. March 30, 1762; d. Sept. 8, 1767.
6. HANNAH, b. March 3, 1764; d. Sept. 1, 1767.
7. LOIS, b. Feb. 17, 1766; m. (1st) in 1794, JONATHAN PERRY. After his death she m. (2d) ASA GREENE; lived for some time at the West and d. June 15, 1830, at Bridgewater, Vt. No ch.
8. JONATHAN, b. March 30, 1768; a physician; m., and settled in St. Armand, Canada, where he d. June 20, 1831. His only son d. when a young man. He had several daughters, one of whom m. —— Clough, and lived at Winooski Falls, Vt.
9. DANIEL, b. March 15, 1771; d. June 26, 1775.

---

* One record says Oct. 26, 1790.

10. HANNAH, b. July 1, 1773 ; m. April 22, 1798, PHINEAS JONES of
Spencer, Mass., a soldier in the Revolutionary War, son of
Dea. Nathaniel* and Eleanor Jones of Charlton. She d. in
Spencer, Feb. 14, 1841. Ch. :

    1. Silas *Jones*, b. Jan. 17, 1799 ; d. in New York, April 25,
1867.

    2. Jonathan Phillips *Jones*, b. Oct. 10, 1800 ; d. young.

    3. Lucy *Jones*, b. Dec. 22, 1802 ; d. Sept. 23, 1804.

    4. Lucy Baldwin *Jones*, b. March 24, 1805 ; d. Sept. 8,
1813.

    5. Eleanor *Jones*, b. July 6, 1807 ; d. Feb. 9, 1830.

    6. Lois Ann *Jones*, b. Jan. 16, 1810 ; after leaving the
common school she was a student for some time at
Leicester Academy, after which she was employed in
teaching school. She was possessed of a strong
intellect and very retentive memory, was a woman of
rare intelligence and decided views, was well informed on subjects of general interest upon which
she was always able to converse freely. She m. Mar.
29, 1843, Rev. David Metcalf. He was author of a
catechism and a work on moral obligation. He d.
Sept. 25, 1884. She d. at her residence in Auburn,
Feb. 23, 1885.

    8. Maria *Jones*, b. Apr. 21, 1816 ; d. Aug. 29, 1834.

    9. Phineas *Jones*, b. Apr. 18, 1819. He commenced his
business career in his native town of Spencer as a
merchant and auctioneer. Being endowed with rare
business talents, and having high aspirations, he
sought a wider field for his labors, and in 1855 removed to Elizabeth, N. J., where he established a
wheel factory. While in that city he was elected a
member of the Common Council. Five years later,
in 1860, he removed to Newark, where after a time
he added to his already very extensive business, the
sale of carriages and sleighs. He was director of
the People's Ins. Co., trustee of the Evergreen
Cemetery Association, a prominent member of the
N. J. Agricultural Society, one of the founders, and
first president, of the Gentlemen's Driving Club. He
was one of the original members of the Board of
Trade, of which he was several times offered the presidency. He was a member of the State Legislature
from Newark, and in 1880 was elected member of
Congress. He served the full term with a high degree
of satisfaction to his constituents, but while residing

* Dea. Nathaniel Jones was b. near Boston ; removed to Worcester and afterwards
to Charlton ; son of Nathaniel Jones.

in Washington, contracted ill health from which he never recovered. In the summer of 1883 he visited New England and Richfield Springs for the benefit of his health, but the trip failed to bring the needed relief. He d. at his home in Newark, Apr. 19, 1884, leaving a wife and six children. He m. (1st) Emeline, dau. of Austin Lamb. After her death he m. (2d) Harriet L. Whittemore who d., and he m. (3d) Laura Hamlett of Manchester, N. H. Of the children there is one son by the first marriage, one son by the second, and four children by the last.

"Mr. Jones was a man of genial manners, and won the respect and confidence of a large circle of friends. In business his integrity was above reproach, and in private and social circles he was characterized by qualities which always command esteem. While in Congress he possessed the regard of his associates to a marked extent."

No. 22.

(V.) Dr. Ebenezer Humphrey Phillips (son of

Jonathan and Rachel: No. 21,) born July 17, 1756; studied medicine with Dr. Thomas Babbitt of Sturbridge, and settled in Charlton. He was regarded as a very skilful physician, and his services were often deemed requisite in the neighboring towns. At the age of fifty he was stricken with a shock of palsy which so paralyzed him that he was unable to walk, or to talk so as to be understood for about two years. On the return of health, he found his memory was so impaired that it was impossible for him to pursue his favorite calling. Being anxious to resume practice, he commenced reading medicine again. After reading for some time, the recollection of it flashed upon his mind; he remembered that he had read it all before, and afterwards was able to attend to the wants of the sick, most of the time, till the very close of his life. He bore arms in the service of his country during the Revolutionary War, and for

E. M. Phillips

some years received a pension. He was influential in forming
a lodge of Masons in Charlton in 1799. In 1806 the Grand
Master of Masons appointed him Deputy Grand Master for
the 6th district, with task assigned to visit the several lodges
in the district from time to time and report their condition to
the Grand Lodge. He held the office of town clerk from 1801
till 1807. He married (1st) 1780, **Ruth Morgan** of Brimfield. She died April 10, 1817, in her 64th year. He married
(2d) **Mrs. Ruth (Towne) Wheelock,*** daughter of Gen.
Salem Towne, Sr. His death, which was caused by another
paralytic shock, took place in Charlton, Dec. 1, 1837. Children, born in Charlton:

1. RUTH, b. Jan. 1, 1788; m. 1808, Dr. P. F. Groves, who was
   surgeon in the army of 1812, and d. in 1814. She d. in 1819.
   Child:

   1. Harriet Morgan *Groves;* d. in 1821.

2. EBENEZER MORGAN, b. Feb. 19, 1792; of Westboro. (No. 23.)

3. HARRIET, b. Nov. 2, 1795;† m. Col. JASON WATERS of Sutton.
   Both died in Philadelphia, leaving two sons and two daughters,
   living there Dec., 1877.

No. 23.

(VI.) **Ebenezer Morgan Phillips** (son of Ebenezer

E. M. Phillips

H. and Ruth: No. 22,) b. Feb. 19, 1792. He was for some
years in early life a clerk in the dry goods business in Boston
and Philadelphia. In 1817 he established himself in Sutton,
Mass., remained there a few years, then removed to Westboro,
Mass., where he resided till his death, continuing in the same
business for a time, and about 1844 became station agent for

---

* Elizabeth Ruth Wheelock, granddaughter of Mrs. Ruth (Wheelock) Phillips, by
first marriage, m. Rev. Daniel Phillips, Congregational clergyman of Chelmsford,
Mass.

† Town record says Nov. 1, 1796.

the Boston & Worcester R. R., which position he held nearly thirty years, resigning it when eighty-one years of age. He possessed considerable musical talent, and was for many years leader of the church choir. He commenced his public singing in Charlton Church, when nine years old, sustaining his part, the alto, alone ; and was connected with a choir nearly all the time for fifty years, until his voice failed from disease in the throat. He was ever a man of few words, but was always a lover and promoter of good morals, and was one of the original founders of the Evangelical Cong. Church and Parish in Westboro, and that, "at a time when most bitter opposition served to root more deeply the principle that led to outward action."

Up to the age of eighty-seven, he was able to superintend his farm, and to work many hours each day in his garden among the flowers, which had ever been his delight. The portrait prepared for this work was from a photograph taken when he was eighty years old. He married Oct. 12, 1818, **Ann Maria Brigham,** born July 14, 1794, daughter of Hon. Elijah and Sarah (Ward) Brigham, and granddaughter of Gen. Artemas Ward. He was one who always made his home happy, and their married life included sixty-one and one-half years. He passed away at half-past one on the morning of May 1, 1880, and she on the 14th of Dec. following. Children :

1. ELIJAH BRIGHAM, b. in Sutton, Aug, 20, 1819. Beginning in

1839, his life thus far has been almost wholly occupied with the management of railroads, and he has held high official connection with no less than eight different railroad corporations, some of them among the most important in the United States.

" He commenced his service as railroad employé at a period when railroads were in their infancy, and has risen in regular order up to his present important rank as president of one of the oldest and most influential railroad corporations in the State. Following his railroad history, it will be seen that in point of date of service he ranks every other railroad superintendent and president in the country. His first service was as clerk in the employ of the Boston and Worcester Railroad Corporation, in October, 1839. In June, 1843, he was advanced to the position of master of transportation, then, as now, an important post, as the increase of freight on our Massachusetts railroads demanded a separate department from that of general superintendent, and the Boston and Worcester Railroad direction was the first to recognize this. As master of transportation he remained until September, 1852, when he was elected, over all others, to the superintendency of the Cleveland and Toledo Railroad, then one of the most advanced railroads of the west; and here it may be pertinent to remark that in the early history of western railroads, the management almost invariably selected for the principal offices those who had been trained on the Boston and Worcester Railroad. This office Mr. Phillips filled satisfactorily till September, 1858, when a change took place in the Boston and Worcester Railroad, and he was requested to return to take the superintendency of that road. This office he held till October, 1865, when the west made another demand, and he was elected president of the Southern Michigan and Northern Indiana Railroad Corporation, the stock being largely held by New England parties. In October, 1870, the Wisconsin Central Railroad started up one of the most important trunk lines of the northwest, and Mr. Phillips was solicited to take charge of its interests, both in construction and in its operation—a trust which he executed with eminent ability as well as satisfaction to his board of directors. In July, 1878, he retired, after arduous service, to obtain needed rest; but he was destined to remain idle but a short time. The Eastern Railroad complication at this time had reached a crisis; a competent president was demanded, and in 1879 Mr. Phillips was the one selected. His record and his services as president of that corporation began a new era in the history of that road. His labors were brilliant and unremitting, and gave him a reputation which could not be disputed, at least, for executive ability and fair independence. Leaving that road, he took the presidency of the narrow gauge road in Missouri, of which he is still president. In November, 1883, after the death of William B. Stearns, president of the Fitchburg Railroad Corporation, the directors cast about for a new president, and, out of a large number to select from, they decided to take Mr. Phillips. He has peculiar qualifications for the office, as he is familiar with all the details of railroad operation and management, and is certainly giving character to this corporation, which is one of the most important in the State." * While at the West he resided in Cleveland, Ohio, Milwaukee, Wis., and Chicago, Ill. Present res. Boston, Mass. He m. Feb. 2, 1845, MARIA REBECCA AYLING of Boston. Children:

1. Henry Ayling, b. in Boston, Aug. 19, 1852; grad. S. B. at the Mass. Institute of Technology, class of 1873; visited Europe in the summer of 1875; architect, 1884, in Boston.
2. Anna Maria, b. in Cleveland, Ohio, Dec. 21, 1856.
3. Walter Brigham, b. in Boston, Mass., April 2, 1864; member of the class of '86, Harvard College.

2. HARRIET MARIA, b. in Westboro, Aug. 8, 1824; m. EDWARD WARREN CLARK, b. in Tewksbury, Mass., son of Oliver Clark. He grad. at Dartmouth College, 1844, and at Andover Theological Seminary, 1847; was ordained to the gospel ministry, Jan. 1, 1850, and at the same time was installed as pastor of the Bethesda Church, Reading, Mass. Subsequently he was settled as pastor in Auburndale, Mass., and at Claremont, N. H.; was for two years chaplain of the Mass. Senate, which office he left to take the chaplaincy of the 47th Mass. Reg. stationed at New Orleans in 1863. Ill health has for many years laid him aside from active service; present residence, Westboro.

Francis Edward Symmes, adopted son, b. in Aylmer, Canada, Sept. 12, 1851, son of Charles C. and Lydia (Clark) Symmes. After the death of his last surviving parent, he was legally adopted and took the name of Frank Edward *Clark*. He grad. at Dartmouth College in 1873, at Andover Theological Sem. in 1876, was ordained and installed pastor of the Williston Church, Portland, Me., Oct. 18, 1876, where he remained until called to the pastorate of Phillips Church, South Boston, where

* *Worcester Spy*, Dec. 9, 1884.

he was installed Oct 16, 1883. He m. Oct 3, 1876, Miss
Hattie E. Abbott of Andover, Mass. Ch. :

> 1. Maude Williston *Clark*, b. in Portland, Maine, Nov. 16, 1877.
> 2. Eugene Francis *Clark*, b. in Portland, Aug. 10, 1879.
> 3. Faith Phillips *Clark*, b. in So. Boston, Nov. 5, 1883, and d. Dec. 13, following.

No. 24.

(V.) **Dea. John Phillips** (son of Jonathan and Rachel :

No. 21,) born June 29, 1760 ; a farmer in Sturbridge ; served
for a time in the American army during the Revolutionary War.
He was deacon of the Baptist Church in Sturbridge for sixty-
four years, represented the town in the Legislature twice,—in
1815 and 1816, and for a considerable time held a commission
as justice of the peace, and his papers contain the records of
twelve or fifteen couples whom he united in marriage. He
married, May 25,* 1785, **Love Perry**, born June 3, 1767,
daughter of Jonathan and Martha Perry of Sturbridge, with
whom he lived sixty-four years, she dying Aug. 8, 1849, at the
age of eighty-two. He lived on the homestead farm, with the
exception of very brief intervals, the whole of his long life,
where he died Feb. 25, 1865, at the extreme age of 104 years
and eight months.

He voted for George Washington at the first presidential
election held in the United States, and for Abraham Lincoln at
the election in Nov., 1864, when 104 years of age, and with one
exception (1860,) at every intermediate presidential election.
Shortly after voting the last time, he received from President
Lincoln the following complimentary letter :

" EXECUTIVE MANSION, WASHINGTON,

Nov. 21, 1864.

" MY DEAR SIR :

" I have heard of the incident at the polls in your town, in which

---

* Town record says May 19.

you bore so honored a part, and I take the liberty of writing to you to express my personal gratitude for the compliment paid me by the suffrage of a citizen so venerable.

" The example of such devotion to civic duties in one whose days have already extended an average life-time beyond the Psalmist's limit, cannot but be valuable and fruitful. It is not for myself only, but for the country which you have in your sphere served so long and so well, that I thank you.

Your friend and servant,

A. LINCOLN."

On the 29th of June, 1860, a large number of his friends and relatives gathered at the Baptist Church in Fiskdale, about four miles from his residence, to celebrate the 100th anniversary of his birth. As a part of the exercises he offered a prayer and made the following address :

" My friends, I give you thanks for this opportunity of seeing so many of you present, and for the attention bestowed upon me ; but I feel unworthy to receive it. As I have been requested to offer prayer on this occasion, I will first make a few remarks. For seventy-five years I have been a professor of religion, and I have endeavored to adorn my profession. I am now an old child—broken down—100 years for you to look upon. I feel that I am a child in knowledge and in everything else. My creed consists of four particular points ; —1st, the goodness of God ; 2d, the divinity of our Saviour ; 3d, the power and reality of revealed religion ; 4th, the depravity of man. Here I stand, a monument of God's goodness."

When about fifty years of age, anticipating the decline of life, he wrote a letter to his oldest son, who was away from home engaged in teaching, requesting the son so to arrange his plans as to come home soon and remain, in order to take care of him in his old age. The son obediently complied with the father's request ; but, after the lapse of upwards of fifty additional years, and while the father was still living, the son jocosely intimated to the compiler of this record, with the usual pleasant twinkle of his eye, that he regarded the arrangement as somewhat premature, and more especially in view of the fact that he hardly needed the strong arm of his son to sustain him till near the close of his protracted life, having retained his native vigor till it seemed uncertain which of the two would be likely first to require an arm of support in their declining years.

He was well formed, strong and vigorous. In his prime, his height was six feet, and, after sixteen years of age, his weight was always about two hundred pounds. At the age of eighty, after having used glasses for thirty years, he was able to leave them off and read without them till within a few years of his death. When in his 100th year he was summoned to Worcester as a witness at court, and was able to recognize his signature and give his evidence with clearness and distinctness. Next to a strong and enduring constitution, his long and even life is attributable to his habits of strict temperance. "His manner of living was always plain and frugal, laboring hard as a farmer, but not to excess, and not to late hours, usually retiring early and rising early. He was temperate in eating, drinking, sleeping, working and in all things."

Children, all born in Sturbridge :

1. EDWARD, b. April 29, 1786. (No. 25.)
2. JOHN, b. Jan. 25,* 1788 ; of Spencer. (No. 26.)
3. HERVEY, b. May 14, 1790; of Wisconsin. (No. 27.)
4. JONATHAN PERRY, b. Sept. 9, 1792 ; of Lake Mills, Wisconsin. (No. 28.)
5. DANIEL, b. Aug. 30, 1795; died Jan. 30, 1796.
6. ELDRIDGE, b. May 24, 1797 ; of Monson. (No. 29.)
7. MARY, b. June 27, 1799 ; d. May 18, 1803.
8. LAURINDA, b. Nov. 18, 1806 ; m. March 31, 1830, EDWARD RICHARDSON, son of Alpheus Richardson, a native of Sturbridge, but resident of Woodstock, Conn. They moved from Sturbridge to Wisconsin in 1858, and now reside (1879) in Ableman, Sauk Co., that State. Ch. :

    1. Sidney Edwards *Richardson*, b. Jan. 8, 1832; grad. at Rochester University in 1853, taught in a Government school of the Cherokee Nation during the two years following ; graduated at Rochester Theological Seminary in 1857, and was settled in the ministry for a few years; but when the Rebellion broke out he joined the Union Army, and was to have been

* Town record says Jan. 21, but the above as kept in the old family record is probably correct.

made Chaplain of an Illinois regiment, but was killed in the battle of Fort Donaldson, Feb. 15, 1862.

2. Harriet *Richardson*, b. Sept. 6, 1833; m. Dec. 28, 1854, Albert Prouty. Present residence, Brimfield, Mass. Ch. :
    1. Charles Albert *Prouty*, b. April 8, 1857.
    2. Mabel Sherman *Prouty*, b. March 15, 1863.
    3. Edward Nathan *Prouty*, b. April, 1868.

3. Adeline *Richardson*, b. April 22, 1837. She and her sister, Ellen J., graduated at the Westfield, Mass., Normal School, and afterwards taught in the district schools of Wisconsin, where they were considered most excellent and able teachers. She m. Nov. 29, 1866, Simeon L. Wells. Present residence, Mauston, Juneau Co., Wisconsin. Ch. :
    1. Dora Laurinda *Wells*, b. Oct. 9, 1867.
    2. Nellie Adeline *Wells*, b. April 9, 1869.
    3. Anna Louisa *Wells*, b. Sept. 21, 1870.
    4. Lucius Stafford *Wells*, b. May 3, 1873.

4. Ellen Jones *Richardson*, b. Sept. 23, 1841 ; m. Feb. 3, 1868, Hosea T. Stockwell; present residence, New Philadelphia, Ohio. Ch. :
    1. Maria Ellen *Stockwell*, b. Aug. 29, 1875.
    2. Julia Jones *Stockwell*, b. July 10, 1878.

5. Edward Phillips *Richardson*, b. Oct. 19, 1847; m. Aug. 29, 1876, Addie J. Pierce. Present residence, Ableman, Sauk Co., Wisconsin. Ch. :
    1. Sidney Ernest *Richardson*, b. Oct. 23, 1878.

9. ADELINE, b. July 3, 1812; m. in 1839, LEWIS W. MARSH, son of Moses Marsh of Sturbridge. He was b. March 17, 1812, on the place still occupied (1878) by his only surviving brother, Simeon F. Marsh, and d. July 17, 1873. She resides at Chicopee Falls, Mass. No ch. :

No. 25.

(VI.) Col. Edward Phillips (son of John and Love : No. 24,) born April 29, 1786 ; for many years one of the most prominent and useful men of his town, being widely known and highly respected, and was continually honored by being called to fill the various town offices,—moderator, selectman, assessor, school committee, and all the minor offices, and was often placed on important committees. In his early life he was employed considerably in teaching school. He was elected three times to represent the town in the State Legislature, held a commission as justice of the peace for about thirty years, and that of coroner as long or longer, and was colonel of the home militia.   When Southbridge petitioned the Legislature for a part of the territory of Sturbridge, which they tried twice, he was sent both times as agent of the town to aid their representative in opposing the petition.   He was elected, in 1832, one of a committee of four,[*] to effect a design for the Worcester Manual Labor High School, an institution out of which grew the present Worcester Academy, and was afterwards one of its trustees.   He was a person of large frame, in his prime upwards of six feet in height, naturally very erect and of dignified bearing ; but he fell, while repairing his house, in 1855, a distance of some fourteen feet and struck on his head, producing an injury of the spine from which he never recovered.   After this he was never able to carry his head erect, and it doubtless had the effect of shortening his life by some years.   He had large clear black eyes and heavy features, but a pleasant countenance.   He was, like other members of the family, inclined to jocularity, was agreeable and courteous in his manners and entertaining in his conversation.

He married April 7, 1812, **Mary Newell**[†] of Sturbridge, born Feb. 14, 1787.   She died Jan. 28, 1866.   He died Dec. 3, 1869, at the homestead previously occupied by his father and grandfather.   Children, all born in Sturbridge :

1. CAROLINE, b. April 14, 1813 ; m. in Sturbridge, May 2, 1838, ABIJAH SMITH LYON, son of Dea. Jonathan Lyon.   He was b. in Woodstock, Conn., April 2, 1805 ; grad. at Brown Univer-

---

[*] This committee consisted of Isaac Davis and Otis Corbett of Worcester, Edward Phillips of Sturbridge, and Otis Converse of Grafton. The details of the plan were wisely left to their discretion, under the general direction that the instruction should be of the first order; that strict moral and religious character should be attained; and that every facility should be afforded for productive labor, to the end that education should be good but not expensive.—Hist. of Worcester. Wm. Lincoln : p. 308.

[†] Mary Newell appears to have been a descendant of Abraham Newell, b. in England, 1584. He and his wife Frances came to America, 1634, landed with six children, one b. on the passage, and settled in Roxbury. Isaac,[1] son of Abraham, m. Eliza Curtis, Dec 14, 1658; d. 1707. Isaac[2] had wife Sarah and seven children. Isaac,[3] b. Feb. 1, 1687-8; m. Dec. 14, 1715, went to Sturbridge.—Newell Gen. J. K. Newell.

Isaac,[3] above, went to Sturbridge, 1737, was the second town clerk and one of the selectmen the same year. Isaac,[4] b. Jan. 1, 1718; m. Ruth Duin about 1746; d. 1790. She was b. 1725; d. 1770. Stephen,[5] b. June 29, 1760; m. Thankful Smith; d. Apr. 11, 1747. She d. Nov. 11, 1811. Their dau. Mary, m. Edward Phillips.

sity in 1837, became pastor of the Baptist Church at North
Oxford; but they afterwards removed to Newport, Minn.,
where she d. July 21, 1871, and he, Sept. 13, the same year.

Ch. :

    1. Edward Phillips *Lyon*, b. Jan. 21, 1840; present residence,
       Newport, Minn.
    2. Mary Annah *Lyon*, b. Dec. 3, 1841; m. Feb. 14, 1867, Rev. Elias
       H. Johnson, now settled in Providence, R. I.
    3. Albert Jonathan *Lyon*, b. July 11, 1848; graduated at the Uni-
       versity of Rochester, in 1871, and followed teaching in
       Minnesota immediately after graduation; graduated at the
       Rochester Theological Seminary in May, 1877, and Sept. 20,
       following, was ordained as Baptist minister and foreign
       missionary. He m. at Northville, Mich., Sept. 5, 1877, Miss
       Lida A. Scott. After his ordination, they sailed for Burmah,
       and immediately after their arrival there, he was taken sick,
       and d. at Bhamo, which was to have been the seat of his
       missionary operations, March 15, 1878.

2. HARRIET NEWELL, b. April 27, 1815; m. Nov. 26, 1840,
EPHRAIM MOULTON; d. April 27, 1848. Child :

    1. Harriet Louisa *Moulton*, b. Nov. 10, 1847; m. Charles Barry
       of Melrose, where they reside. Ch. :
       1. Charles Gardner *Barry*, b. Aug., 1877.

3. MARY ANN, b. Oct. 23, 1817; married May 19, 1839, WILLIAM
H. RICE of Sturbridge. He died Oct. 31, 1875. She was
living 1885. Ch. :

    1. Ella Antoinette *Rice*, b. Aug. 28, 1844; m. Joaquin M. Delgado,
       a native of Cuba, and now a resident of the city of St.
       Domingo, on the island of that name. He is a large sugar
       planter, and started the first plantation in St. Domingo. Ch. :
       1. Marina E—— *Delgado*, b. May 21, 1875.
       2. Joaquin M—— *Delgado*, b. Sept., 1877; d. young.
       3. Phillips Mario *Delgado*, b. Apr. 1, 1880.
    2. Arthur William *Rice*, b. July 14, 1846; m. Flora E. Holt of
       Bridgewater, Vt.; present residence, Stoneham, Mass.
    3. Louis Phillips *Rice*, b. April 26, 1849; m. Nellie A. Perry of
       Sturbridge, where they reside. Ch. :
       1. Mary A—— *Rice*, b. Aug. 6, 1876.
    4. Edwin Addison *Rice*, b. Nov. 7, 1852; present residence,
       Sturbridge; m. Ella Boucher of Pittsfield.

4. MARIA LOUISA, b. Nov. 22, 1820; m. Nov. 25, 1841, JABEZ H.
WESTGATE. For a considerable time previous to the death of
her parents, they resided with them at the homestead in Stur-

bridge ; but since their decease they have removed to Malden, Mass., where they continue to reside, 1885.   No children.

5. EDWARD HARRISON, b. Jan. 22, 1824 ; d. in Sacramento, Cal., Nov. 11, 1850.

6. EDWIN ADDISON, b. Feb. 20, 1827 ; m. Jan. 23, 1862, NELLIE DOUGLAS of Milwaukee, Wis.   She d. Jan. 18, 1863, aged 25 years. He d. in Pensacola, Fla., March 1, 1870. Child :

> 1. Percy Douglas, b. Oct. 20, 1862; d. young.

No. 26.

(VI.) **John Phillips** (son of John and Love : No. 24,) born Jan. 25, 1788 ; a millwright and wheelwright in Spencer, Mass. He married (1st) **Catherine Lamb** of Brookfield, Mass., daughter of Oliver Lamb. She died April 25, 1835. He married (2d) **Mrs. Madelia (Gilmore) Pickett** of Conn. He died in Spencer, Jan. 31, 1875. Children, all born in Spencer (by first marriage) :

1. DANIEL, b. May 10, 1813 ; d. June 4, 1838.

2. MARY, b. Dec. 11, 1816 ; d. May 24, 1837.

3. CHARLOTTE, b. Aug. 29,* 1818 ; m. in Leicester, Mass., May 25, 1842, JONAS L. WARREN ; d. May 12, 1869. Ch. :

> 1. Jennie *Warren*, b. April 1, 1843 ; m. January 8, 1862, Marshall Fuller of Leicester. She d. Nov. 17, 1866. Ch. :
>
>> 1. Arthur W. *Fuller*, b. Oct. 4, 1864.
>> 2. Geo. H. *Fuller*, b. June 20, 1866.
>
> 2. Mary C. *Warren*, b. Aug. 31, 1845 ; m. in Leicester, Jan. 18, 1866, William Graham. Child :
>
>> 1. Jennie W. *Graham*, b. in Leicester, May 20, 1871.
>
> 3. Aamasa *Warren*, b. Oct. 3, 1847 ; m. in Upton, Mass., Aug. 4, 1870, Emma Peaslee. Lived in Springfield. Child :
>
>> 1. Charles F. *Warren*, b. Feb., 1876.
>
> 4. Charles W. *Warren*, b. July 16, 1850 ; d. Oct. 25, 1871.

4. BETSEY ANN, b. Aug. 28, 1820 ; d. in Charlton, Oct., 1845.

5. REBECCA, b. April 26, 1823 ; d. Dec. 6, 1825.

6. ALFRED LORENZO, b. Dec. 16, 1827 ; m. SARAH McDUFFEE. Residence, Spencer. Ch. :

> 1. Celia Fanny, b. June 17, 1861 ; d. Sept. 11, 1863.
> 2. George Clark, b. July 20, 1863.
> 3. Etta Maud, b. Nov. 26, 1868.

---

* Town record says 28th.

7. THEODORE, b. Feb. 16, 1831 ; d. July 15, 1836.

(By second marriage) :

8. GEORGE PERRY, b. Dec. 14, 1841 ; enlisted July 19, 1862, in the war of the Rebellion ; wounded Sept. 19, 1864 ; discharged April 19, 1865. He was adopted by Baxter Clark, and his name was changed Sept. 2, 1862, to GEORGE PERRY CLARK. He m. JULIA A. KEITH. Child :

      1. Hattie M. *Clark*, b. Feb. 15, 1872.

No. 27.

(VI.) **Hervey Phillips** (son of John and Love : No. 24,) born May 14, 1790. He was a teacher in the early part of his married life, went to live in the northern part of New York State, and about 1853 bought a farm in northern Wisconsin. He never accumulated any considerable property, but "was a man well calculated to lead in political, as well as religious, circles." He married **Betsey Leach,** a descendant of the Allens of Sturbridge. He died at Big Spring, Wisconsin, Aug. 17, 1855. Children :

1. EMELINE ; m. ——— RUSSELL. She d. soon after, leaving one son, Arthur *Russell.*
2. LOUISA ; a noble woman, strong, self-reliant, of sound judgment, who devoted herself for years, with the most unselfish devotion, to an invalid mother and the family in general. Late in life she married ·——— RUSSELL, her deceased sister's husband.
3. HENRY HARRISON, m. and residing at Big Spring, Wisconsin. Ch. :
   1. William.
   2. Herbert.
   3. Minnie.
4. JANE.
5. ANGELINE.

No. 28.

(VI.) **Jonathan Perry Phillips** (son of John and Love : No. 24,) born Sept. 9, 1792. He served an apprenticeship to Squire Upham to learn the blacksmith's trade. After

serving his time and reaching his majority, he started for Oneida
Co., N. Y., on horseback, his sole capital being his horse, and
twenty-five dollars in money. At Whitestown, N. Y., he became
acquainted with **Sophronia Joslyn** (daughter of John Joslyn, formerly of Tyringham, Mass., of Norman French descent),
to whom he was married Jan. 17, 1817. After a few years
they removed to Canastota, Madison Co., N. Y., where he
carried on a large business, in blacksmithing and wagon-making,
and achieved a handsome property. In Oct., 1849, the family
removed to Lake Mills, Jefferson Co., Wisconsin, where he
lived, with the exception of a year or so, at Madison, Wis.,
until his death, Sept. 21, 1865. She died Feb. 23, 1884. His
daughter, Mrs. H. P. Eaton, to whom the compiler is indebted
for this record of her father's family, writes :

"He was a man of sound judgment, even temper, strong
affections and friendships, universally beloved and respected,
always greatly interested in all matters of public interest.
Judge Spencer of Syracuse, N. Y., recently told my brother
that the first person he ever heard urge the necessity of free
schools and a thorough education of all classes, was our father.
He was an earnest anti-slavery man from the beginning, a man
of broad intelligence, who kept his interest in all the great
questions of the day, up to the day of his death.

"Our branch has the light brown hair which our father
inherited from his mother's side of the house ; though some of
us take the dark brown hair from the Joslyn side. All of us
have many strong Phillips traits in common ; among them a keen
appreciation of wit and humor. All are inveterate jokers, as
was our father, and all dearly love a good horse,—true to the
Greek origin of our name. None of us care much for glitter or
general society ; we are strong in our prejudices, likes and
dislikes. It is interesting to trace heredity extending even to
chirography. I have been surprised to find with the majority
of us such strong resemblances in penmanship to others and
remote members of the Phillips family." Children :

1. John Franklin, b. in Whitestown, N. Y., Oct. 9, 1817; m. in
    Lake Mills, Wis., April 4, 1755, Minerva C. Butterfield,

dau. of Oliver Butterfield, formerly of Allegany Co., N. Y.
He d. May 3, 1862. Child :

    1. Cora Frances, b. Sept. 20, 1856 ; m. George Ferry, architect, of
        Springfield, Mass., in 1880. Child :

            1. Robert Phillips *Ferry*, b. in Milwaukee, Wis., Nov.,
               1882.

2. ADELIZA L———, b. April 14, 1820 ; d. Sept. 22, 1827.
3. ALBERT JOSLYN, b. in Whitestown, Feb. 18, 1822 ; m. in Cana-
    stota, Jan. 13, 1848, LAURA JANE MENZIES, of Scotch descent.
    In 1855 he removed with his family from Herkimer, N. Y., to
    Madison, Wis., and subsequently to Chicago, Ill. Child :

    1. George Albert, b. Oct. 25, 1849 ; m. in Chicago, Sept. 20, 1877,
        Amelia Margaret Bergh, of German descent. Ch. :

            1. Grace May Bergh, b. Nov. 15, 1878.
            2. Laura Jane, b. Nov., 1881 ; d. Mar. 6, 1884.

4. CHARLES HENRY, b. in Whitestown, Feb. 21, 1824 ; m. at
    Pompey Hill, Onondaga Co., N. Y., July 15, 1857, MARY
    ELIZABETH BUTTERFIELD, descended by her mother from the
    Haynes family of Worcester Co., Mass. He d. Jan. 1, 1879.
    No ch.

    Respecting his character, &c., his sister fondly writes :—
" My brother Charley was one of the very best specimens of
the Phillips family that I ever met.   All that I could say would
not do him justice nor convey to you an idea of what a grand
good man he was ; genial, witty, of sound judgment, of broad
charity, one of ' God's own men,' as I've heard others call
him.   I have often remarked, and so have others, his strong
resemblance in figure and appearance to Wendell Phillips of
Boston.   He was the recognized leader of the Republican
party in his county.   He served several terms in the Assembly,
and was State Senator-elect at the time of his death.   The
Democratic party have a majority in that county of about
1600, but he was elected by over 1500 majority.   He was
indefatigable in working for the educational interests of the
town and county, and is deeply mourned throughout the State.
He had kept the farm upon which the family settled in 1849,
and had become a large stock raiser, making a specialty of
Alderney cattle and carriage horses."

5. ELMIRA, b. in Canastota, N. Y., April 21, 1826 ; m. (1st) Feb.
    15, 1844, WILLIAM W. KENNEDY, merchant, of Scotch-Irish

descent—his mother a Livingstone. He d. in the spring of 1850, after which she, with her son, joined her father in Wisconsin, where she m. (2d) Dec. 1868, Rev. J. H. JENNE, a presiding elder in the Methodist denomination. Child :

1. Charles William *Kennedy*, b. Jan. 19, 1845; entered the navy in 1861; grad. at the Naval Academy, Newport, R. I., in 1864; Lieut. Commander, commissioned Mar. 26, 1869; d. at Las Vegas, New Mexico, Nov. 29, 1883. A brother officer wrote :— " He was a most efficient officer, and his death was a sad loss to his friends and to the Navy." Another, a Commodore in the Navy said :—" He was a most charming and cultivated gentleman." He m. in Sept., 1873, Harriet Hall, granddau. of Ex-Gov. Hiland Hall of Vermont. Ch. :

     1. Charles Phillips *Kennedy*, b. June, 1875.
     2. Nat Hall *Kennedy*, b. Nov., 1876.
     3. Robert Livingstone *Kennedy*, b. Feb., 1878.

6. MARY ADELINE, b. May 17, 1828; married July 13, 1848, DANIEL A. SEEBER, lawyer, of Holland-Dutch descent; now. of Waterloo, Jefferson Co., Wis. Ch. :

1. Frank A. *Seeber*, b. in Waukegan, Ill., July 4, 1849; a physician in Iowa; m. 1874, Emma Langdon. Ch. :

     1. Mary Phillips *Seeber*.
     2. Robert Thomas *Seeber*.

2. Fred. Austin *Seeber*, b. at Lake Mills, Wis., March 23, 1851; m. in Janesville, Wis., March, 1877, Miss Sarah Byrne, of English descent. She d. Dec. 19, 1879. Child :

     1. Sarah Byrne *Seeber*, b. Dec. 19, 1879.

3. George Phillips *Seeber*, b. Feb. 4, 1853.
4. Claude Valentine *Seeber*, b. in Waterloo, Feb. 14, 1867.

7. EDWIN, b. in Canastota, July 19, 1830; d. Aug. 21, 1831.
8. WILLIAM PERRY, b. in Canastota, Dec. 26, 1833; a lawyer by profession, but gave up his practice in Kansas, on account of the ill health of his brother Charles, and since 1861 has been associated with him until his brother's death at Lake Mills. Unmarried.
9. HARRIET, b. in Canastota, Oct. 18, 1838; m. June 19, 1858, GEORGE BOARDMAN EATON,* of Welsh-English descent, eldest son of Geo. W. Eaton, LL. D., late president of Madison University, Hamilton, N. Y. By profession a civil engineer,

---

* His mother was a Boardman, b. in Conn.

but since 1861 has been connected with the inspector's department of the New York Custom House.   Ch. :

 1. Charles Phillips *Eaton*, b. in New York City, May 13, 1863:
  Entered the Cadet Eng. Corps of the Naval Academy, Oct. 1,
  1879; grad. Naval Cadet, June, 1883.

 2. Mira Louise *Eaton*, b. in New York City, April 19, 1865.

No. 29.

(VI.) **Eldridge Phillips** (son of John and Love: No. 24,) born May 24, 1797; a blacksmith by trade, and followed the trade as long as he lived.   He settled in Monson, Mass., where he owned a residence, on the main street of the village, and where he was buried.   He married **Betsey Butterworth.**   On the 29th of August, 1848, as he was riding in his sleigh with his wife, in the neighboring town of Palmer, and crossing the railroad track, they were struck by a passing train and both killed instantly.   Children :

 1. ALBERT MORGAN, b. in Brimfield, Mass., July 19, 1821; m.
  1843, LAVINIA MIRRICK ; residence, Monson.

 2. SARAH BUTTERWORTH, b. in Brimfield, Aug. 12, 1823; m. June
  10, 1845, by Rev. Alfred Ely of Monson, to SIDNEY H. HALL ;
  residence, Burke, near Madison, Wis.   Ch. :

   1. Charles Henry *Hall*, b. in Monson, March 16, 1846; graduated
    at University of Wisconsin, 1870, and at Hahnemann Med.
    College, Philadelphia, 1876; a practising physician in Madi-
    son, Wis.; m. May 18, 1877, Carrie Norton.

   2. Mary Elizabeth *Hall*, b. in Monson, Aug. 13, 1847.

   3. Sarah Anna *Hall*, b. in Palmer, Mass., Aug. 30, 1849; d. in
    Burke, Wis., March 18, 1862.

   4. Hattie A. *Hall*, b. in Madison, Wis., Nov. 7, 1854; d. in Burke,
    April 6, 1878.

   5. Frances Marion *Hall*, b. in Madison, June 12, 1857.

   6. Jane Maria *Hall*, b. in Madison, July 29, 1859.

   7. Alice Electa *Hall*, b. in Burke, June 1, 1862; d. Sept. 25, 1863.

   8. Lucy Lincoln *Hall*, b. in Burke, April 12, 1865.

 3. WILLIAM BUTTERWORTH, b. in Monson, Aug. 20, 1830; lumber

dealer in Chicago, and manufacturer of sash, doors, blinds, &c.; m. Oct. 11, 1856, Miss MARION GOSS, of Chicago, whose parents were from Massachusetts, her father of Leominster, and her mother a daughter of Capt. Abbott of Brookfield. Children, all born in Chicago:

1. Jessie, b. July 26, 1857.*
2. Daniel Eldridge, b. Aug. 18, 1859; d. March 25, 1860.
3. William Abbott, b. Jan. 18, 1861.
4. George B., b. Dec. 25, 1863; d. Jan. 29, 1864.
5. Charles, b. Aug. 31, 1870.

No. 30.

(IV.) **Lieut. Israel Phillips** (son of Joseph and Ruth: No. 20,) born in Oxford, Aug. 17, 1737; but that part of the town in which he lived being set off in 1778, he became a citizen of Auburn, or Ward as it was first named; a soldier in the French war, 1758; died Feb. 28, 1800. He married, Sept. 18, 1760, **Huldah Towne,** born Nov. 2, 1737, eighth child of Jonathan Towne;† ceremony solemnized by Rev. John Campbell, first settled minister of Oxford. She continued to live on the homestead with her son, Simon, whom she outlived, or died near the time of his decease. She is described by those who remember her, as a very thin, light and wiry person, an estimable woman, and one who instructed those under her care in the precepts of the Bible. Children, all born in Oxford (now Auburn):

1. RUTH, b. Sept. 25, 1761, d. July 17, 1783.
2. MARTHA, b. Sept. 24, 1763; m. EBENEZER PRAY, who served in the army of the Revolution. She d. Nov. 25, 1852. Child:
   1. Ebenezer *Pray ;* went to Maine.

---

* In 1871 or 1872, Miss Jessie Phillips and two other young ladies, all representatives of the Phillips family, in different public schools of Chicago, each won a gold medal. One of the others was Miss Cora F., daughter of John Franklin Phillips, and the third, a Miss Phillips, a more distant relative.

† Jonathan Towne was b. at Topsfield, Mass., Mar. 11, 1691, and in 1714 resided at Oxford, where he was deacon of the church, and where he d., 1771. He was son of John and Mary (Smith) Towne, and a descendant, in the fourth generation, of William Towne who was of Salem, " 11, 8 mo., 1640."—*Hist. and Gen. Register.* Vol. 21, p. 218.

3. SIMON, b. Jan. 6, 1766 ; a farmer in Auburn ; m. 1791, REBECCA
    SCOTT of Leicester. He d. in the autumn of 1817. Ch. :

    1. Huldah, b. 1796; m. Oct. 2, 1816, James Marble of Millbury;
        went to Augusta, Oneida Co., N. Y. Ch. :

        1. Joel Phillips *Marble*, and five others whose names
            have not been ascertained.

    2. Simon, b. Feb. 3, 1800; a carpenter by trade; m. Eveline Sar-
        gent of Leicester, and settled in Greece, N. Y., where he d.
        Dec. 23, 1878;—" not a wrinkle in his face or a gray hair on
        his head." Ch. :

        1. ———; d. in infancy.
        2. Martha Louise; m. James Field of Greenfield, Mass.;
            resides (1878) in Greece, N. Y.
        3. Charles Follinsby; d. at eleven years of age.
        4. Elizabeth Sarah; m. John Wilson of Rochester, N. Y.;
            d. 1875.

4. JOHN, b. May 2, 1768 ; a farmer in Auburn in 1800.
5. ISRAEL, b. April 7, 1771 ; of Greenfield. (No. 31.)
6. RUFUS, b. Aug 31, 1773 ; m. May 5, 1796, DILLA PITTS of
    Auburn. He was a blacksmith in Worcester, where he died in
    1802. She survived him many years, and died at Deer Isle,
    Me. Ch. :

    1. Leonard; a farmer in Sullivan, Tioga Co., Penn. He m. there
        and d. about 1865 or 1866, leaving five daughters.
    2. Melinda, m. 1821, Juno Metcalf, and went to Deer Isle, Maine,
        where she d.

7. DANIEL, b. March 1, 1776 ; of Charlton. (No. 41.)

No. 31.

(V.) **Israel Phillips** (son of Israel and Huldah : No.
30,)born April 7, 1771 ; a farmer in Greenfield, Mass., to which
place he went about 1790. He bought a piece of wild land,
covered with the original forest, where he settled, living the
first few years in a log house, and continued to live on the same
place till the close of his life. He died Feb. 3, 1844. He m.
1791, **Mercy Bascom,** daughter of Dea. Moses Bascom of
Greenfield. It was his practice for several winters during the
early part of his married life to teach school, taking his pail of
dinner and leaving his wife alone in the house, three-fourths
of a mile from any neighbors, in the midst of the forest, which

at that time was not clear of wild beasts, going two or three miles to the school-house, and returning at night. Owing to their straitened circumstances their boys were put out to work, where they could earn their living quite young. Children, all born on the homestead in Greenfield :

1. ALVAH CLESSON, b. May 6, 1795 ; of Wyoming, Pa. (No. 32.)
2. ISRAEL, b. Sept. 1, 1797. (No. 33.)
3. JOHN TOWNE, b. May 26, 1799 ; of Laurens, N. Y. (No. 34.)
4. RUFUS SEVERANCE, b. Nov. 10, 1801. (No. 35.)
5. ELVIRA, b. Oct. 14, 1804 ; m. SETH MANN of Gill, Mass. She
   d. in Gill, Sept. 12, 1865. No children.
6. NOBLE PHILANDER, b. April 19, 1807. (No. 36.)
7. EZEKIEL LYSANDER, b. July 16, 1809 ; of Brattleboro, Vt.
   (No. 37.)
8. ALONZO DANIEL, b. Feb. 9, 1812. (No. 38.)
9. MOSES BASCOM, b. July 11, 1814 ; of Falls, Wyoming Co., Pa.
   (No. 39.)
10. HULDAH, b. Nov. 27, 1816 ; d. April 19, 1820.
11. SIMON CADY, b. May 8, 1819 ; of Gill. (No. 40.)

No. 32.

(VI.) **Alvah Clesson Phillips** (son of Israel and Mercy : No. 31,) born May 6, 1795. He went to Wyoming, Penn., where he followed the occupation of clothier and wool carder, but after a time, received a commission as justice of the peace with power to hold jury trials. At first he received his commission from the Governor, but was afterwards elected by the people, and was continued in this office till his death. The amount of his legal business soon became so extensive that he was compelled to give up his former occupation, and devote himself wholly to his new calling. Incessant application to this business, confinement in the impure air of the court room, and want of sufficient exercise, seriously and permanently injured his health, which he made repeated but unsuccessful efforts to regain. He was, writes one of his children, "a man of no ordinary ability." He died in Wyoming, Oct. 8, 1840. He m. **Ann Chapin,** who was born Sept. 16, 1794, daughter of

Solomon and Catharine Chapin of Wyoming (then New Troy),
Luzerne Co., Penn.   She died in Northmoreland, Wyoming
Co., Nov. 10, 1865.   Children :

1. MARY S., b. in Wyoming, April 13, 1818; m. Dec. 19, 1837,
    GORDON PIKE ; residing (1878) in Northmoreland, Penn. Ch. :

    1. Ruey *Pike*, b. Oct. 31, 1838.
    2. Emily Gordon *Pike*, b. Dec. 13, 1845.

2. ISAAC S., b. Sept. 13, 1820 ; m. May 22, 1851, LOUISE WOOD-
    HOUSE ; residence, Chicago, Ill. Ch. :

    1. Lillie C——, b. Aug. 10, 1853; singing (Feb. 1878) with the
        Hutchinson family in Philadelphia.
    2. Harry; deceased.
    3. Chapin.
    4. Fred.

3. JOHN, b. March 27, 1822 ; d. Dec. 6, 1831.
4. ROBERT CHAPIN, b. Feb. 3, 1825. A soldier of the Union army
    in the late Southern war, now a farmer in Northmoreland,
    Penn. He m. in 1870, AMELIA REED. Ch. :

    1. Hattie, b. June, 1871.
    2. Annie, b. 1873.
    3. Robert C——, b. 1875.

5. DIANA R——, b. April 1, 1827 ; m. March 7, 1847, ABEL
    MARCY ; residence, Tipton, Mo. Ch. :

    1. Beverly *Marcy*, b. July 31, 1848.
    2. Justin *Marcy*, b. Jan. 11, 1852.

6. CAROLINE HOSMER, b. Oct. 10, 1829 ; m. May 12, 1853, S——
    GALE SMITH ; residence, Northmoreland, Penn. Ch. :

    1. Charlie Wesley *Smith*, b. Sept. 29, 1854; d. in Northmoreland,
        Oct. 9, 1863.
    2. Maggie Dewit *Smith*, b. in Northmoreland, Dec. 5, 1863.
    3. Dorrie Chapin *Smith*, b. in Northmoreland, Dec. 31, 1865.
    4. Annie May *Smith*, b. in Northmoreland, Feb. 10, 1872.

7. HARRIETTE W——, b. Nov. 19, 1833 ; m. June, 1859, E.
    L. UNDERWOOD.   She d. in Northmoreland, Jan., 1874.
    Ch. :

    1. Frank *Underwood*, b. Aug. 4, 1860.
    2. Fred. *Underwood*, b. Aug. 18, 1862.
    3. Oran *Underwood*.
    4. Eva *Underwood*.

Truly yours
Israel Phillips

8. FRANCES E———, b. Jan. 2, 1838; m. Nov. 27, 1856, THEO-
DORE HATFIELD. She d. in Northmoreland, Oct. 23, 1858.
Child, dau.:

    1.   Frank E ——— *Hatfield*, b. Oct. 22, 1857; residing in Pittston,
        Luzerne Co., Penn.

No. 33.

(VI.) **Israel Phillips** (son of Israel and Mercy: No.
31,) born Sept. 1, 1797.
He left his home when
about twelve years of age,
and after one or two years
spent with his uncles, Daniel and Simon, went to
Leicester to learn the trade of card-maker; but the company
failed before his time expired, and we next find him laboring at
his trade at South Hadley, Mass., and later at Lansingburg,
N. Y. He was the first stage driver on what was called "the
east side mail line" from Springfield to Brattleboro, Vt., driving from South Hadley to Springfield. The first three years of
his married life were spent in Greenfield; then he moved to
Hartford, Conn., and took charge of a card factory, for two years
at a salary of two hundred dollars a year. He then removed to
Springfield, and with others there commenced the manufacture
of cards under the firm name of Bowdoin, Phillips & Co.
Four years after, the company obtained a charter under the
name of the Springfield Card Manufacturing Co., of which he
continued as the superintendent. He was chosen 1st Lieut. of
the Springfield Horse Guards, and commissioned by Gov. Levi
Lincoln, and was twice chosen delegate from Springfield to the
Democratic State Convention. His health failing, in 1830, he
sold out his interest in the card company, and moved on to a
farm in Greenfield. In 1835, having regained his health, he
removed to Willimansett, near Springfield, as superintendent
of the Willimansett Manufacturing Co., of which the late Hon.

Stephen C. Bemis was agent and manager, and served in the employ of Mr. Bemis and his sons in various positions, more or less every year, for upwards of forty-five years. For two years he had charge of a hardware store for Mr. Bemis in Troy, N. Y., with a $10,000 stock of goods; but this enterprise proved a failure, and fortune set him down at poverty's gate. So reduced was he at this time, the spring of 1843, that, with wife, six children and all his earthly possessions, he left the city for his native town on a one-horse wagon. This was a heavy blow to bear; the cloud that overshadowed him was black indeed, but he passed through the trial manfully. Possessed with a remarkably hopeful spirit, good health and strong hands, he entered anew the great battle of life, fortune smiled, and he not only kept the wolf from the door, but earned and still enjoys an easy competency. His employer, the late Mr. Bemis of Springfield, was once heard to remark to a friend, "I have great confidence in the honesty of Mr. Phillips, why! I would trust him with *millions* of *uncounted gold.*" In religion, a strong believer in the final restoration to peace and happiness of the whole family of man; in politics, a staunch Jacksonian democrat; a Free Mason sixty years.

His son, Dea. Charles C. Phillips, to whom the compiler is indebted for the greater part of this sketch, wrote in 1878, "he is nearly eighty-one and has just returned from a commercial trip embracing the New England States and the State of New York. He is probably the oldest traveling agent and the best known of any in the country, having been on the road some thirty-five years." After the above was written he continued to travel for two or three years, but has since retired from the road, and has been residing with his daughter Caroline, at his homestead in Greenfield, where 1885, he was still enjoying a comfortable life. The above autograph was written when he was eighty-seven years of age. The portrait prepared for this work is from a photograph taken at the age of eighty.

He married **Dorothy Sage,** born in Berlin, Conn., Feb. 22, 1797, died in Bernardston, Mass., Feb. 15, 1866. Her parents were Capt. Oliver Sage, who died in Greenfield, Sept.

2, 1859, aged 90, and Mary (Denio) Sage, who died in same place, Nov. 13, 1854, aged 83. Children:

1. DOROTHY DENIO, b. in Greenfield, May 18, 1817; m. in Springfield (now Chicopee) EDMUND R. BROWN, a native of the latter place, a machine card maker; from 1864 to 1879 a commercial traveler; present residence, Deerfield. Janitor and librarian of the Dickinson High School since its opening in 1879. Ch.:

    1. William Phillips *Brown*, b. in Hartford, Conn., July 16, 1840; in a Regiment of Engineers from New York, having enlisted at the commencement of the war of the Rebellion and served till after the surrender of Gen. Lee, at the close of the war; d. suddenly in Fitchburg, Mass., Aug. 14, 1869.
    2. Anna Adelaide *Brown*, b. in Pittsburg, Penn., March 23, 1842; m. Jan. 16, 1868, Charles H. Robinson of Springfield. At the beginning of the war of the Rebellion, he enlisted in the first regiment that went from Massachusetts, and served throughout the war. Present residence, Lynn, Mass. Child:
        1. Lewis Taylor *Robinson*, b. Oct. 20, 1868.

2. MARY ANN, b. in Greenfield, Dec. 20, 1818; m. in same place, May 7, 1833, ZORA ATHERTON, farmer; removed to Gill, Mass., about 1838. She d. after a short illness, Dec. 8, 1880. Ch.:

    1. Alonzo *Atherton*, b. in Greenfield, 1836; m. Mariah Seaver of Shelburne, Mass.
    2. Mary *Atherton*, b. in Greenfield, 1838; m. ——— McElwain of Montpelier, Vt.
    3. William *Atherton*, b. in Gill, 1840; a soldier of the Union army in the late Southern war; wounded at Fair Oaks, Va., shot through the thigh; m. Augusta Brooker of Greenfield.
    4. Ralph *Atherton*, b. in Gill, 1842; a soldier of the Union army in the late Southern war, and lost his right arm in the service; wounded at Fair Oaks, Va.; m. Alma Bascom of Gill.
    5. Isabell *Atherton*, b. in Gill, 1844; m. Henry Tyler of Greenfield.
    6. Elizabeth *Atherton*, b. in Gill, 1846; m. Gilbert Stacy of same place.
    7. Oliver *Atherton*, b. in Gill, 1848; m. Rose Scott of Bernardston. She died 1876.
    8. Harriet *Atherton*, b. in Gill, 1850.
    9. Abbie *Atherton*, b. in Gill, 1852.
    10. Carrie *Atherton*, b. in Gill, 1854.
    11. Charles *Atherton*, b. 1860; d. 1864.

3. HARRIETTE E———, b. in Greenfield, Aug. 5, 1820; in 1878 of Beloit, Wis.; m. in Windsor, Conn., May 5, 1839, ANSON

6

B. STONE, a farmer. He died in Newark, Wis., Feb. 15, 1863, aged 50 years, 4 mos. Ch.:

1. William Anson *Stone*, b. at Willimansett, Mass., July 21, 1841; in 1878 of Chicago, Ill. At President Lincoln's first call for volunteers he enlisted in the 1st Wis. Reg., Co. F, for three months, and, at the expiration of that time re-enlisted in the 74th Ill. Reg., Co. D, and remained until discharged at the end of the war. He m. in Beloit, Wis., Aug. 31, 1862, Julia A. Stillwell. One son.

2. Ella Annetta *Stone*, b. in Chester, Mass., March 13, 1847; d. in Greenfield, Aug. 28, 1848.

3. Eddie Clarence *Stone*, b. in Chester, Aug. 21, 1851; in 1878 of Beloit, Wis.

4. Elna Carrie *Stone*, b. in Branford, Conn., June 29, 1854; m. in Newark, Wis., March 18, 1871, Frank L. Hayden; residing, 1878, in Beloit, Wis.

4. WILLIAM P————, b. in Hartford, Conn., Jan. 24, 1822; d. in Springfield, Mass., April 24, 1839.

5. CHARLES CLESSON, b. in Springfield, Mass., June 2, 1823; a farmer and painter, of Greenfield, and deacon for six years of the 1st (Orthodox) Church. He was a soldier of Co. A, 52d Reg., Mass. Vol. Militia, and served under Gen. Banks in 1862 and 1863, was at the capture of Port Hudson, La., was wounded in the face by the explosion of a rebel torpedo soon after entering the place. For eighteen years prior to 1862 he was identified with the Democratic party; was delegate to one of its County and three of its State Conventions. He has of late years been in hearty sympathy with the temperance reform movement; was one of the first in his county to move for the organization of a Union Sunday School Association; was for ten years at the head of the County Committee on Sunday Schools; has been treasurer and a director of the Franklin Co. Bible Society from its organization in 1874. He m. in Greenfield, April 28, 1846, ADELINE BASCOM, dau. of Chester and Dorcas (Bissell) Bascom, and gr. dau. of Joseph Bascom. No ch.

6. JOHN HANCOCK, b. in Springfield, Mass., Jan. 20, 1826; of Springfield; agent of *Phillips' Felting Works*, manufacturers of fire-proof and indestructible boiler and pipe coverings. He m. (1st) in Guilford, Conn., Apr. 16, 1851, ABBIE LOPER, dau. of James S. Loper. She d. Feb. 13, 1870, and he m. (2d), Aug. 31, 1876, Mrs. JULIA A. PICKETT of New Haven,

wid. of Charles Pickett. Ch., by first marriage, several of whom died :

1. Fred Kendall, b. at Plainville, Conn., Oct. 4, 1854; at present, 1885, with the Turner & Seymour Mfg. Co., of Torrington, Conn., and N. Y., as western agent; m. Elizabeth Scully of Waterbury, Conn. She d. March, 1880. Ch. :

    1. Harry, b. Oct 10, 1877.

2. George Lyman, b. in Trenton, N. J., Jan. 20, 1864; m. Miss Katie Scofield of South Norwalk, Conn.

7. CLARISSA C———, b. in Springfield, March 20, 1828 ; m. in Greenfield, Nov. 6, 1852, LEWIS W. TAYLOR, agent; res., Pittsfield. No ch.

8. HENRY DWIGHT, b. in Springfield, March 22, 1830 ; learned the fresco, sign and banner painting business in Springfield; settled in New Haven, Conn., in 1856 ; established himself in business in 1859, and has built up one of the largest and most successful painting establishments in New England. He enlisted in Co. D, 2d Reg., C. N. G. in 1859, and, after filling all the subordinate positions in the company, was elected Captain in 1874, which position he held until 1879, when he resigned ; has held many responsible political positions in the Democratic party ; is a member of the Masonic, Odd Fellows, Knights of Pythias and B. P. O. Elks, orders. He m. June 25, 1851, LOUISE ANN JACKMAN of Westfield, Vt. Ch. :

1. Willie, b. in Springfield, Feb. 14, 1852; d. Feb. 16, 1852.
2. Lillian Louise, b. in Springfield, Oct. 7, 1853; d. in New Haven, Jan. 4, 1862.
3. Frank Henry, b. in Cazenovia, Madison Co., N. Y., Dec. 28, 1855; house painter and paper hanger, of New Haven; m. June 25, 1876, Nellie McKeon of Saybrook, Conn. Ch. :

    1. Frank Raymond, b. May 18, 1878.
    2. Mary Louise, b. Jan. 30, 1881.
    3. Lillian Allena, b. Dec. 27, 1882.
    4. Edith Lyle, b. Oct. 12, 1884.

4. Fred, b. in New Haven, Feb. 16, 1858 ; d. July 20, 1858.
5. Jennie Louise, b. in New Haven, May 19, 1863 ; d. Feb. 14, 1864.
6. Charles Raymond, b. in New Haven, March 11, 1864 ; in business with his father; "a very clever artist, and shows great skill with the brush."
7. Emma Isabel, b. in New Haven, Aug. 4. 1868 ; d. Aug. 18, 1868.

9. LEWIS L———, b. in Greenfield, Sept. 20, 1832 ; a resident of Springfield ; m. in Greenfield, 1859, ANNIS M. BARTLETT. Child :

    1. Jennie, b. in Springfield, June 1, 1860; m. J. A. Hennick. She d. in Springfield, Jan. 18, 1881.

10. CAROLINE E———, b. in Greenfield, June 20, 1835 ; m. Jan. 3, 1866, MOSES BASCOM PHILLIPS, son of Ezekiel L. and Laura A. Phillips. Child :

    1.· Alva Israel, b. in Greenfield, April 13, 1874.

11. GEORGE C———, b. in Springfield, Oct. 10, 1838 ; a farmer in West Springfield ; m. (1st) in Greenfield, Aug. 4, 1859, MINERVA FAIRMAN. She d. May 29, 1867, and he m. (2d) Miss MARY FRANCES CLEMENT of New Hampshire. Ch., by first marriage, all born in Greenfield :

    1. Frederic T———, b. April 14, 1860; d. Sept. 1, 1865.
    2. Clara May, b. Sept. 20, 1864.
    3. Nellie, b. March 29, 1867; d. Oct. 1, following.

No. 34.

(VI.) **John Towne Phillips** (son of Israel and Mercy : No. 31,) born May 26, 1799 ; went to Laurens, Otsego Co., N. Y., where he followed the trade of clothier and wool carder for about thirty years, then sold out and was afterwards one of a company that built a large cotton mill. He was prospered in business and became a man of considerable pecuniary means. He was one of the pillars of support in the Methodist Society of that place, for the benefit of which it was his habitual practice to contribute liberally. He m. Sept. 7, 1823, **Mary Sheldon** of Bernardston, Mass. He died May 27, 1877.

Children :

1. ELVIRA C———, b. in Laurens, Feb. 10, 1825 ; m. April 5, 1850, ELIJAH HUBBELL.
2. MARY M———, b. in Laurens, March 10, 1828 ; d. in same place, Dec. 1, 1851.

No. 35.

(VI.) **Rufus Severance Phillips** (son of Israel and Mercy : No. 31,) born Nov. 10, 1801 ; a farmer in Greenfield, and an accurate land surveyor, his services in the latter capacity being very often solicited by people in his own and neighboring towns. He was considerably occupied in town business, and held the office of assessor for several years. He was regarded by those familiar with him as a great mathematician, who declared it to be impossible to catch him in a mistake in any problem. One who served on the board of assessors with him said he was the best man at figures he ever saw. He occupied the homestead where his widow still resides, 1883. The family has held possession of this place for ninety years. He married Nov. 1, 1843, **Sally Page** (or **Paige**) of Leyden, Mass., born April 30, 1814, daughter of Paul and Sally (Crumb) Page. He died in Greenfield, July 2, 1875. Children:

1. ARTHUR, b. Nov. 1, 1844; a soldier of the Union army in the late Southern war; residing, 1878, in Gill. Married CLIMENA ROBERTS of Gill. Child:

    1. Halbert, b. Jan. 4, 1874.

2. SARAH, b. in Greenfield, Jan. 4, 1848; m. EDGAR THAYER of Hinsdale, N. H., a Union Soldier in the late Southern war; residing, 1878, in Amherst, Mass. Child:

    1. Glenroy *Thayer*.

3. MILLARD FILLMORE, b. in Greenfield, Oct. 22, 1850; living, 1883, at the old homestead.

4 and 5. Two sons who died young.

No. 36.

(VI.) **Noble Philander Phillips** (son of Israel and Mercy: No. 31,) born April 19, 1807; a shoemaker in Bernardston, a farmer in Gill and in Greenfield, where he now resides, 1885. He married in Vernon, Vt., 1830, **Nancy Ann Kenny.** She died June 30, 1881. Children:

1. HULDAH JANE, b. May 25, 1831; d. March 8, 1847.

2. ELLEN ANJELINE, b. Dec. 5, 1832; in 1885 of Santa Rosa, Cal., having lived in California about twenty-five years; m. April 14, 1859, ALVAH W. PARK. He d. in Santa Rosa, Apr. 1, 1884. No ch.

3. ALONZO MARTIN, b. Oct. 14, 1834; d. April 14, 1835.

4. CLEMENT COOLEY, b. Feb. 2, 1836; in 1885 of Portland, Oregon, having been many years extensively engaged in the

manufacture of doors, sash and blinds ; m. (1st) in that place, 1864, CECELIA MCKAY. She d. May 16, 1865, leaving one child. He m. (2d) 1867, LIZZIE JOHNSON. Ch. (by first marriage) :

   1. Alva.

(By second marriage) :

   2. Edward W———, b. Oct. 25, 1868; d. Aug. 13, 1869.
   3. Alida C———, b. June 13, 1870.
   4. Nellie E———, b. May 18, 1872.
   5. Anna E———, b. Oct. 24, 1874; d. same day.
   6. Wilber, b. Sept. 26, 1875.
   7. Leslie, b. Sept. 13, 1878.
   8. Herbert, b. Apr., 1881.

5. NANCY ANN, b. April 17, 1838 ; m. April 14, 1863, JOB G. PICKETT, a respectable farmer of Greenfield, where they reside. Ch. :

   1. Frank Noble *Pickett*, b. Feb. 23, 1864.
   2. Ellen Anna *Pickett*, b. Nov. 13, 1868.

6. DWIGHT MARTIN, b. May 18, 1840 ; a respectable farmer of Greenfield ; m. March 11, 1873, ELLA COBB. He d. Oct. 17, 1880.

7. NEWTON, b. Jan. 27, 1843 ; of West Thompson, Conn.; served in the war of the Rebellion in the 52d Reg., Mass. Volunteers ; m. March, 1866, ELIZA CHASE. Ch. :

   1. Alice, b. Dec. 17, 1866.
   2. Walter, b. Dec. 11, 1867.
   3. Willie, b. Dec. 26, 1870.
   4. Maud Adelaide, b. Dec. 23, 1884.

8. ELVIRA SOPHIA, b. Oct. 25, 1845 ; m. April 12, 1871, EBER N. LARRABEE, justice of the peace and wealthy farmer of Greenfield. Ch. :

   1. Clara *Larrabee*, b. May 9, 1872.
   2. Anna *Larrabee*, b. June 25, 1874.
   3. Lizzie *Larrabee*, b. Feb. 17, 1878.
   4. Hart *Larrabee*, b. Dec. 4, 1880.

9. CHARLES NOBLE, b. April 7, 1848 ; of Greenfield; m. 1873, PHEBE CLARK. Ch. :

   1. Henry, b. July 24, 1874.
   2. Dona Jane, b. Aug. 27, 1876.
   3. Carrie Bell, b. Jan. 6, 1879.
   4. Leon D———, b. Apr. 18, 1881,
   5. Herbert, b. Aug. 17, 1883.

No. 37.

(VI.) **Ezekiel Lysander Phillips** (son of Israel and Mercy: No. 31,) born July 16, 1809 ; a machinist in Brattleboro, Vt. ; m. Jan. 27, 1832, **Laura A. Holden.** He died in Brattleboro, March 25, 1842. She died June 6, 1852. Children, all born in Brattleboro :

1. HENRY OSCAR, b. April 21, 1833 ; residing, 1878, in Laurens, Otsego Co., N. Y. ; m. Jan. 28, 1854, MARIETTA MULKIN. Ch. :
    1. Carrie, b. in Laurens, May 28, 1856.
    2. Mary Brooks, b. in Laurens, April 18, 1861.
    3. John F———, b. in Hartwick, N. Y., Feb. 4, 1864.
    4. Henry Oscar, b. at Richfield Springs, N. Y., April 28, 1868.
    5. Stearns Spencer, b. in Laurens, Sept. 21, 1876.

2. RICHARD LYSANDER, b. April 20, 1835 ; in 1878 of Greenhorn, Pueblo Co., Col. ; has lived mostly at the West, having left his Massachusetts home in his youth and never since returned. He served during the war of the Rebellion, from the commencement to the close of the war, in Company C, 6th Kansas Cavalry ; was Lieut., commanding company for two years of the time. He m. LAURA B. MARSHALL, who was born in Salem, Columbiana Co., Ohio, Feb. 12, 1843, and d. at Twin Springs, Linn Co., Kansas, Jan. 24, 1872, dau. of J. C. and H. T. Marshall. He d. 1883. Ch. :
    1. Frank E———, b. at Twin Springs, April 1, 1863 ; d. at Mound City, Kansas, July 8, 1863.
    2. Horace A———, b. at Twin Springs, Sept. 22, 1864.
    3. Homer M———, b. at Fort Scott, Kansas, May 22, 1867.
    4. Lizzie H———, b. at Fort Scott, June 6, 1870 ; d. June 7, 1870.

3. JOHN FRANKLIN, b. July 14, 1837 ; a resident, 1885, of Chicago, Ill., and paymaster of the Chicago, Rock Island and Pacific R. R. He m. Jan. 1, 1867, REBECCA M. WEBSTER, who was b. Jan. 8, 1845. Ch. :
    1. Charlotte Louise, b. July 2, 1871.
    2. Robert Howard, b. May 3, 1873.
    3. Ernest LeRoy, b. July 7, 1877.

4. MOSES BASCOM, b. June 19, 1839 ; a farmer in Greenfield ; served in the war of the Rebellion in Co. I, 21st Reg., Mass. Volunteers ; was disabled while in service. He m. in Greenfield, Jan. 3, 1866, CAROLINE E. PHILLIPS, dau. of Israel and Dorothy Phillips. Ch. :
    1. Alva Israel, b. in Greenfield, April 13, 1874.

5.   ALVA CLESSON, b. April 14, 1842; sergeant in Co. E, 10th
     Reg., Mass. Volunteers, was wounded at the battle of Gettys-
     burg, July 3, 1863, and died of the wound Oct. 3, following,
     in the hospital.

No. 38.

(VI.) **Alonzo Daniel Phillips** (son of Israel and
Mercy: No. 31,) born Feb. 9, 1812; an accomplished and
popular hotel keeper, which business he followed for thirty
years, and lived successively in Springfield, Mass., Brattleboro,
Vt., Hartford, Conn., Athol and Fitchburg, Mass. For a time
in the early part of his life he was employed in the service of
the late Hon. Stephen C. Bemis of Springfield. He married
Mary A. Robinson, born at West Springfield, Feb. 15,
1818, daughter of Joel and Anna (Bartlett) Robinson. He died
in Greenfield, May 3, 1863. Children:

1.   SMITH ROBINSON, b. at Willimansett, Mass., Jan. 14, 1837; a
     member of the Mass. Legislature from Springfield in 1874,
     being elected without an opposing vote. When the resolutions
     of censure against Hon. Charles Sumner were rescinded by
     that assembly, he was active in securing that result, and was
     one, appointed with others, to deliver to the Hon. Senator the
     welcome document, stating that the vote of censure had been
     rescinded. He was also one of the Committee appointed by
     the Legislature to proceed to Washington, after the death of
     the lamented Senator, and receive his body. He m. in Mon-
     tague, Mass., June 19, 1859, IDA M. BISSELL, daughter of
     John W. and Sophia (Cushman) Bissell. He d. in Springfield,
     Oct. 7, 1877. Child:

     1.   Isanella S——, b. in Montague, Aug. 3, 1860.

2.   ALONZO DANIEL, b. in Brattleboro, Vt., Aug. 31, 1838; went
     to Kenosha, Wis., in Oct., 1856, and to Portage City, Wis.,
     July, 1857, and in Dec. same year went 'to Prairie du Chien,
     where he was telegraph operator and clerk in the railroad
     freight office until Aug. 1, 1875, when he was appointed
     freight and ticket agent, which position he has since occupied.
     He m. in Boscobel, Wis., Oct. 11, 1861, MARY A. COPE, b. in
     Athens, Penn., Aug. 19, 1846, dau. of Thomas V. and Eliza-
     beth Cope. Children, all born in Prairie du Chien:

    1.   Frederic Charles, b. Dec. 20, 1863.
    2.   Frank Henry, b. Jan. 5, 1866.
    3.   Inez May, b. Sept. 30, 1871.

3. CHARLES OSCAR, b. in Brattleboro, Vt., Aug. 5, 1840 ; an officer during the war of the Rebellion in the 4th Mass. Cavalry, as was also his younger brother, and both were at different times members of the staffs of Generals Terry and Weitzel. He m. ELLEN E. PENDLETON, daughter of Dennis B. and Nancy (Robinson) Pendleton. He died Jan., 1877, from disease, the foundation of which was laid while he was in the service of his country. Children :

    1.   William Harry, b. Nov. 23, 1868.
    2.   Louis Agassiz, b. Aug. 14, 1870.
    3.   Edith Ryerson, b. Aug. 16, 1873.

4. HENRY MOSES, b. in Athol, Mass., Aug. 11, 1845 ; an officer during the war of the Rebellion in the 4th Mass. Cavalry ; in 1878 treasurer of the Phillips Manufacturing Co., Springfield. In the summer of 1881, he, with his wife and son visited Europe. Representative from Springfield in 1880 and '81 ; mayor of Springfield in 1883, '84 and '85. He m. Dec. 1874, JULIA B. ALEXANDER, daughter of Henry Alexander of Springfield. Child :

    1.   Henry Alexander, b. Sept., 1875.

5. MARY ANNE, b. in Athol, Feb. 23, 1847 ; m. JOHN A. FIELD, son of Robert R. and Eliza O. Field. Child :

    1.   Henry Alonzo *Field*, b. in Milford, Mass., Aug. 8, 1870.

6. EMMA LUCY, b. in Fitchburg, Mass., Dec. 23, 1854 ; m. C. A. BROWN, son of Lewis and Abigail Brown.

No. 39.

(VI.) **Moses Bascom Phillips** (son of Israel and Mercy : No. 31,) born July 11, 1814 ; a cloth dyer and dresser by trade, and partner in a factory in Falls township, Wyoming Co., Penn., where he accumulated a handsome property, and continued in this business till the failure of his health and the destruction of his factory by fire, after which, by the advice of his physicians, he bought a farm near Keelersburg, Wyoming Co. Owing to the loss of health he was unable to labor on his farm, yet managed it successfully by means of hired help. "His education was good for his opportunity. He was remarkable for his taciturnity, for months never speaking any unnecessary words, a good citizen and an honest, honorable, man." He married (1st) **Josephine T. Hartley,** daughter of Wm. Hartley of Glenwood, Wyoming Co., Penn. She died in the Spring of 1849, leaving a son a few days old. He married (2d) Oct. 20, 1858, **Jane Harris,** born Feb. 18, 1814, an estimable lady, living in 1878, in Pittston, Penn. Her parents were Isaac Harris of Pleasant Valley, Dutchess Co., N. Y., and Nancy (Wickes) Harris from Morrisville, Del. Co., N. Y. He died July 23, 1865. Child:

1. CHARLES H———, b. March 6, 1849; m. 1876, Miss HARRIET WILSON.

No. 40.

(VI.) **Simon Cady Phillips** (son of Israel and Mercy: No 31,) born Aug. 8, 1819; a millwright of Gill, Mass. He married Jan. 27, 1847, **Rossy Sophia Ballard** of Gill, b. in that place March 13, 1820, daughter of Amaziah Ballard. She died in Gill, Nov. 9, 1874. Children:

1. EMMA JOSEPHINE, b. in Gill, Feb. 7, 1851; living, 1878, in same place.
2. CLESSON BALLARD, b. in Gill, March 29, 1853; teacher of penmanship and book-keeping in Philadelphia.
3. EDWARD SIMON, b. in Deerfield, Mass., Nov. 13, 1854; of Bureau, Ill.; station agent for the Chicago, Rock Island and Pacific R. R. The three children above mentioned have all been teachers.

No. 41.

(V.) **Daniel Phillips** (son of Israel and Huldah: No. 30,) born March 1, 1776; a farmer in Charlton, Mass., to which place he moved in Nov., 1800. Previously to this he worked for Rev. Samuel Austin of Worcester. He died Monday morning, March 27, 1848. He was six feet in height and had large features. During the last seven years of his life he was afflicted with lameness and protracted suffering, and unable to do any work. For the greater part of this time he could walk only with the aid of crutches. He was a respected citizen, highly esteemed for his reliability and general integrity. He married (1st) 1798, **Hannah Small,** daughter of Capt. Samuel and Mrs. Mary Small of Sutton (now Millbury). She died June 14, 1798, aged 26. He m. (2d) Aug. 28, 1800, **Jemima Dennis** of Charlton, born April 27, 1776, daughter of Dea. Jonathan and Mehetabel Dennis. She died, and he m. (3d) Dec. 27, 1807, **Abigail Dresser** of Charlton, born Aug. 17, 1775, daughter of Asa and Abigail (Wheelock) Dresser, and granddaughter of John* and Sarah Dresser. She died (buried April 17th) 1816. He m. (4th) Dec. 19, 1816, **Lucy Harwood** of Charlton, born Feb. 22, 1787, daughter of Gershom and Susanna (Wyman) Harwood, and granddaughter of Solomon and Sarah Harwood. Her father was a Revolutionary soldier. She had the reputation of being an excellent dairy woman, her butter and cheese always being prized as first class. In confirmation of this, she at one time received a testimonial from Hon. Charles Allen of Worcester, who had long been one of her customers, in the form of a valuable present, accompanied by a highly complimentary letter. She was very large, and weighed at sixty years of age, two hundred and forty pounds. To the children who were entrusted to her care immediately upon entering this household, she ever acted the part of a faithful mother. Soon after the death of her father, in 1826, Mr. Phillips bought the farm near the centre village, which had been owned and occupied by the Harwood family for about seventy-five years, and they moved on to it in 1828, and here they both died. She died Wednesday, Feb. 10, 1875. Children, all born in Charlton (first three by second marriage, last four by third marriage) :

1. CURTIS, b. Sept. 10, 1801. (No. 42.)
2. CLARISSA, b. Aug. 18, 1803 ; m. April 6, 1831, JOSIAH UPHAM of Dudley, Mass. She d. Jan. 4, 1833. He m. a second wife by whom he had three ch. He d. July 18, 1883. Child :
     1. Daniel Phillips *Upham*, b. in Dudley, Dec. 30, 1832; learned the carpenter's trade in Oxford, Mass., but not long after left

---

* John Dresser was son of Richard Dresser of Thompson, Conn.

this occupation and was for some years employed in the service of the Adams Express Company in Hartford, Conn., and in New York City. He afterwards engaged in mercantile pursuits in the latter place, and later in Arkansas, to which place he went in 1865. He was extremely quiet and unassuming in his general conduct, but he met with that bitter opposition which has too often been the lot of the northern emigrant to the south. Consequently the unsettled state of the community led him to enter actively into political and military life. When attempts were made in 1868 and 1869 to revolutionize the State Government, he was appointed to the command of the State Militia, with title of Major-General. During this trying period his life was hunted by the outlaws of that region, and he received several bullet wounds in attempts made to assassinate him. After this he was clerk of the Chancery Court for five years. He was United States Marshal from 1876 to 1880 for the western district of Arkansas, which includes the Indian Territory, and comprises a larger area than any other district, and in the amount of business done, money expended and responsibility cast upon the officers of the Court, said to be the most important in the United States. At the close of his term of office in 1880, the *Arkansas Republican* said of him: " Gen. Upham has managed the Marshal's office of his district better than it has ever been managed. A better, more able, honest and efficient officer does not live."

" Upham is a man of pure private and public character; a man who can be used by no one. . . . . . . His character, ability and peculiar fitness for this position are known and admitted by all. The way he has administered the office for four years has forced praises and commendations from even the unwilling. He—with the aid of a judge and district attorney who have been faithful—has given the people of the Indian country peace and security against the efforts of interlopers, murderers, outlaws and villains of all kinds, until life and property are measurably secure in that country."

For a number of years he was in the practice of purchasing at the east and transporting to Arkansas choice animals of pure Jersey stock, for the growth and development of which that section seems to have a peculiar fitness, and his herd and those of his customers included some of the best specimens of breeding stock of this kind which could be obtained in New England. After retiring from the position of U. S. Marshal, his health commenced to fail and he came on a trip to New England, hoping to recuperate amid the scenes of his native town; but, though struggling manfully against disease, he continued slowly to decline and died at the homestead in Dudley, Nov. 18, 1882. He m. Miss Lucy K. Nash

of Oxford, who faithfully stood by him and shared with him
the trials and anxieties of that dark and uncertain period
when his life was kept in jeopardy; and her constant sympathy and kind ministrations continued unabated till the
close of his life. Since his death she has resided in Little
Rock.

3. AUSTIN, b. June 17, 1805 ; d. young.
4. DANIEL, b. July 2, 1809 ; of Hartford, Conn. (No. 43.)
5. ABIGAIL, b. Feb. 12, 1811 ; m. April 25, 1833, SAMUEL P.
HICKS of Charlton, b. in Sutton, Nov., 1805, son of Elijah*
and Nancy (Leland) Hicks. She was for many years a con-
sistent and beloved member of the Congregational Church in
Charlton, an affectionate and devoted wife, a kind and faithful
parent. She died after a long illness, Nov. 13, 1858. Since
her death he has resided in Worcester. Children, all born in
Charlton :

1. Austin Prescott *Hicks*, b. Aug. 3, 1834; d. Feb. 17, 1853.
2. John Warren *Hicks*, b. Oct. 18, 1836; d. March 6, 1837.
3. Abigail Louisa *Hicks*, b. March 29, 1838; d. Sept 21, same year.
4. Lewis Wilder *Hicks*, b. Nov. 20, 1845; graduated at Yale
College in 1870, at Hartford Theological Seminary in 1874.
He preached in July, August and Sept., 1871, in Canaan. Me.,
and Sept. 10, 1874, was installed over the Congregational
Church in Woodstock, Vt.,† where he continued to labor
with good results for seven years. In 1881 he removed to
Wethersfield, Conn., where he was installed Sept. 14th, and
has since continued to be pastor of the Congregational
Church in that town—a church which claims to be the oldest
in the State. His labors have usually given a high degree of
satisfaction, which has been repeatedly expressed by the
liberality of his parishioners. His public addresses show
scholarship and research, and several of them, delivered on

---

* Elijah Hicks was a descendant of —— Hicks of Cambridge, who, with his
brother John, who settled in Charlestown, and another brother who settled in
Rehoboth, came to this country with their father. John, of Charlestown, went to
assist in taking up the bridge, to prevent the British from crossing, on their way
to Concord, and was shot and killed. —— Hicks [1] of Cambridge removed to
Sutton, was a carpenter, and framed the first meeting-house in that town, where
some of his descendants are now to be found. His son Samuel,[2] m. Elizabeth Leland,
who is said to have been a descendant of John Leland, chaplain to King Henry VIII.
She d. in Charlton, Sept. 16, 1834, aged 94. Their son. Elijah,[3] m. Nancy Leland,
above, removed to Charlton about 1810, to Worcester, 1848, where he d. July 6, 1857,
aged 75 years, 2 months. She d. Aug. 15, 1854, aged 69.

† The pastorate in this place was occupied about ten years earlier by Dr. Jonathan
Clement, who married another member of the Watertown Phillips family.

occasions of unusual interest, have been published.* He m.
(1st) July 2, 1874, Kate Curtis, daughter of Dr. J. S. Curtis
of Hartford, Conn. She d. Nov. 3, 1876.. He m. (2d) June
18, 1878, Elizabeth H. Barrett, dau. of Judge —— Barrett
of Woodstock, Vt. Child by first marriage :

 1. Edward Phillips *Hicks*, b. in Woodstock, Aug. 3, 1875.

6. Moses Dresser, b. May 15, 1813 ; of Worcester. (No. 44.)
7. Austin Towne, b. Aug. 26, 1815. (No. 45.)

No. 42.

(VI.) **Curtis Phillips** (son of Daniel and Jemima : No.
41,) born Sept. 10, 1801 ; an industrious and economical farmer
of Charlton, but during the later years of his life a resident of
Southbridge. A man of scrupulous honesty, extremely unassuming, and in his use of language, conscientiously cautious,
deliberate and truthful. By his habits of honesty and truthful-
ness he always held the respect of his acquaintances. He died
at his birthplace in Charlton, June 3, 1880. He m. April,
1828, **Lucy Dodge** of Dudley, who died Oct. 28, 1859, aged
55. Children, all born in Charlton :

 1. Edwin, b. June 6, 1829 ; a miller, grain merchant and farmer
  in Charlton, and an extensive land holder. In 1870 he established a grist-mill on Cady brook, about one-fourth mile from
  his house, and entered at first gradually, and after a few years
  extensively into the grain business. In this business he has
  met with encouraging success, and enjoys the reputation of an
  honorable dealer. In 1881, he built a large dam, five hundred
  feet in length, one-fourth mile lower down, and erected a commodious building for a grist-mill and saw-mill. In 1883, he
  bought a tract of seventy-five acres of land with the purpose
  of flowing it as a reservoir, thereby largely increasing the
  capacity and the value of his privilege. His grain goes principally to the Southbridge market, three miles distant. He
  owns and occupies the same farm and house which were occupied by three generations of his ancestors, the first of whom

---

* His printed discourses include the following: Address at the funeral of Mrs.
Abigail Crossman Hazen, Woodstock, Jan. 1, 1879. Address at the funeral of Solo-
mon Woodward, Woodstock, May 3, 1879. Address at the funeral of Mrs. Mary Ann
Wentworth Williams, Nov. 9, 1879. Sermon at the dedication of the Cong. Church,
Bridgewater, Vt., Sept. 2, 1880. Sermon at the dedication of the Cong. Chapel,
Woodstock, Oct. 31, 1880. Letter of resignation of the pastorate of the Cong.

Daniel Phillips

was Dea. Jonathan Dennis, one of the two first deacons of the Congregational Church in Charlton, who here made an opening in the original forest and broke the untilled land. He m. 1862, ADELIA L. PLIMPTON, b. in Southbridge, August 1, 1833. Children, all born in Charlton :

    1. Lillian Dora, b. March 4, 1865.
    2. Alice Adelia, b. June 28, 1866.
    3. Everett Curtis, b. April 3, 1874.

2. MARY LUCY, b. April 8, 1832 ; m. MARTIN HERSEY of Spencer. One child.

3. CLARISSA MELINDA, b. April 20, 1834 ; d. in Southbridge, May 6, 1873.

4. EMILY, b. Dec. 2, 1839 ; m. JOHN D. PAINE ; resides in Dudley. One child.

No. 43.

(VI.) **Daniel Phillips** (son of Daniel and Abigail : No.

41,) born July 2, 1809 ; went to Westboro in 1829, and carried on butchering and other business, which not proving remunerative, he removed to Hartford, Conn., Oct., 1841. Here he engaged in the express business, then in its infancy, and which grew during his connection with it to the very extensive proportions which it attained in later years. His business efforts were here rewarded with abundant success. He was the Hartford agent of the Adams Express Company for several years following its incorporation, but for some years past has not been actively engaged in that business. For many years he has been prominently identified with several of the principal banking, insurance, manufacturing, educational and benevolent institutions of Hartford, and has been the firm and helping friend of the important religious and charitable enterprises of the city and community, ever watching carefully for the best interests

---

Church, Woodstock, June 19, 1881. Discourse at the re-dedication of Wethersfield Church, April 29, 1883. Poem, "At Antietam," delivered at Wethersfield, May 30, 1884. Sermon, "Seven Spiritual Stages," in the Wethersfield Cong. Church, Sunday, Oct. 26, 1884.

of the city and the institutions with which he has been connected. Being one of the first to engage in the express
business, it is perhaps, not too much to say that the implicit
confidence which the general public have in the express companies of the day, is owing, in no small degree, to the firm and
honorable business principles which it was his constant object
to initiate into the system at its commencement. On many
occasions he has been elevated to positions of trust by the votes
of the citizens of Hartford ; he represented the city in the General Assembly at New Haven during the session of 1854, and
was Alderman in 1859. He has been director or trustee of each
of the following companies and associations, several of which
positions he continues to occupy : Hartford Savings Bank and
Building Association, City Fire Ins. Co., Charter Oak Life Ins.
Co., Hartford Steam Boiler Ins. Co., Orient Fire Ins. Co.,
American National Bank, Mechanics Savings Bank (also vice-
president of the latter), National Screw Co., Weed Sewing
Machine Co., Willimantic Linen Co., Theological Institute of
Conn., Hartford Female Seminary, Hartford Branch of the Am.
Tract Society, and Cedar Hill Cemetery. He was a member of
the building committee for the erection, in 1869, of the magnificent business block on Main Street, of the Charter Oak Life
Insurance Co. He was one of the signers of the call for the
first Republican mass meeting ever held in Connecticut, and
which resulted in the formation of the Republican party of that
State. Ever since that time he has been a member of that party,
an out-spoken advocate of its principles, and usually a firm
and ardent supporter of its candidates. Being a man of warm
heart and genial disposition, and of a peculiarly practical
benevolence, he has gained a great number of friends among
all classes who will cherish the memory of his many deeds
of kindness. More than one is able to say that the business
and social standing to which he has happily attained, is owing
largely to the encouragement which he received in earlier days
from Mr. Phillips. But those who have the best claim to the
affections of their fellow-men are sometimes the ones who suffer
the heaviest blows at the hands of Providence, and so it has

been with him. He and his wife have been blessed with five
happy children, but they have been removed by death, at intervals of some years, till all are gone. He married April 6,
1836, **Mary M. Forbush** of Westboro, born Feb. 10, 1812.
Children :

1. MARY HELLEN, b. in Westboro, April 21, 1838 ; d. in Hartford,
    Aug. 19, 1843.
2. DANIEL AUSTIN, b. in Westboro, Feb. 14, 1840 ; d. in Hartford,
    March 22, 1861. He was of quick and clear mind, of good
    judgment, accurate in forming conclusions, and with an apti-
    tude for business which was more than an average for those
    of his age. He was of a somewhat humorous disposition, a
    pleasant and jovial companion, and had a large number of
    warm friends. For considerable time previous to his death, he
    was clerk in the office of the Adams Express Co. in Hartford.
3. HENRY CURTIS, b. in Hartford, Sept. 24, 1843. He was in the
    service of the Adams Express Co. for several years as mes-
    senger on the railroad between Hartford and Providence, and
    in various other capacities. Failing health compelled him to
    give up active employment. He was generous and hopeful in
    his nature, a cheerful and pleasant companion. He d. July
    31, 1882. He m. April 8, 1878, ADDIE GILBERT of Hartford,
    b. April 8, 1846, dau. of Milo M. and Caroline Gilbert. No
    children.
4. ALICE MARIA, b. in Hartford, Sept. 16, 1848. In the summer
    of 1864 she crossed the Atlantic in company with her father
    and other friends, and visited with much gratification the prin-
    cipal points of attraction in Great Britain, France, Germany
    and Switzerland. She d. while on a visit to friends in Albany,
    N. Y., Jan. 29, 1865. She was noticeable for her amiable
    qualities, being possessed of a lovely countenance, a winning
    manner and a sweet disposition. She was a light in the house-
    hold, and a gentle and confiding friend among her associates.
5. CHARLES WILLIE, b. in Hartford, July 3, 1852 ; d. after a brief
    sickness, May 16, 1870. Of an agreeable and confiding
    disposition, he seemed to gain the affection of all with whom
    he came in contact, as well as the perfect confidence of his
    employers. Previous to his last sickness he was employed as
    clerk in the office of the Charter Oak Life Insurance Co. The
    estimation in which he was held by his employers may be shown

7

from the fact, that, during the morning of the funeral the office of the company was closed, and the officers, directors and clerks attended the funeral in a body, wearing the badge of mourning.

No. 44.

(VI.) **Moses Dresser Phillips** (son of Daniel and Abigail : No. 41,) born May 15, 1813.   Not being of a sufficiently robust constitution to endure the labors of the farm, he left the paternal homestead, Sept. 18, 1832, being nineteen years of age, and went to Worcester, then a thriving village of four thousand inhabitants, where he engaged as a clerk in the bookstore of Clarendon Harris.   In 1835 he went into partnership with William Lincoln, Esq., and with him followed the business of bookseller and publisher for some years.   But desiring a larger field for his labors, he removed his trade, about the year 1845, from Worcester to Boston, where, till the close of his life, he was principal partner in the firm of Phillips, Sampson & Co., whose extensive transactions in the book trade gained for them a world-wide reputation, the amount of their business, part of the time, being regarded as second only to one other establishment of the kind in America.   Thus he raised himself by his own exertions, in a little more than twenty-five years, from the humble position in which he first entered business, to the head of the first publishing house in Boston ; and he became the founder of the *Atlantic Monthly*, a magazine unexcelled in the branch of literature to which it is devoted. The accumulating cares of busines, greatly increased by the financial pressure of 1857 and 1858, and by the death of Mr. Sampson, his chief partner, produced too severe a strain upon his constitution, and he gradually sunk under the weight thus brought to bear upon him.   He was a man of genial ways, of firm and honest principles and noble sentiments, which characteristics won for him a large number of friends.   In the years 1852 and 1853, he was a member of the Worcester Board of Aldermen.   Perhaps his character and abilities may best be shown by the following resolutions and statements made on the occasion of his death, by men who were familiar with his business life. At a meeting of the booksellers and publishers of Boston, held for the purpose of taking some action in regard to his death, the following resolutions were unanimously adopted :

" *Whereas*, we have learned with regret, of the death of our friend and co-laborer, Mr. Moses D. Phillips ; therefore

"*Resolved*, That we have always recognized in him the character of an honest, faithful man ; that we cherish his memory with respect, and that in his death we have lost an intelligent and useful member of the trade.

Resolved, That we close our places of business during the funeral services."

One said of him : " He became favorably known for his intelligence, excellent judgment, and executive abilities. In comparatively a short time the firm gained a high reputation at home and abroad. The deceased was much respected by the whole community, and was highly esteemed by a large circle of friends."

Another remarked : " He was a man remarkable for his modesty, industry, honesty and nobleness of heart ; was amiable, faithful and reliable. Those who knew him well, agree that he had a genial spirit, a fund of ready anecdote, and great kindness of heart."

Another wrote : " After almost daily business transactions with Mr. Phillips and his firm, for about fifteen years, it is but truth and justice to say, that he always thoroughly understood what he wanted, gave his orders concisely, managed everything methodically, was always ready to assist in removing difficulties and smoothing the path, and never placed obstacles in the way ; was always courteous and agreeable, even when most pressed by his multitudinous engagements. And during the whole period, no matter under howsoever trying circumstances (and no doubt they were often presented), he never lost his good temper or spoke to us an unkind word. Amidst a multiplicity of calls in attending to so large a business, he was always attentive and social to the caller, and had a ready fund of anecdote, or story, or humor, to make pleasant the dreary path of daily toil and care. He was to be envied while living, and his memory will be fondly cherished, we doubt not, by hundreds, if not thousands, of persons who had no kinsman's claim, but who enjoyed the broad comprehensive and practical view he took of the subjects discussed with those whose daily walk brought them into his society. As a business man he was a model."

He continued his residence in Worcester till 1856, when he changed it to Brookline, four miles from his place of business, where he died after a protracted illness, August 20, 1859. His remains were taken to Worcester and buried in Rural Cemetery. He married April 10, 1838, **Charlotte Foxcroft,** born in Worcester, 1812, daughter of John and Charlotte (Heywood) Foxcroft.*   Children :

1. CATHERINE FISKE, b. in Worcester, Jan. 7, 1839 ; d. Jan. 10, 1842.

2. SARAH FOXCROFT, b. in Worcester, April 6, 1841 ; living in Brookline, 1885.

3. JOHN FOXCROFT, b. in Worcester. Dec. 14, 1842 ; a resident of Brookline ; in 1861 he entered the store of J. A. & W. Bird & Co., importers of drugs and chemicals, Boston, and after being constantly employed by them for upwards of twenty years, serving with zealous faithfulness in different capacities, but principally as cashier, he became a partner in the firm.

4. CHARLOTTE HEYWOOD, b. in Worcester, Nov. 15, 1848; of Brookline, 1885.

5. EDWARD HALE, b. in Boston, Jan. 26, 1852 ; has been for several years in the employ of J. A. & W. Bird & Co., Boston ; resides at Cottage Farms. He m. Apr. 19, 1879, ELIZABETH

---

* Daniel Foxcroft was mayor of Leeds, 1666; d. in England, Aug. 6, 1694. Francis,[1] son of Daniel, was of Cambridge, Mass.; m. Oct. 3, 1682, Elizabeth, dau. of Dep. Gov. Danforth. She d. July 4, 1721, aged 56, and he Dec. 31, 1727, aged 70. "He was a gentleman by birth, and of a worthy family in the north of England; was just and upright in all his business." Francis[2] (son of Francis[1]), was b. Jan. 26, 1694; of Cambridge; grad. at Harv. Coll., 1712. "First Justice of the Court of General Sessions of the Peace, and inferior Court of Common Pleas for the County in which he lived," 1737 to 1764. He m. Nov. 5, 1722, Mehitable Coney, had ten sons and five daus., one of whom appears to have m. Judge Samuel Phillips of Andover. He d. Mar., 1768, aged 73; his wife, Mehitable, d. at Andover, May 4, 1782, aged 79." Judge Foxcroft occupied the paternal mansion, and in his will expressed a strong desire that it should be retained in the family." Francis[3] (son of Francis[2]), b. Nov. 15, 1744; grad. at Harv. Coll., 1764; an eminent physician of Brookfield, Mass., where he m. May 5, 1768, Sarah, dau. of Dr. Jabez Upham. He d. Feb. 15, 1814, aged 69; his wife, Sarah, d. in Claremont, N. H., Apr., 1827. John[4] (son of Francis[3]), b. Nov. 27, 1785, in Brookfield; grad. at Harv. Coll., 1807; a merchant in Worcester, where he d. July 24, 1824. He m. May 26, 1811, Charlotte, dau. of Capt. Daniel Heywood of Worcester. She d. in Brookline, Jan. 12, 1862, aged 69. Eight of the Foxcroft name have graduated at Harv. Coll.

Austin T Phillips

PIDGE ROBINSON, b. in Hallowell, Me., Nov. 19, 1856. Her
parents were Wm. Shaw Robinson, b. in Norway, Me., Feb.
11, 1796, living, 1885, in Worcester, Mass., and Eunice
(Sampson) Robinson, b. in Leeds, Me., 1812; m. Nov. 1,
1847. Mrs. Robinson d. Dec. 6, 1881. Ch. :

   1. Alice Elizabeth, b. in Brookline, Feb. 9, 1880.
   2. Charlotte Foxcroft, b. in Brookline, May 26, 1883.

No. 45.

(VI.) **Austin Towne Phillips** (son of Daniel and Abigail : No. 41,) born
Aug. 26, 1815; for
forty years a judicious and enterprising farmer in Charlton; prudent and exact in the management
of his business affairs, scrupulously honest in his dealings,
always cherishing a tender desire to promote the highest interests of his family, a liberal supporter of the church and society,
the ardent friend of education, temperance and every enterprise
calculated to benefit the community.

It was the custom of the late Judge Charles Allen of Worcester, to depend upon him annually for a supply of butter,
and he and his father, counting the few years in which his
father preceded him, furnished that family with table butter
for fifty-one years in unbroken succession. He came into possession of the farm previously owned by his father, and, by
persistent industry, energy and economy, greatly aided and
encouraged in his efforts by his frugal and devoted wife, added
to the original farm of fifty acres upwards of fifty more, some
of it containing valuable woodland. In 1878, having sold the
homestead farm two years before, he removed to Auburn,
where he has since resided. The portrait was taken at the age
of sixty-nine. He married Jan. 1, 1843, **Abigail Willis**,
born in Charlton, Sept. 6, 1820, daughter of Hiram and Dolly

(Merritt) * Willis, and granddau. of Jabez Willis, a native of Windham, Conn., who died in Charlton, Dec. 6, 1846, aged 85, and Achsah (Comins) Willis.† Children:

1. ALBERT MERRITT, b. in Charlton, Oct. 9, 1843 ; attended school

Albert M. Phillips.

part of the time in 1860, '61 and '62, at Nichols Academy, Dudley, and afterwards, one term at the Academy in East Greenwich, R. I. ; taught school in Uxbridge in the winter of 1861–2 ; removed to Auburn, 1878 ; farmer in Charlton ; land surveyor and justice of the peace in Auburn ; town assessor 1882, 1883 and 1884. He collected and arranged the material for the "Phillips Genealogies." He m. Oct. 18, 1882, MARY CHARLOTTE SIBLEY, b. in Auburn, Oct. 18, 1847, dau. of Stephen‡ and Charlotte Read (Pierce).§ Sibley. Ch. :

1. Clara Willis, b. in Auburn, May 13, 1884.

---

* Dolly Merritt was a descendant of Col. Moses Marcy of Sturbridge (now Southbridge), b. Apr. 18, 1702, son of John Marcy of Woodstock, Conn. Moses Marcy was the first representative from his town to the General Court, the first citizen who received the appointment of justice of the peace, and held the most important town offices for many years, being moderator in 72 town meetings, selectman 31 years, town clerk 18 years, treasurer 8 years. He owned 400 acres of land where Southbridge village now stands, and made the first improvement of water power on the Quinebaug river, in the present limits of Southbridge. He was gt.-gd.father of Gov. William L. Marcy of N. Y.; d. Oct. 9, 1777. He m. 1723, Prudence, b. Aug. 9, 1702, dau. of Edward Morris of Woodstock, whose father was of Roxbury, and a member of the Governor's Council.—*Ammidown's Hist. Collections.* Their dau., Dorothy Marcy, b. Nov. 18, 1723; m. Capt. Richard Dresser, b. Sept. 22, 1714, first town clerk of Charlton, son of Richard Dresser of Thompson, Conn. Their dau., Chloe Dresser, b. Sept. 4, 1767; m. Capt. Henry Merritt of Charlton, b. June 5, 1767, son of Henry Merritt; and their dau., Dolly Merritt, b. May 9, 1797, d. Feb. 11, 1885; m. Hiram Willis, b. Dec. 19, 1794, d. June 12, 1864.

† Achsah Comins, b. in Charlton, Sept. 22, 1763; d. Mar. 31, 1838, dau. of Reuben and Mary Comins. Reuben was son of Jacob, who d. Apr. 18, 1762, aged 60, and grandson of John Comins, who d. Apr. 10, 1751, aged 83, probably in Oxford (now Charlton).

‡ Stephen Sibley, b. in Auburn, July 26, 1805, son of Solomon and Sally (Stockwell) Sibley. Solomon, b. Nov 17, 1769, was son of Timothy and Annè Sibley of Sutton, Mass., and grandson of John and Zeruiah Sibley. John was one of the first settlers in Sutton, b. in Salem, Sept. 18, 1687, said to have been son of the immigrant ancestor.

§ Charlotte Read Pierce was dau. of Luther Pierce, who m. Clarissa Read, or Reed, dau. of Thomas and Martha (Park) Reed. John Read, the immigrant ancestor, removed from England in 1630, and settled in Rehoboth, Mass.; farmer. His son

2. DANIEL WILLIS, b. in Charlton, Sept. 8, 1850 ; an attractive
    boy of honesty and truthfulness, giving promise of future
    usefulness, an excellent scholar, and beloved by all who knew
    him.   He d. after a few days sickness, Jan. 6, 1863.

John[1] was of Rehoboth, and his son Samuel[2] of Mendon; and his son Samuel[3] of
Uxbridge, Mass. His son Daniel[4] of Uxbridge, m. Sarah Taft of that town. Their
son Thomas[5] m. Martha Park, an intellectual and refined lady. The progenitor of
this branch of the Park family was Edward Park,[1] a merchant in London, Eng.
His son Henry,[2] also a merchant there; his son Richard,[3] a resident of Mendon,
Mass., whose son Thomas,[4] also lived there; his son Edward,[5] same place; his son
Nathan,[6] lived in Uxbridge, and his dau. Martha m. Thomas Reed of Uxbridge, as
stated.—Hist. of Morrison Family. L. A. Morrison, p. 97.

GENEALOGY OF THE FAMILY

OF

EBENEZER PHILLIPS,

OF SOUTHBORO, MASS.

No 46.

(I.) **Ebenezer Phillips,** the ancestor of a great number who bear the family name, was a resident of Southboro, Mass. Respecting his history, it is much easier to tell what is not known concerning him, than to relate any of the events of his life. Diligent research and repeated inquiries have failed to reveal either his parentage, his birthplace, or the length of time he lived in Southboro. A copy from the town record gives no earlier date concerning this family than 1745. His will, in which he mentions his wife **Mary,** was dated Nov. 20, 1745, and proved Aug. 21, 1746, showing his death to have occurred between those two dates.* A written obligation, dated Feb. 25, 1742–3, and beginning as follows, shows him to have been a resident of Stoneham :

"Know all men by these presents that I, Ebenezer Phillips of Stoneham, in the County of Middlesex, in the province of Massachusetts Bay, in New England, yeoman, am holden and stand firmly bound and obliged unto Ephraim Wood of Southboro, in the County of Worcester, in the province aforesaid, yeoman, in the full and just sum of two hundred pounds, old tenor value."

---

* Mr. Abner S. Phillips of Bondville, Vt., in writing to the compiler, says : "My father had the records of the first of the Phillipses who came to this country, but they were destroyed by a little roguish girl about sixty years ago. The Phillipses left a large amount of property in England, choosing rather to leave their property than to be deprived of the privilege of enjoying their religion." Mr. A. S. Phillips also has in his possession other papers and relics, including a sword, once the property of his ancestors.

Respecting his age at the time of his death, it may be inferred that he was past middle life, as two of his children were married before his death, and the others soon afterwards.* Children :

1. SAMUEL ; of Athol. (No. 47.)
2. EBENEZER. (No. 55.)
3. JOHN ; m. May 3, 1749, HANNAH BROWN. Ch. :
    1. Sarah, b. May 1, 1750.
    2. Jonathan, b. Feb. 22, 1752.
4. MARY ; m. Sept. 12, 1745, NATHANIEL NICHOLS of Framingham.
5. JOANNA ; m. June 25, 1746, JONATHAN FAY.

No. 47.

(II.) **Samuel Phillips** (son of Ebenezer, senior, of Southboro : No. 46,) born June 22, 1726, birthplace not known ; married **Martha Newton,** and removed, probably as late as 1771 or later, to Athol, Mass., where he died Feb. 4. 1810.† He and four of his sons were soldiers in the Revolutionary War. His will was dated June 4, 1793, and presented to probate by Seth Phillips, executor, May 17, 1810. Children, all born in Southboro : ‡

1. SAMUEL, b. May 10, 1748 ; m. JOANNA ——— ; d. 1791.
   Child :
       1. Zedekiah, b. June 29, 1772.

---

* Andrew Phillips, 1659, mentioned in "Wyman's Charlestown Genealogies," pp. 740 to 747, had a son Andrew, who m. Sarah Smith, Nov. 11, 1685, and had ch., Andrew, Ebenezer, Joanna and Samuel. Of these, Ebenezer was b. 1695, and m. Mary Smith. This, taken in connection with the fact that Ebenezer Phillips of Southboro, 1745, had a wife, Mary, and ch. Samuel, Ebenezer and Joanna, and a gr.-son, Smith Phillips, and that at one time, 1743, he was of Stoneham, which was set off from Charlestown, points firmly towards the Charlestown, or Boston, families of this name for the origin of Ebenezer Phillips of Southboro. It would indicate that Ebenezer of Southboro, was the same as Ebenezer, son of Andrew, and guided by these statements only, we should reasonably arrive at this conclusion; but in this we are doomed to disappointment, unless there is an error in the record, or the printed copy, such as does not seem probable, for it is stated farther along that Samuel was administrator to his bro. Ebenezer, age 28, July 11, 1723. Whereas, Ebenezer of Southboro was living more than twenty years later.

† One record says he died Feb. 3. Another says he was born July 3, 1732, but is evidently wrong. The same says his wife was born June 11, 1736, and died Feb. 3, 1818. This date of her birth is wrong, and perhaps should be 1726 instead of 1736.

‡ The twelve children are all reported from the town records of Southboro as "born to Samuel Phillips and Martha, his wife."

2. SARAH, b. Dec. 2, 1749 ; d. Dec. 10, 1749.

3. ANDREW, b. Dec. 26, 1750 ; m. (1st) SARAH FAIRBANKS, who
    d. Oct. 16, 1793 ; m. (2d) in 1798, MARY SMITH, who d. about
    1820. He resided in Marlborough, N. H., till after the birth
    of his children, then in Chesterfield, N. H., and d. very
    suddenly, Nov. 26, 1822, at the home of his daughter, Mrs.
    Jackson. He had been out from home that day, and on return-
    ing, seated himself in a chair before the fire, when he died
    almost instantly, and was buried on the day appointed for his
    third marriage. " He was a farmer in comfortable circum-
    stances, and a man of good strong common sense." Ch. :

    1. Martha, b. Aug. 28, 1778 ; m. Enoch Jackson; d. Dec. 24, 1858.
        Eight children.
    2. Experience, b. Nov. 6, 1788; d. Oct. 6, 1802.

4. ZEDEKIAH, b. Feb. 7, 1753 ; d. Feb. 21, 1754.

5. JEDEDIAH, b. Dec. 20, 1754 ; of Medway. (No. 48.)

6. JOHN, b. May 3, 1757 ; of Chesterfield, N. H. (No. 51.)

7. NATHANIEL, b. Apr. 15, 1759 ; of Fitzwilliam, N. H. (No. 52.)

8. JOSIAH, b. May 11, 1761.

9. ELIJAH, b. Jan. 23, 1764 ; of Fitzwilliam, N. H. (No. 53.)

10. MARY, b. March 20, 1766 ; m. ———— BALL, and lived in Athol.

11. JASON, b. Dec. 1, 1768 ; married and had a family of children.
    Some of the earlier portion of his life was occupied in roving
    about, but later he settled down and spent his last days with
    his son Eden, in Alexandria, Jefferson Co., N. Y.   Dexter
    Phillips of New Salem, Mass., is another son.

12. SETH, b. June 10, 1771 ; of Athol. (No. 54.)

No. 48.

(III.) Jedediah Phillips (son of Samuel of Athol: No.
47,) born Dec. 20, 1754; settled at East Medway, Mass. ;
married (1st) Miss Sarah Bullen; after her death he married (2d) Miss Charlotte Bacon of Franklin. He was in
service in the Revolutionary War, for which he afterwards
drew a pension. He died at East Medway, Jan. 25, 1847.
Children, all by first marriage, and all born in Medway :

1. JOHN, b. July 12, 1775 ; d. Nov. 22, 1857 ; m. and had three
    children :

    1. John ; married ; no ch.

    2. Jedediah; d. unmarried.
    3. Abigail; d. unmarried.
2. MARY, b. Feb. 3, 1779 ; d. Dec. 30, 1861.
3. LYDIA, b. June 3, 1781 ; d. July, 1857.
4. RACHEL, b. Aug. 9, 1783 ; d. 1862.
5. OLIVER, b. June 10, 1786. (No. 49.)
6. JOSIAH, b. Aug. 8, 1788. (No. 50.)
7. SALLY, b. March 3, 1791 ; d. March 3, 1871.
8. CATHERINE, b. June 8, 1793 ; d. April 13, 1795.
9. JEDEDIAH, b. March 2, 1796 ; d. March 2, 1800.

No. 49.

(IV.) **Oliver Phillips** (son of Jedediah of Medway : No.
48,) born June 10, 1786 ; m. (1st) Dec. 1, 1808, **Hannah
Richardson.** After her death he m. (2d) about April 1,
1860, **Mrs. Irene (Richardson) (Turner) Hawes,** who
died about March, 1873. He died March 14, 1880. Children,
all born at East Medway :

1. AMANDA, b. March 31, 1809 ; m. JOHN BARBER of Rockville,
    Mass. ; d. July 18, 1834. Had one child, a daughter, who m.
    W. Francis Bacon, and d. several years ago.
2. ELISHA RICHARDSON, b. April 5, 1811 ; m. Nov. 13, 1835,
    ELIZABETH DANIELS of E. Medway, sister of Ellis Daniels.
    He lived about a year and a half in Holliston, and afterwards
    a few years at E. Medway. " Consumption, death's messen-
    ger, released the weary suffering body, and the bright spirit
    went up to the beautiful home which Jesus has prepared for
    those who love and serve him." He d. Aug. 27, 1852. Ch. :
        1. Elizabeth, b. Jan. 25, 1837.
        2. (Adopted July, 1844), Amanda, 2d daughter of Ellis and Sarah
            Daniels. She d. Nov. 29, 1867.
3. SARAH, b. Sept. 13, 1813 ; m. Nov., 1834, ELLIS DANIELS of
    Medway ; d. July 3, 1844. Ch. :
        1. Joseph L. *Daniels*, member of the 16th Regiment, Mass. Vols.;
            d. while in service in Virginia, Feb. 13, 1863.
        2. Sarah E. *Daniels;* d. Nov, 29, 1848, aged about twelve years.
        3. Amanda *Daniels*, b. April 23, 1842; adopted by E. R. Phillips,
            as stated.
        4. Hannah *Daniels;* d. in infancy, Aug. 12, 1844.

4. HANNAH, b. Nov. 23, 1816; m. Jan., 1838, TIMOTHY BULLARD
    of E. Medway; living, 1880, in Westboro, Mass. Five
    children, all living.

5. OLIVER FRANCIS, b. Jan. 8, 1829; living on the homestead in a
    house one hundred and fifty years old; m. April 14, 1855,
    MERCY PENNIMAN ADAMS. Ch., born in Medway:

    1. Edward Adams, b. Jan. 30, 1857.
    2. Mary F., b. Nov. 15, 1861; m. Feb. 16, 1881, Stuart McLees of
        Norfolk, and d. Nov. 19, same year.

No. 50.

(IV.) **Dea. Josiah Phillips** (son of Jedediah of Medway: No. 48,) b. Aug. 8, 1788; m. **Sally Morse** of North
Wrentham (now Norfolk); died Nov. 14, 1857. Children, all
born in Medway:

1. SARAH B———, b. Jan. 18, 1812; m. JOHN SMITH of Medway.
    Ch.:

    1. Sarah Jane *Smith*, b. Oct. 17, 1831; d.
    2. John Emerson *Smith*, b. April 1, 1835; d.
    3. John Milton *Smith*, b. Jan. 25, 1837; d.
    4. Sylvia Elethea *Smith*, b. Aug. 27, 1839; d.
    5. Leander Brayton *Smith*, b. Jan. 21, 1841; d.
    6. Martha Ann *Smith*, b. Aug. 31, 1843; d.
    7. Abner Mason *Smith*, b. Jan. 27, 1845.
    8. Clara Angenette *Smith*, b. Dec. 7, 1848.
    9. Alice Maria *Smith*, b. Aug. 30, 1849.
    10. George Emerson *Smith*, b. Oct. 5, 1850.

2. JOSIAH E———, b. March 20, 1815; d. 1838.

3. MARTHA A———, b. Jan. 22, 1817; m. BRAINARD ROCKWOOD
    of Milford, Mass. Ch.:

    1. Waldo *Rockwood*; d.
    2. Wallace *Rockwood*.
    3. Henry *Rockwood*.
    4. Josiah *Rockwood*; d.
    5. David *Rockwood*.
    6. Sabra *Rockwood*.
    7. Frank *Rockwood*.

No. 51.

(III.) **John Phillips** (son of Samuel of Athol: No. 47,)
born May 3, 1757; a farmer in Chesterfield, N. H.; not having
much of this world's goods, "he possessed a fund of mirth,

was full of joke and catch." He died Sept. 7, 1842. He m.
(1st) **Huldah Ansden,** who died Nov. 5, 1785, in her 26th
year. He m. (2d) **Mrs. Mary Henry,** widow of Wm.
Henry. Children (by first marriage) :

1. ———, a son, name not given, who d. at about eleven years of
    age.
2.. BETSEY; m. JOSHUA STRATTON of Athol, Mass., and d. "not far
    from 1855."
3. CLARISSA, b. Nov. 3, 1783; m. Jan. 18, 1807, WILLIAM NEW-
    HALL; res. in Chesterfield a few years, then moved to Hinsdale,
    N. H. She d. March 13, 1867.
4. HULDAH, b. Oct. 29, 1785; m. WILLIAM HILDRETH.
    (By second marriage) :
5. SALLY, b. Jan. 14, 1787; m. ABEL FISK of Chesterfield.
6. EDEE, b. Nov. 31, 1789; d. at Youngstown, N. Y. Unmarried.
7. MARTHA; m. JASON DAVIS of Chesterfield; moved to Youngs-
    town, N. Y., where she d.

No. 52.

(III.) **Nathaniel Phillips** (son of Samuel of Athol:
No. 47,) born April 15, 1759; a resident of Fitzwilliam,
N. H.; died Sept. 23, 1838. He m. **Mary Bailey,** who
died September 6, 1844, "aged 86 years, 3 months, 15 days."
Children :

1. ISABEL, b. Nov. 25, 1779; d. Aug. 28, 1861.
2. ANDREW, b. Aug. 10, 1784; m. NANCY MAY of Milton, Mass.,
    and lived in Boston, where they both d. He d. Jan. 1, 1822.
    Ch. :
    1. William; d. in Boston.
    2. Sally; m. George Olmsted; living, 1880, in Fitzwilliam.
3. SUSANNAH, b. July 13, 1786; d. May 5, 1868.
4. NAOMI, b. March 7, 1789; d. Aug. 11, 1850.
5. JEDEDIAH, b. Jan. 23, 1792; d. Feb. 6, same year.
6. DANIEL, b. March 6, 1793; d. April 12, 1795.
7. PATTY [? MARTHA], b. Nov. 5, 1795, living, 1880.
8. RUTH, b. Aug. 20, 1798; m. ABEL DUNTON; living Aug., 1880,
    in Fitzwilliam. Ch. :
    1. Jonas *Dunton* ; d. Feb. 6, 1817, aged 4 months, 1 day.
    2. Abel *Dunton,* b. March 31, 1820.

3. Lucy *Dunton*, b. Jan. 10, 1822.
4. William *Dunton*, b. May 19, 1824; a soldier in the war of the Rebellion in Co. A, 2d N. H. Reg. He received a shocking wound in the face, which disfigured him for life, and lay eight days on the battle-field without food; living, 1880, in Fitzwilliam.
5. Asahel *Dunton*, b. Oct. 24, 1826.
6. George *Dunton*, b. June 18, 1832.
7. Sylvender *Dunton*, b. July 4, 1834; d. March 7, 1859.
8. Mary *Dunton*, b. Oct. 19, 1837.
9. ———, name not given.

No. 53.

(III.) **Elijah Phillips** (son of Samuel of Athol: No. 47,) born Jan. 23, 1764; of Fitzwilliam; m. **Lydia Brigham,** daughter of Levi Brigham of same place. He died in Fitzwilliam, May 9, 1841. Children:

1. BELINDA, b. May 20, 1796; d. Aug. 13, 1798.
2. LUCY, b. Jan. 14, 1798; d. Oct. 4, 1805.
3. ELIJAH, b. April 6, 1800; d. Sept. 6, 1805.
4. RUFUS BRIGHAM (Deacon), b. June 7, 1802; d. Feb. 5, 1882, in Fitzwilliam, not having been able to do any work or walk a step for fifteen years, yet, as he stated in a letter to the compiler a year before his death, "all wisely ordered." He m. MARY WOODWARD, daughter of Jacob and Mercy Woodward of Marlboro, N. H. Ch., all born in Fitzwilliam.
    1. Susan M———, b. Oct. 24, 1832; m. May 18, 1853, Charles L. Taft of Fitzwilliam. She d. Sept. 26, 1884.
    2. Edward P———, b. June 22, 1837; served in the Union Army one year, in the war of the Rebellion; teacher of vocal music, 1878, in St. Albans, Vt.
    3. Mary, b. March 28, 1840; m. Dec. 18, 1861, Chester Marsh of Windsor, Vt.
5. MARIA, b. July 20, 1804; d. Oct. 30, 1821.
6. GARDNER, b. Nov. 27, 1806; m. PERMELIA CARPENTER, and settled in Westminster, Vt. He d. in Keene, N. H., Dec. 23, 1870. Ch.:
    1. Julia A———, b. in Keene, Nov. 13, 1840; m. Albert Cooper; now (1885) of Allston, Mass. Ch.:
        1. Ella Hattie *Cooper*, b. Apr. 29, 1874.
        2. Albert Lewis *Cooper*, b. Mar. 22, 1876; d. Dec. 5, 1884.
        3. Alfred Earl *Cooper*, b. Feb. 1, 1879.
        4. Alice Louisa *Cooper*, b. Apr. 22, 1881.

2. Hattie S——, b. in Keene, Oct. 27, 1842; in 1880, of Westminster, Vt.; m. Alfred P. Ranney.
3. Fannie M——, b. in Keene, Feb. 12, 1845; of Westminster.
4. Eliza J——, b. in Walpole, N. H., June 15, 1847; d. in Keene, Sept. 16, 1865.
5. John G——, b. in Walpole, Dec. 24, 1850; of Westminster.
6. Lydia D——, b. in Westminster, Nov., 1853; d. May 9, 1856.
7. Herbert, b. in Westminster, Dec. 9, 1858.

7. ELIJAH, b. April 11, 1809; killed by Indians in Dover, Ill., June 18, 1832.

8. ALMOND, b. Oct. 9, 1811; m. KEZIAH ALLEN of Fitzwilliam. They had two sons and two daughters. One of the sons, Leslie A., is a physician in Boston.

9. LEVI, b. Jan. 30, 1814; m. (1st) SUBMIT TAFT of Fitzwilliam, and settled in Manchester, Vt. She d. in 1860, and he m. (2d) Mrs. MARY BISSELL. Ch. (by first marriage):

    1. Helen, b. in Fitzwilliam, Aug., 1837; d. in Winhall, Vt., 1843.
    2. George Henry, b. in Fitzwilliam, Dec. 14, 1839; a sergeant in the war of the Rebellion, in Co. C, 14th Vt. Reg.; was in the battle of Gettysburg; now of E. Arlington, Vt. He m. Susan M. Webb of Sunderland, Vt. Ch.:
        1. George Edward, b. in Arlington, Oct. 23, 1871.
        2. Reuben Lewis, b. in Arlington, July 19, 1877.
    3. Elmer Elijah, b. in Fitzwilliam, Aug. 8, 1841; a soldier in Co. C, 14th Vt. Reg., participated in the battle of Gettysburg; graduated at Middlebury Coll. in 1868; principal since 1876 of English and Classical Schools in Lambertville, N. J., and Waterbury, Conn. He m. May 10, 1870, Miss Ellen E. Carpenter of Norwich, Conn., a graduate, in 1865, of Mt. Holyoke Female Sem. He removed to Brooklyn, N. Y., in 1884.
    4. Lewis Winslow, b. in Manchester, Vt., Dec. 5, 1845; killed on the Cheshire R. R., near Keene, N. H., Oct. 21, 1876. He m. Mattie Carter of Keene.

(By second marriage):
    5. Harriet, b. in Winhall, Vt., 1863; d. in Manchester, Vt., 1868.

10. WINSLOW, b. Jan. 19, 1817; always resided in Fitzwilliam; m. in same place, April 21, 1847, SUSAN BENT, b. in Fitzwilliam, Dec. 30, 1825, daughter of Hyman and Levinah (Allen) Bent. Hyman Bent was b. in Sudbury, Mass., Sept. 17, 1788, and d. Dec. 21, 1872. Levinah Allen was b. in Fitzwilliam, July 15, 1797. Ch., all b. in Fitzwilliam:

    1. Herbert Wendell, b. March 18, 1851; d. Sept. 29, 1853.

2. Arthur Lynmore, b. Sept. 7, 1854; res. Winchendon, Mass. He
   m. Oct. 7, 1878, Hattie Marie Kieth, in Jaffrey, N. H. Ch. :
   1. Goldie Augusta, b. Dec. 14, 1879.
3. Wilber Henry, b. Feb. 8, 1856.
4. Chester Herbert, b. May 27, 1868.

No. 54.

(III.) **Seth Phillips** (son of Samuel of Athol : No. 47,)
born June 10, 1771; resided in Athol; m. **Ruth Allen** of
Royalston, Mass. He died in Athol, Oct. 10, 1852. Children :

1. EPHRAIM, b. June 22, 1795; d. Sept. 7, 1812.
2. ASA, b. Feb. 27, 1797; d. June 28, 1798.
3. SMITH, b. Feb. 17, 1799; d. Feb. 27, following.
4. SETH, b. Dec. 24, 1799; d. April 3, 1808.
5. ASA WILSON, b. Jan. 2, 1802; d. Dec. 21, 1818.
6. JAMES HARVEY, b. Oct. 19, 1803; d. July 29, 1805.
7. SOPHRONIA IDELIA, b. Dec. 31, 1805.
8. AARON JONES, b. June 29, 1809. In the spring of 1839 he
   went to Winhall, Vt., where he bought a tract of land in the
   wilderness, built a log house and cleared up a farm. He
   labored industriously and reared a large family. About 1867
   he sold the farm and removed to Londonderry. He died in
   Winhall, Nov. 26, 1880. He m. SUSAN WALKER of Athol.
   Children :
   1. Elvira W——, b. in Athol, Nov. 24, 1834; m. May 12, 1853,
      Richard Hews of Peru, Vt., where she d. Aug. 20, 1866.
   2. George Henry, b. in Athol, May 3, 1836; a sergeant in Co. C,
      14th Vt. Reg. in late war; now of Putney, Vt. He m. Nov.
      29, 1864, Miss Hellen M. Barrus.
   3. Lucy J——, b. in Athol, Aug. 17, 1837; m. June 6, 1867, John
      G. Barnard of Winhall; res. Londonderry.
   (The six following were born in Winhall :)
   4. Lydia A——, b. Nov. 9, 1839; m. Jan. 28, 1864, Warren J.
      Sheldon.
   5. Charles Abner, b. April 12, 1841; a soldier in the late war, in
      Co. C, 14th Vt. Reg. He with his brother Geo. H. were in
      the battle of Gettysburg.
   6. Martha J——, b. Feb. 17, 1843; m. April 19, 1865, Samuel A.
      Shattuck.
   7. Seth A——, b. Oct. 4, 1845; d. Oct. 12, 1849.
   8. Amos J——, b. Sept. 8, 1849; d. Sept. 11, 1852.
   9. Sumner B——, b. June 28, 1852.

8

9. JONAS ALLEN, b. Oct. 8, 1811 ; m. and buried his wife and two
small children ; two children living, 1880, a daughter and a
son.

10. ABNER SMITH, b. Oct. 29, 1814 ; of Bondville, Vt.   He m.
LUCINDA HARWOOD, b. in Athol, Mass., June 21, 1819,
daughter of David and Rebecca A. (Reed) Harwood.   She
died May 21, 1882, from the effect of injuries received about
two weeks before, caused by her horse running away.   Ch. :

   1. Lucy Melissa, b. in Athol, Nov. 6, 1845; in 1885 of West
Townshend, Vt. ; m. Charles H. Stratton.   Three children.

   2. David Abner, b. in Athol, Oct. 4, 1848; d. at the place of his
residence, Factory Point, Manchester, Vt., on the morning
of Sept. 1, 1881.   He was a young man of good habits, faithful in everything which he undertook, and always ready with
a pleasant word for every one.   He taught many how they
should be prepared to become living stones in that spiritual
temple, that house not made with hands, eternal in the
heavens.   But in the midst of his usefulness, when buds of
hopeful promise were just bursting into fruition, when
seemingly he could least be spared, he was called from his
temporal labors to eternal rest.   He was a member of Pacific
Engine Co., and of Adoniram Lodge, F. & A. M., both of
which orders attended his funeral in a body.   He m. Cleora
E. Cressey.   Ch. :

      1. Florence C———, b. at Factory Point, Oct. 6, 1875.
      2. Mabel L———, b. in Winhall, June 11, 1877; d. Jan.
4, 1879.
      3. Lettie M———, b. at Factory Point, Aug. 7, 1879.

No. 55.

(II.)   **Ebenezer Phillips*** (son of Ebenezer, senior, of
Southboro : No. 46,) resided in Southboro, but appears to have
lived later in neighboring towns.   He married **Hannah Lis-
comb** (or **Lyscom**).   Children : †

1. RUTH, b. May 27, 1745.

---

* A coincidence of names between some of the children of Ebenezer Phillips, Jr.,
of Southboro, and those of Ebenezer Phillips, b. Weston, 1722 (son of Samuel, and
gt.-grandson of Rev. Geo. of Watertown), has led some to conclude that the two
were identical, and it is so given in a lately published historical work; but this is
evidently erroneous.   The dates are widely at variance, and such a conclusion is con-
trary to the most authentic records and best preserved traditions of this family.   It
is certain that his grandchildren styled him Ebenezer Phillips, Jr. (son of Ebenezer
of Southboro), and his son of the same name, Ebenezer Phillips, 3d.

† The records of this family seem to have been much neglected, which made it
difficult to give a complete and correct genealogy.   It is believed, however, that the

2. HANNAH, b. Jan. 12, 1746-7.
3. MARY; m. April 5, 1769, DANIEL HUNT of Holliston.
4. SUSANNAH, b. Nov. 20, 1749.
5. EBENEZER, b. Feb. 23, 1752. (No. 56.)
6. SMITH, b. in Hopkinton, Mass., July 11, 1761.

No. 56.

(III.) **Ebenezer Phillips** (son of Ebenezer, Jr. of Southboro: No. 55,) born Feb. 23, 1752; described by his descendants as a man of great muscular development and marvellous strength, six feet two inches in height. It is related of him, that, on one occasion, when drawing several barrels, filled with cider, from the mill, the cart accidentally tipped up and precipitated the barrels into the road. This was repeated after he had carefully lifted the barrels into the hind end of the cart, and then, in the heat of the excitement occasioned thereby, he grasped the barrels by the chine, one at a time, and lifted them with agility and apparent ease over the side of the cart. Some of his descendants, for several generations, have inherited to a considerable extent, his muscular development and strength, if not his gigantic frame. He was a soldier in the war of the Revolution, participated in the battle of Bunker Hill, and was by the side of Gen. Warren when that distinguished hero fell. Late in life he drew a pension.* Among his descendants there has generally been manifested considerable natural talent for vocal music. He lived in Sutton (now Millbury) and Grafton, and died in Grafton, June 5, 1834. He married **Rachel Gale** of Sutton (now Millbury). Children:

1. SILAS, b. Oct. 27, 1775; of Rutland, N. Y. (No. 57.)
2. EZRA, b. March 9, 1778; of Shrewsbury; d. April 5, 1861.
   He m. ANNIE WHEELOCK, who d. Aug. 5, 1860. Ch.:
   1. Ann, b. Jan. 8, 1810; m. Ira Shepard of Worcester, and lived in Shrewsbury.

---

above, though lacking in dates and general information, is correctly given. The birth of Mary was a little in doubt, and possibly should have been placed after that of Susannah. One account says, Hannah, wife of Ebenezer Phillips, was b. April 29, 1722, 3d child of Israel Lyscom of Marlboro.

* Charles L. Phillips of Washington C. H., Ohio, a gt.-grandson, informs the compiler that he has in his possession the sword which once belonged to the above Ebenezer.

2. Sarah, b. Mar. 3, 1812; m. L. Hodges of Warren, and went to Richmond, Ohio.
3. Mercy, b. Sept. 23, 1815; m. Obed Chickering of Shrewsbury.
4. Hannah, b. Jan. 5, 1817; m. James Flannigan, of Irish birth.
5. Ezra, b. Dec. 22, 1819; m. Merinda M. Warren of Shrewsbury, where he resides.
6. Silas, b. Feb. 23, 1821; m. Lucy Bartlett of Shrewsbury, and went to Sturbridge, Mass.
7. Tyler, b. Oct. 12, 1823; d. in Shrewsbury, March 24, 1838.
8. Henry b. Aug. 30, 1827; m. Martha Roods of Grafton; d. Aug. 25, 1860.
9. Harriet, b. Oct. 24, 1830; m. James C. Keyes of Worcester.

3. EBENEZER. (No. 63.)
4. HANNAH; m. JOSIAH WARD, and d. in North Brookfield.
5. JOSIAH; of Watertown, N. Y. (No. 64.)
6. MARY; m. JOSHUA BARNARD of North Brookfield, and d. in Ohio, Nov., 1859, aged 74.
7. ELIZABETH; m. OLIVER WARD of North Brookfield, where she d. April 13, 1864.
8. JOHN, b. 1789. (No. 65.)
9. MERCY; m. WILLIAM AYRES; lived in North Brookfield and Smithfield, R. I., and d. in Worcester, June 23, 1866. Ch.:
    1. William W. *Ayres*, b. in N. Brookfield, March 12, 1813; m. Emily J. Fishback.
    2. John Phillips *Ayres*, b. in Smithfield, Oct. 31, 1818; d. June 4, 1819.
    3. Lucy H. *Ayres*, b. in Smithfield, Jan. 5, 1820; m. Charles C. Foster. Children:
       1. Charles A. *Foster*, b. in Grafton, May 12, 1845; residence, Brooklyn, N. Y.; m. Flora E. Goodnow.
       2. James M. *Foster*, b. in Grafton, Nov. 3, 1847; dentist of Hoboken, N. J.; d. in that place May 19, 1879.
10. SARAH; unmarried; d. May 24, 1871, aged 77.
11. TYLER; d. young.
12. ABIGAIL; unmarried; d. in Grafton, Jan. 30, 1878, aged 78.

No. 57.

(IV.) **Silas Phillips** (son of Ebenezer of Grafton: No. 56,) born Oct. 27, 1775; a farmer; settled in Rutland, Jefferson Co., N. Y., in the spring of 1805. He was among the early settlers of Jefferson Co.; collector of taxes in Rutland for eighteen years, and the people of the town expressed their confidence by electing him to other positions of honor and trust. "For many years he was a worthy member of the M. E. Church, and at the time of his death showed strong evidence that he was prepared for a bright and happy entrance into the spirit world." He died Aug. 29, 1850. He married **Lucretia Scott** of Ward (now Auburn), Mass. She died May 1, 1852, aged seventy-six. Children :

1. CLARENDON, b. in Auburn, May 18, 1799. (No. 58.)
2. CLARISSA, b. in Oakham, Mass., Jan. 19, 1801 ; m. her cousin, HOSEA B. PHILLIPS, son of Ebenezer and Sarah (Lathe) Phillips. She d. in Washington, D. C., Jan. 29, 1873.
3. ELIZABETH, b. in Oakham, Nov. 2, 1802 ; d. Nov. 2, 1871 ; unmarried.
4. SILAS GALE, b. in Oakham, March 23, 1804 ; of Champion, N. Y. (No. 59.)
5. CATHERINE, b. in Rutland, Jefferson Co., N. Y., Sept. 1, 1805 ; m. Oct. 28, 1838, WILLIAM L. WILCOX. He d. near Natural Bridge, N. Y., June 28, 1873, aged seventy-six.
6. LUCRETIA, b. Sept. 13, 1807 ; d. Nov. 17, 1808.
7. JOSIAH, b. Sept. 11, 1810. (No. 60.)
8. JERUSHA, b. May 20, 1813 ; m. Jan. 6, 1834, JOSIAH JOHNSON, b. in Buckland, Mass., Nov. 11, 1806, in 1879, of Black River, N. Y.
9. MARY J——, b. Sept. 27, 1815 ; m. July 4, 1838, CLARK CROOK of Champion, N. Y., where they had a fine residence, and where they both died, he May 22, 1874, and she May 25th following.
10. DAVID, b. May 6, 1818 ; of Gage's Lake, Ill. (No. 61.)
11. EBEN, b. Oct. 27, 1821 ; of Natural Bridge, N. Y. (No. 62.)

No. 58.

(V.) **Clarendon Phillips** (son of Silas of Rutland : No. 57,) born May 18, 1799 ; married Feb. 20, 1829, **Barbara Ann Wilcox**; died March 25, 1857. She died Nov., 1848. Children :

1. LUCRETIA, b. in Rutland, Feb. 14, 1831.
2. HIRAM, b. March 30, 1833 ; mason by trade, of Natural Bridge ; m. (1st) June 12, 1860, MARCIA JANE CLARK, who was b. June 9, 1843, and d. Aug. 15, 1865, leaving two children. He m.

(2d) Aug. 8, 1867, SARAH JANE CRANKER, b. April 11, 1845.
Ch. (by first marriage) :

1. Margaret Ellen, b. July 13, 1861.
2. Susan Emma, b. March 11, 1863.

(By second marriage) :

3. Lydia, b. Aug. 26, 1868.
4. George, b. Nov. 3, 1869.
5. Asaph, b. July 4, 1871.
6. Clara Jane, b. Jan. 9, 1873.
7. Catherine Amelia, b. April 15, 1877.

3. CALISTA, b. Feb. 24, 1837; d. Nov. 18, 1872.
4. ELIZABETH, b. May 28, 1839 ; d. June 17, 1878.
5. DAVID, b. Oct. 4, 1841 ; d. Nov. 28, 1873.
6. NELSON, b. May 30, 1843 ; of Black River ; removed to Adams, N. Y.
7. CATHERINE, b. August 10, 1845 ; m. June 29, 1862, ALLEN SANFORD KILBURN, a carpenter and joiner, of Champion. Ch. :

1. Albert Jerold *Kilburn*, b. Feb. 18, 1867; d. March 23, 1872.
2. Coraetta Blanche *Kilburn*, b. July 5, 1870.
3. Hubert Allen *Kilburn*, b. Oct. 1, 1875.

8. SARAH REBECCA, b. Aug. 15, 1847 ; m. April 9, 1868, JOHN SMITH DAVIS, a farmer, of Natural Bridge, b. May 17, 1846. Ch. :

1. Nelson Garie *Davis*, b. Oct. 30, 1870.

No. 59.

(V.) **Silas Gale Phillips** (son of Silas of Rutland : No. 57,) born March 23, 1804 ; a farmer of Champion, N. Y. ; married Dec. 15, 1836, **Abigail Woodward**. He died in Champion, Oct. 21, 1876. Children :

1. JOHN LANE, b. Aug. 10, 1841 ; a farmer, occupying the homestead farm ; m. Sept. 22, 1869, SARAH JOSEPHINE PEEBLES. Ch. :

1. Leona Blanche, b. Feb. 5, 1871.
2. Edward S——, b. April 23, 1877.

2. ERWIN WILLIAM, b. March 3, 1852.
3. ROSE ADALAIDE (adopted), b. Jan. 25, 1850 ; m. Nov. 25, 1875, DUANE A. PEEBLES.

No. 60.

(V.) **Josiah Phillips** (son of Silas of Rutland : No. 57,) born Sept. 11, 1810 ; married Feb. 20, 1839, **Lorene Crook.** Children :

1. ORRIN, b. May 29, 1842 ; m. June 3, 1869, JULIA I. MANCHESTER, b. Jan. 31, 1848. Ch. :
    1. Joel Wilber, b. Dec. 28, 1871 ; d. Aug. 14, 1872.
    2. Anna Bertha, b. Aug. 5, 1873.
    3. Mabel Emogene, b. May 30, 1875.
2. LUCY ANN, b. Sept. 7, 1843 ; m. July 4, 1865, JOHN BARBER ; living, 1879, in Champion.

No. 61.

(V.) **David Phillips** (son of Silas of Rutland : No. 57,) born May 6, 1818 ; married Dec. 25, 1845, **Emily S. Porter,** born Dec. 3, 1819 ; residence, Gage's Lake, Lake Co., Ill. Children :

1. SARAH JANE, b. Sept. 10, 1846 ; m. Dec. 23, 1868, JARED O. BLODGETT, b. Feb. 22, 1838. Ch. :
    1. Emma L. *Blodgett*, b. Jan. 13, 1870.
    2. George D. *Blodgett*, b. Aug. 22, 1871.
    3. Phillips J. *Blodgett*, b. Oct. 2, 1874.
    4. Valnet M. *Blodgett*, b. March 28, 1877.
2. FRANK P———, b. Dec. 24, 1848.
3. CLARK J———, b. Nov 4, 1851.
4. DAVID S———, b. Dec. 12, 1854.
5. MYRON H———, b. Jan. 6, 1857.
6. EMMA G———, b. April 3, 1862.
7. MARY M———, b. Aug. 13, 1865.

No. 62.

(V.) **Eben Phillips** (son of Silas of Rutland : No. 57,) born Oct. 27, 1821 ; enlisted Aug. 1, 1864, in the 186th Reg., N. Y. Vols. As a brave and true soldier he served till the close of the war of the Rebellion, having thoroughly experienced the vicissitudes and dangers of camp life and battlefield, and was honorably discharged June 9, 1865. Residence,

Natural Bridge, N. Y. He married May 4, 1858, **Apalonia Amanda Becker.** Children, five living 1879 :

1. SILAS GALE, b. April 20, 1859.
2. CATHERINE APALONIA, b. Nov. 12, 1861.
3. ALBERT ALONSO, b. Oct. 1, 1863.
4. MARY JANE, b. Oct. 11, 1865.
5. LEWIS R——, b. Jan. 4, 1868.

No. 63.

(IV.) **Ebenezer Phillips** (son of Ebenezer of Grafton : No. 56,) born in Sutton;* a cooper by trade; m. **Sarah Lathe.** Children :

1. HOSEA B——, b. in Grafton, Aug. 20, 1801; m. CLARISSA PHILLIPS, daughter of Silas (No. 57) and Lucretia (Scott) Phillips; he d. Oct. 3, 1861. Ch. :

    1 and 2. ——, daughters; names not given; both married; residence, Washington, D. C.

    3. Charles L——, b. in Rutland, N. Y., March 3, 1827; lived in Grafton, Mass., a year and a half, in Washington, D. C., eighteen years, and since 1868 in Washington, Ohio. Although no mention is given of enlisting as a regular soldier, the time in which he was engaged in the service of his country some two years or more seems to have been full of wild adventure. He assisted with his team to convey Gen. McDowell's camp equipage from Washington to Centerville at the time of the first battle of Bull Run, and was close by headquarters during the battle. He soon after went on one of the government transport steamers, and was on the water for two years. The boat on which he was employed was sunk near Fortress Monroe, but after four weeks was raised and fitted up, and he was again employed on the same steamer. He m. (1st) Dec. 24, 1849, Julia Melotte, b. 1828. She d. Sept. 14, 1851, and he m. (2d) Jan. 24, 1852, Cornelia D. Wright, b. Aug. 2, 1831. Ch. :

        1. Corah C—— C——, b. Feb. 8, 1853.
        2. Lewis C——, b. April 2, 1855; a druggist in Washington, Ohio.
        3. Sarah Elizabeth, b. March 29, 1858; d. Sept. 16, 1861.
        4. George William, b. Feb. 28, 1861.

* One account says he was born in 1777, another says 1779. Another says he died Aug., 1859. According to probate records, Sarah Phillips of Grafton, widow of Ebenezer Phillips, made her will in Grafton, March 19, 1852; will proved Nov. 7, 1854.

2. George W———, b. in Grafton, Aug. 18, 1804 ; m. Maria L. Tucker ; residence Grafton. No children.
3. Sarah C———, b. June 1, 1809 ; d. young.
4. Sarah Ann, b. July 19, 1813 ; m. Moses L. Batcheller ; d. May 3, 1877.
5. Robert William, b. in Grafton, Feb. 7, 1816 ; of Sutton ; m. Mary Batcheller.

No. 64.

(IV.) Josiah Phillips (son of Ebenezer of Grafton : No. 56,) born Jan. 2, 1782, in Grafton, Mass. ; m. Huldah Pike, and emigrated, probably about 1820, to Watertown, N. Y. ; a blacksmith and scythe maker ; emigrated in May, 1854, to Wayne Centre, Ill., where he died Nov. 29, 1858, aged seventy-seven. Children :

1. Eliza Ann, b. in Millbury, Mass., Jan. 3, 1818 ; m. A. Danforth ; residence, Philadelphia, Jefferson Co., N. Y.
2. Mary Jane, b. in Brownville, Jefferson Co., N. Y., Nov. 17, 1823 ; m. in Champion, N. Y., Jan. 10, 1844, James B. Babcock ; res., 1885, Nugent, Iowa ; emigrated to Ill., 1854, and to Iowa, 1868.
3. William Nelson ; of Albany, Oregon. (No. 64a.)

No. 64a.

(V.) William Nelson Phillips (son of Josiah of Watertown, N. Y. : No. 64,) b. Dec. 30, 1825 ; an officer in the late war, adjutant of the 105th Ill. Volunteers. He married Lucy J. Taylor of Charlton, Saratoga Co., N. Y. ; res. Albany, Oregon. Children :

1. William Irving, b. in Charlton, N. Y., July 20, 1847 ; a soldier of the Union Army, in the 23d Ill. Reg. ; grad. Wheaton Coll., Wheaton, Ill., 1873 ; grad. at Chicago Theological Sem., 1876 : Congregational minister at College Springs, Iowa ; publisher and treasurer 1885, of the National Christian Association, Chicago, Ill., whose avowed object is : " To expose, withstand and remove secret societies, Freemasonry in particular, and other anti-Christian movements, in order to save the churches of Christ from being depraved, to redeem

the administration of justice from perversion, and our republican government from corruption."

He m. 1876, Mary Dana Bissell, b. Dec. 13, 1849, at Norwalk, Indian Territory, five miles westerly from Wheelock, dau. of Lewis Bissell, b. in Melborn, Canada, July 29, 1819, and Mary Jackson (Dickinson) Bissell of Deerfield, Mass., where her family lived many years. Lewis Bissell and his wife were missionaries of the American Board to the Choctaw Nation, where he went in the fall of 1844. He was son of Austin and Clarissa (Stacy) Bissell of Wardsboro, Vt. Austin Bissell was b. Sept. 26, [1787?]; she was b. Nov. 18, 1793, and d. in Wardsboro. "They were both Christians." Ch. :

     1.   Carrie; d. at College Springs, Sept. 24, 1877.
     2.   Paul Bissell, b. Jan. 7, 1879.
     3.   Walter Irving, b. Apr. 3, 1880.
     4.   James Edwin, b. May 13, 1881.

2.   MARY ROSETTA, b. in Antwerp, N. Y., Jan. 13, 1849; m. JOHN A. SEDGWICK; res., Oak Park, Cook Co., Ill.

3.   CHARLES ELLIOTT, b. in Antwerp, Feb. 11, 1850; d. Apr. 25, 1876, in Lombard, Ill., leaving a widow.

4.   JAMES EDWIN, b. in Antwerp, May 13, 1851; grad. at Ann Arbor, Mich., Law School; a lawyer in Wheaton, Ill.; m. EMMA SAYER.

5.   GEORGE HOLLISTER, b. in Antwerp, N. Y., March 12, 1853; residence, Channahon, Ill.

6.   STANLEY HERBERT, b. in Wayne, Dupage Co., Ill., April 26, 1855; of Forest Grove, Oregon (Pacific University); m. in Portland, Oregon, Oct. 15, 1879, EMMA LOUISE SPENCER, b. in San Francisco, Cal., Nov. 25, 1854, dau. of George H. Spencer of Eng., cousin to Herbert Spencer of Eng. Ch., born in Forest Grove:

     1.   Irving Spencer, b. May 4, 1881.
     2.   Mary Louise, b. April 14, 1884.

7.   JULIA ADELAIDE, b. in Wayne, Ill., March 23, 1857; residence, Oak Park, Ill.

8.   LUCY ELLA, b. in Wayne, Ill., Aug. 22, 1860; m. Oct. 3, 1883, CHARLES HENRY CAUFIELD, cashier of Oregon City Bank; res., Oregon City, Oregon. Ch. :

     1.   Edna Jane *Caufield*, b. Nov. 19, 1884.

9.   MERRIL DANFORTH, b. in Wayne, Ill., Oct. 13, 1861.

10.   MINNIE E———, b. in Wayne, Ill., Nov. 18, 1863 ; d. in same place.
11.   HOMER JOSIAH, b. at Downer's Grove, Dupage Co., Ill., Nov. 7, 1869.
12.   HAROLD HENRY, b. at Downer's Grove, Ill., March 31, 1871 ; d.
13.   HENRY SPENCER, b. in Worthington, Minn., May 7, 1874.

No. 65.

(IV.)   **John Phillips** (son of Ebenezer of Grafton : No. 56,) born 1789 ; married **Catharine Lathe;** resided in Grafton and died there July 4, 1862, in his seventy-third year. Children, all born in Grafton :

1.   CATHARINE, b. Apr. 7, 1807; m. Jan. 20, 1827, CHARLES LELAND HEYWOOD.   She d. July 30, 1840.   Ch. :
    1.   Catharine Amelia *Heywood*, b. 1828; m. A. R. Briggs, of San Francisco, Cal.
    2.   Charles Phillips *Heywood;* of Hannibal, Mo.
2.   JOHN GALE, b. June 8, 1809 ; of Quidnick, R. I. ; m. (1st) in Sutton, Mass., SALLY NEWTON ; (2d) in Providence, R. I., SUSAN TEW.   He d. May 5, 1882.   Ch., by first marriage :
    1.   Ansel Porter; m. (1st) Elizabeth Smith of Providence; (2d) Isabella Randall of same.   He d. in Kansas City, July 17, 1882, aged about forty-eight.   Ch., by first marriage :
        1.   Florence, b. about 1860.
    2.   Sarah Isabella; m. Gerritt Smith, a distinguished electrician, of New York City.   She d. 1866, aged thirty-one.   No ch.
    3.   John Ebenezer; d. young.
    4.   John Ebenezer; d. young.
    5.   Margetta; d. at six or seven years of age.
    6.   Charles Heywood, b. Aug., 1845, railroad agent in Kansas and New Mexico; m. Annie Hall of Wickford, R. I.
    7.   Jane; d. when about two years old.
3.   ELBRIDGE GERRY, b. March, 1815 ; of Blackstone, Mass ; m. DORCAS MONROE, of that place.   He d. Oct. 12, 1882.   No ch.
4.   BENJAMIN LATHE, b. Nov. 20, 1817 ; inventor, of Providence ; he invented the eccentric engraver, an ingenious and highly valued device much used in preparing rolls for the printing of calicoes ; d. July 8, 1862, only a few days after his father.

He m. Oct. 31, 1839, ADELINE BROWN BACON. Ch., born in Grafton :

   1. Willard Jerome, b. Apr. 6, 1841; of Providence, where he d. March 10, 1885; m. Eleanor Carlisle, July 2, 1866. Ch. :

      1. Benjamin Anthony, b. June 24, 1868.
      2. Ann Elizabeth, b. Sept. 2, 1870.
      3. Eleanor Louisa, b. July 4, 1873.
      4. Sarah Margaret, b. Feb. 6, 1876.
      5. Walter Lyon, b. June 4, 1880.
      6. William Robert, b. July 21, 1883; d. June 1, 1884.

   2. Ann Maria, b. Jan. 26, 1843; m. June 23, 1863. Miles G. Merry; of Lonsdale, R. I. Ch. :

      1. Mary Gracie *Merry*, b. Mar. 11, 1874.

5. ANDREW SMITH, b. May 8, 1825 ; of Providence. (No. 66.)
6. JEROME ; d. before maturity.

No. 66.

(V.) **Andrew Smith Phillips** (son of John of Grafton : No. 65,) born May 8, 1825 ; of Providence, R. I. ; the first engineer at the Point street bridge, commencing in 1873 and is still employed there, 1885. This bridge was one of the first worked by steam in New England. He married Sept. 16, 1845, **Roxana Minerva Drake** of Shrewsbury, Mass. She was born in Northbridge, Mass., June 13, 1828, daughter of Jonathan Heyden, and Anne Bruce (Stone) Drake, and grand-dau. on her father's side, of Francis Drake of Shrewsbury, and on her mother's side, of Daniel, and Anne (Bruce) Stone of Shrewsbury. Children :

1. WALTER POLK, b. June 14, 1846 ; of New York City. (No. 67.)
2. KATE MINERVA, b. in Grafton, Feb. 1, 1851 ; m. Jan. 16, 1873, CHARLES HENRY BOGLE. She d. in Providence, Dec. 21, 1876. No. ch.

No. 67.

(VI.) **Walter Polk Phillips** (son of Andrew Smith of Providence : No. 66,) was born in Grafton, Mass., June 14, 1846. He is almost entirely self-educated, having left school at the age of twelve years. After the premature close of his school days the

Walter G. Phillips

ensuing two years were devoted to service on a farm, when, being fourteen years of age, he entered the employ of the American Telegraph Company, at Providence, R. I., as a messenger boy. Here his aptitude and devotion to duty were made apparent and he soon became a valuable operator. In 1867, he being then barely twenty-one years of age, we find him the acknowledged head of the telegraphic profession as a skilled and rapid manipulator. In that year he performed the greatest telegraphic achievement on record, viz: "receiving," that is, copying from sound, in a clear, legible hand, 2,731 words in sixty minutes, a feat which has never been equalled. This performance called forth the hearty personal recognition of the inventor of the Morse telegraph, Prof. Samuel F. B. Morse, who presented Mr. Phillips with a handsome testimonial; and, on April 27th of that year (the seventy-eighth anniversary of the great inventor's birth), he penned a strong and flattering autograph letter to young Phillips, acknowledging the wonderful perfection he had reached. In 1870, Mr. Phillips became the managing editor of the *Providence Daily Herald,* and the marked ability with which he conducted that paper attracted the attention of many of the leading state officials, and earned for him the enduring friendship of numerous men of mark. In 1872, Mr. Phillips founded the *Attleboro Chronicle,* and by his ability and untiring energy not only made it a flourishing concern in Attleboro, but placed it on the news-stands of the larger neighboring cities. The *Chronicle* passed from his hands in 1875, when he entered the service of the Associated Press in its New York office. Although Mr. Phillips entered the latter service as a subordinate, he was, ten months thereafter, promoted to the important position of principal assistant to James W. Simonton, who is at the head of all the far-reaching machinery of this powerful organization.

On the fourteenth of June, 1878, his thirty-second birthday, Mr. Phillips was placed at the head of the Washington bureau of the Associated Press, a position of much influence, honor and emolument. He is also Superintendent of the Associated Press telegraph line, and under his immediate direction or wise counsels, vast improvements have been introduced during the past four years. Among these improvements may be mentioned the "Phillips system of Steno-telegraphy," which doubles the capacity of wires without the aid of any expensive machinery. This system has been introduced on the Associated Press circuits with pronounced success, and is probably destined to come into general use for the rapid transmission of business on public lines, at an early day.*

Between 1872 and 1875 he wrote some remarkably clever sketches — studies of by-gone telegraphic heroes—which, in 1876, were published in book form, together with a series of non-telegraphic stories. His entrance to "the sacred guild of authors" was greeted with many flattering notices from the press, and was succeeded by large sales, several editions of the book being rapidly called for.

In addition to his present duties, he is constantly writing verses,† sketches and editorial articles for literary, telegraphic or other scientific papers, and he is at present engaged on a novel illustrative of a New England boy's life. Indeed, he has been a prolific writer for newspapers for the last ten years, under the pen names of "Gilbert Slowboy," "Maurice McLeod," and finally "John Oakum," which is now the widest and most favorably known.

While to bespeak for Mr. Phillips at present, a place beside the very foremost of our leading writers of the present day would be premature, it is no exaggeration to say that his language and his descriptions, whatever they bear upon, are as pure and as clear as those of authors whose style is accepted as a standard, even if they have not pretended to so wide a range, and that there is much promise in him for his maturer years. The world to him, notwithstanding his extreme earnestness and numerous well balanced and settled convictions, is a

---

* When Mr. Simonton died, in 1882, Mr. Phillips retired from the Associated Press and assumed full charge as General Manager of The United Press, which, under his direction during the past two years, has won recognition as a legitimate and powerful rival of the Associated Press. His headquarters are in New York, and his home is in Plainfield, N. J.

† The verses at the close of this sketch, which have been widely copied, illustrate his poetical efforts.

school. He is always open to discuss freely the merits of
"the points" in his efforts, excellent as those points may be;
promptly profits by successes and failures alike; is always
thankful for suggestions and sensible criticism touching his
literary work, weighs them all carefully, and acts readily upon
them when good ones are made. This is a quality which, of
itself alone, must tend greatly toward final success. Another
of his qualities is untiring industry. While busily engaged, in
one capacity, in supervising the collection and distribution of
reliable and unbiased, but necessarily uninspiring commonplace
news and statistics, we find him on the other hand, in a different
capacity, commenting on the same and drawing the appropriate
lesson therefrom for the public, just as naturally and easily as
though the latter occupation were the only duty which circumstances had imposed upon him. His published sketches show
that they are the deductions of one possessing a habit of close
observation, a keen sense of humor, and one who is at the same
time a shrewd but mirth-loving man of the world. He "turns
out" a pathetic incident, or invests solid sober counsel with all
the charm of half-earnest but penetrating pleasantry with equal
adroitness; and his writings, pathetic or "light," are ever
replete with shrewd and wholesome suggestions.

In his literary treatment of the telegraphic profession—a field
where some of his earliest triumphs were won—there is not one
competitor to approach him.—As a far-seeing critic he has
proved himself fearless and just, yet so good-natured, that his
victims can never muster up feelings of resentment, but rather
profit by his lecturing. Nor is his strength as a writer confined
to prose. His poetical efforts are well represented. The
estimation in which Mr. Phillips is held by the telegraphic
profession is best determined by the numerous spontaneous
outbursts which greet him in the journals, published by that
interesting and generally intelligent fraternity. Many poetical
offerings have been made to him by his admirers, which, although they evince a lusty appreciation of Mr. Phillips, are
hardly worth more than bare mention.

He refers to his native town in "Oakum Pickings," as

follows :—"Away up among the hills and dales of Massachusetts, where the Blackstone winds brightly in the sunlight a
mere brook ; where the atmosphere is as clear and fragrant as
nectar ; where, of all the world, the trees and the earth are
of the greenest possible tint ; where the robin sings in the
sweetest strains at morning ; where the bluejay is the bluest;
where the whippoorwill chirps in tones of the most melancholy
sweetness at night ; where the moon shines the softest ; where
the stars twinkle the merriest ; and where everything around,
in our opinion at least, is primitive, beautiful and smiling, we
were born and passed together our dear, dreamy, delicious days
of boyhood."—Pierce's History of Grafton.

CURFEW BELLS.

By John Oakum.
Naples, 1870.

A grand old hymn sang those village bells,
　Which I heard in the golden past ;
Their cadence was mellow, but clear and high
And I hear them again 'neath the starlit sky !
　And a spell o'er my soul is cast.

I stand again midst whispering trees,
　And their murmur a story tells
Of wonderful valor, of love and fame,
While I listen with longings too sweet to name
　To the song of those evening bells.

There are thoughts I fancied were gone for aye,
　But they come trooping back to-night ;
There are unspoken hopes and visions rare,
A locket of gold and a ringlet of hair
　And a face of wondrous light.

Loved forms return at this curfew hour,
　And dreams which ended in sadness ;
Old memories, sweeter than breath of June,
Scent of faded flowers and a long lost tune,
　Which chasten my hours of gladness.

Ring out, oh ! bells of the by-gone years,
  Your voices are dearer to me
Than all musical strains on earth beside,
  As your mellow tones reach me at eventide
  From over the shimmering sea.

He married Apr. 15, 1866, **Francena Adelaide Capron,** of Attleboro', b. May 15, 1847, dau. of Virgil Henry and Nancy (Dunham) Capron. The mother of V. H. Capron was a Bates, and a lineal descendant of John Carver, who came over in the *Mayflower*, and who was the first Governor of Plymouth Colony. Children, all born in Providence, R. I. :

1. IRVING ADDEMAN, b. Nov. 15, 1869 ; d. in Providence, Sept. 14, 1874.
2. ALBERT DICKENS, b. Sept. 4, 1871.
3. EUGENE DUNBAR, b. Aug. 17, 1874 ; d. Sept. 16, 1874.

9

JOHN PHILLIPS,

OF DUXBURY, MASS., 1638.

There was one, John Phillips of Duxbury and Marshfield, at a very early day. The records of his family are meagre, scattering and unsatisfactory. It is evident that no record was kept by him, for we are informed by the Plymouth Colony Records that John Phillips of Marshfield, and Faith Doty of Plymouth, signed a marriage contract by making their marks, Feb. 23, 1666 [1667 N. S.]. He was doubtless the progenitor of a large family which appears to include those given under Nos. 70 to 89 of this work. After referring to various writers whose accounts are sometimes conflicting, the following statements appear to be the most nearly correct:

No. 68.

John[1] **Phillips,** born in England, 1602, where he married. He came to Duxbury as early as July, 1638, and bought a house and land there of Robert Mendall, Oct. 19, 1639, "payments to be made yearly, every first day of Oct., at the house of Mr. Winthrop, in Boston." After 1643 he lived in Marshfield, where he was highway surveyor in 1655, and constable in 1657. July 31, 1658, his son John was killed by lightning.[*] He married for second wife, July 6, 1654, widow **Grace Holloway,** and she with their son Jeremiah were killed by lightning,

---

[*] "Being at work in the meadow, making hay, a tempest suddenly arose and he immediately started for the nearest house. Having entered he sat down between the door and the chimney, when the lightning struck the chimney, and descending, passed out the door, knocking him lifeless on the ground."—*Mather MSS.*

June 23, 1666.* He married (3d) Mar. 14, 1667, **Faith Doty** of Plymouth. She died prior to July 10, 1677. One account says he died in 1677, but this may be a mistake referring to the time of her death, for another says he probably died Oct., 1691, almost ninety years old. Children :

1. JOHN ; killed by lightning as stated.
2. SAMUEL ; m. and had a family.
3. JEREMIAH ; killed by lightning at ten years of age.
4. HANNAH.
5. JOSEPH ; said to have been killed in the Rehoboth fight, 1676.
6. BENJAMIN.† (No. 69.)

No. 69.

Benjamin² Phillips (son of John,¹) born 1658 ; married **Sarah Thomas.** Children :

1. JOHN, b. 1682 ; m. PATIENCE STEVENS, 1710.
2. JOSEPH, b. 1685.
3. BENJAMIN, b. 1687.
4. THOMAS, b. 1691 : probably the same who m. MARY SHERMAN and went to East Bridgewater.
5. JEREMIAH, b. 1697.
6. ISAAC, b. 1702.

Compare these names with the marriages in Marshfield given below.

---

* The account is related in a letter from Rev. Samuel Arnold of Marshfield, to Rev. Mr. Mather of Boston, 1683, and given by Winsor as follows : There were, at the house of John Phillips, fourteen persons. " Instantly a terrible clap of thunder fell upon the house and rent the chimney, and split the door in many places, and struck most of the persons, if not all." Three were " mortally struck with God's arrows, that they never breathed more." They were the wife of Mr. Phillips, and his son, aged about ten years, and one, **Wm.** Shertley [Shurtleff], " who had a little child in his arms, which was wonderfully preserved." This Shertley had just before been burnt out of his own house, and with his family, was at this time, " a present sojourner at said Phillips'."—*Mather MSS.*

† Mitchell, in his History of Bridgewater, mentions Benjamin as son of John² who was killed by lightning, and grandson of John¹ of Duxbury, 1638; but Savage, vol. 3, p. 412, gives information indicating that Benjamin was son of John¹ of Duxbury by second marriage, which is much more probable.

The following fragmentary records, if they could be satisfactorily placed, would probably show a connection with the above family in a majority of cases :—

NATHANIEL PHILLIPS m. Joan White, Jan. 16, 1635, both of M. Dea. Elisha m. Mary Wadsworth, July 1, 1756. Susanna m. Abner Russell, Dec. 24, 1764. Amos m. Priscilla Seabury, Dec. 24, 1778. Asa m. Clynthia Southworth, Oct. 5, 1769. Sarah m. Gideon Dawes, 1771. Bethiah m. James Basset of K., Oct. 14, 1773. Hannah m. Jesse Curtis, July 28, 1774. Benjamin m. Olive and had Joseph, Nov. 13, 1797.—Dux. Rec.—Hist. of Duxbury, Winsor, pp. 291, 292.

JOHN PHILLIPS m. Grace Holloway (widow) July 6, 1654. Benjamin m. Sarah Thomas, Jan. 12, 1681. John m. Ann Torrey, Apr. 3, 1677. John m. Patience Stevens, Feb. 16, 1710. Joseph m. Mary Eames, July 19, 1711. Benjamin m. Eleanor Baker, Jan. 16, 1716-17. Thomas m. Mary Sherman, Feb. 23, 1725. Bethiah m. Ichabod Washburn of Plymouth, June 2, 1725. Isaac m. Sarah White, Jan. 25, 1727.—Marriages in Marshfield.—*Hist. and Gen. Reg.*, pp. 348-352.

WILLIAM PHILLIPS (from Easton) m. 1718, one account says Jan. 16, 1716, Hannah, dau. of John Pryor, and d. 1743; he lived in Hanson probably (then Bridgewater), and his dau. Lydia m. Joseph Pettingill, 1746. Mary, perhaps also dau. of the above, m. Ezra Warren, 1752. Caleb was in Bridgewater, 1738. Eliphalet, thought to be son of Caleb, m. Mary, dau. of David Howard, 1762, and had ch. Eliphalet, 1765. Mary, 1768, Caleb, 1770, Hannah, 1771; he d. 1773, and his wid. m. Seth Harris. Hannah m. Benjamin Leonard, Aug. 15, 1715. Cyrus B. m. Lucretia Barrett of E., 1819. Samuel of Norton, m. Lydia Bassett, 1726. Ebenezer of E. m. Jemima Packard, 1802. William m. Mara Kingman, 1795. Capt. John m. Bridget Southworth, 1749. Rebecca of Plymouth, m. Zadock Packard, 1799. Lewis m. Polly Goodspeed, 1795. — Hist. of Bridgewater. N. Mitchell, pp. 270, 271.

GENEALOGY OF
THOMAS PHILLIPS,
OF DUXBURY, MASS.

No. 70.

(I.)   **Thomas Phillips** was of Duxbury, Mass., and died Dec. 17, 1759, aged 81. His mother's name was Mary. His wife, **Rebecca,** who is supposed to have been Rebecca Blaney* of Boston, died March 4, 1761, aged 80. Continued efforts have been made by some of his descendants to retrace the family to a more remote ancestry, but, so far, it is believed, without much success. It is thought that he was a descendant of John Phillips of Duxbury, 1638. Children :

1. REBECCA ; m. 1725, Philip Chandler.
2. THOMAS ; m. JEDIDAH ———, who d. Jan. 8, 1741. He d. Nov. 11, 1778, aged 73. Ch. :
    1. Mary, b. Jan. 29, 1731.
    2. Rebecca, b. May 18, 1732; m. July 31, 1771, Thomas Dawes.
    3. Abigail, b. Apr. 1, 1733.
    4. Thomas; m. 1771, Abigail Chandler. Ch. :
        1. Abigail, b. 1774.
        2. Rebecca.
        3. Luther.
        4. Mary.
        5. Chandler,
        6. Silvia.
3. JOHN, b. 1707; d. Mar. 16, 1791, aged 84. He m. MARY ———, who d. Mar. 21, 1791, aged 82.
4. SAMUEL, b. 1709 ; d. Nov. 26, 1734.
5. BLANEY. (No. 71.)

No. 71.

(II.)   **Blaney Phillips** (son of Thomas of Duxbury : No. 70,) born in Duxbury, 1712 ; resided in Duxbury, where he was constable or collector, 1745, and in Pembroke (now Han-

---

* Thomas, son of widow Mary Phillips (unknown) of Plymouth, housewright, m. Rebecca Blaney, at Boston, Dec. 31, 1702—Wyman's Charlestown Gen., p. 747.

son), and died in the latter place in 1800. He married May 23, 1733, **Christian Wadsworth.** Children :

1. SAMUEL, b. May 9, 1734 ; d. young.
2. BLANEY, b. July 3, 1736 ; removed to Fitchburg, Mass.   He m. MARY ———, who d. July 20, 1773.   Ch. :
    1. Olive, b. Jan. 24, 1763 ; m. 1782, Robert Sampson, son of Robert.
    2. Eunice, b. Sept. 29, 1764 ; d. young.
    3. Samuel, b. Aug. 5, 1766.   (No. 74.)
    4. Eunice, b. June 30, 1768.
    5. Mary, b. Nov. 8, 1769.
    6. Huldah, b. Dec. 5, 1771.
3. SAMUEL, b. May 2, 1738 ; d. Sept. 18, 1756.
4. CHRISTIAN, b. Apr. 7, 1740.
5. MERCY, b. March 10, 1742 ; d. Sept. 16, 1744.
6. MERCY, b. Oct. 6, 1744 ; m. 1762, MARK PHILLIPS of E. Bridgewater ; d. 1816.
7. SETH ; removed to Fitchburg.   Seth Phillips was one of the company of minute-men who marched from Fitchburg to Concord, Apr. 19, 1775.
8. LOT.   (No. 72.)
9. BETTY.

No. 72.

(III.) **Lot Phillips** (son of Blaney of Pembroke : No. 71,) born 1748 ; resided in Pembroke (now Hanson) ; m. **Diana Howland.** Children :

1. EZRA.   (No. 73.)
2. MEHITABLE, b. May 12, 1783 ; m. EBENEZER KEENE.
3. LYDIA, b. Apr. 7, 1786 ; m. ——— HOLMES.
4. SALLY, b. June 11, 1788 ; m. BENJAMIN BARKER.
5. DIANA, b. March 7, 1791 ; m. JOSEPH ALLEN.
6. CHRISTIAN WADSWORTH, b. Sept. 2, 1793 ; m. CYRUS MONROE.
7. BLANEY, b. Nov. 30, 1795 ; married.

No. 73.

(IV.) **Ezra Phillips** (son of Lot of Pembroke : No. 72,) born Oct. 21, 1779 ; of Hanson, Mass. ; married (1st) **Mehitable Allen** ; (2d) **Lucy Chamberlain** ; (3d) **Mrs. Nabby (Pratt) Phillips.** Children (by first marriage) :

1. EZRA, b. Oct. 10, 1810 ; of the firm of E. Phillips and Sons,

manufacturers of iron, copper, zinc and tinned tacks and shoe nails, South Hanover, Mass. He m. CATHERINE HITCHCOCK TILDEN, b. Oct. 1, 1807. Ch., all born in Hanson :

    1.   Calvin Tilden, b. March 3, 1836; a member of the Mass. Legislature in 1873, a member of the committee of arrangements at the dedication of the soldiers' and sailors' monument, Hanover, in 1878, an occasion which brought together 1500 people. He m. Oct. 31, 1865, Maria E. Josselyn.

    2.   Catherine, b. May 14, 1842; d. Dec. 30, 1843.

    3.   Morrill Allen, b. Feb. 27, 1844.

    4.   Charles Follen, b. April 21, 1846; fitted for the profession of law in the Boston University Law School, and was admitted to the bar.

    5.   Alfred Tilden, b. Nov. 16, 1849; d. March 5, 1850.

  2.   MEHITABLE ALLEN, b. Dec. 22, 1811 ; m. CHARLES BEALS.

(By second marriage) :

  3.   LUCY PRATT, b. May 30, 1818; m. NATHAN MONROE ; d.

  4.   GEORGE, b. July 7, 1824 ; m. BETHIA HATHAWAY ; both deceased.

(By third marriage) :

  5.   LOT, b. Feb. 13, 1841 ; m. SARAH E. BARKER.

No. 74.

(IV.) **Samuel Phillips** (evidently son of Blaney, Jr. of Fitchburg : No. 71,) was born in Duxbury about 1765.* He married **Hannah Bolton** and went to Searsmont, Maine, where he died about 1850. Children :

  1.   POLLY ; m. HIEL HOWARD.

  2.   BETSEY ; m. MARTIN CARY.

  3.   JAMES, b. at Searsmont; resided there till 1856 ; d. at Montville, Me., 1861. He m. MARY PRESCOTT. Ch., all born at Searsmont :

    1.   Charles, b. 1839 ; m. Caroline Brown.

    2.   George, b. 1841 ; d. 1866 ; m. Almeda Grinnell.

    3.   James A——, b. 1843 ; d. 1864.

---

* His grandson, Franklin F. Phillips, who favored the compiler with this record of his family, writes : " Grandfather Samuel's grandparents must have emigrated to this country from England. My uncle Solomon P. has a wallet which Grandfather gave him, saying that originally it was his grandmother's, who was a Scotch woman. The wallet has on it in large gilt letters the name ' London.' " Probably the emigration from England took place much earlier than supposed by Mr. F. F. P. The Scotch woman referred to appears to have been Rebecca Blaney, who m. Thomas Phillips at Boston, 1702.

    4. Nellie M———, b. 1846; m. (1st) George I. Parker who d., and she m. (2d) B. F. Cochran; res. Crete, Neb.

    5. Alvin, b. 1848; m. Minerva Pierce; res. Auburn, Me.

    6. Franklin F———, b. 1852; grad. Bates Coll., 1877; A. M., 1880; principal of Rockland High School, and one of the State assayers, 1881. He m. Julia A. Lyman. Ch.:

        1. Florence M———, b. in Lewiston, Me., Feb. 2, 1879.

        2. Franklin F———, b. in Rockland, Me., Nov. 17, 1880.

4. HANNAH; m. JESSE HARRIMAN; d.

5. WARREN; m. SARAH WALLS; lived in Illinois; d.

6. SAMUEL; d. in infancy.

7. SOLOMON; m. LOUISA GRAY; living, 1881, at South Gardiner, Me.

8. HARRIET; m. JEREMIAH LEWIS.

GENEALOGY OF
THOMAS PHILLIPS
OF

MARSHFIELD AND EAST BRIDGEWATER, MASS.

No. 75.

(III. [?]) **Thomas Phillips** came from Marshfield, and settled in East Bridgewater about 1735. His nativity is not clearly established, but he was probably born 1691, son of Benjamin Phillips who married Sarah Thomas, and grandson of John of Duxbury, 1638. He married Mrs. MARY EAMES SHERMAN, the widow of John Sherman, daughter of Mark Eames and granddau. of Anthony Eames of Marshfield. Children:

1. LYDIA; m. 1749, ZEBULON CARY.
2. THOMAS. (No. 76.)
3. ABIAH; m. 1761, BENJAMIN TAYLOR. She d. 1800, aged 70.
4. MARK, b. 1736. (No. 78.)
5. DEBORAH; supposed to have married LEVI WADE in 1766.

No. 76.

(IV.) **Thomas Phillips** (son of Thomas of Marshfield: No. 75,) born in Marshfield; married 1755, **Mary Hatch,** dau. of David Hatch, and resided in East Bridgewater. He died of small-pox at Spectacle Island, Boston Harbor, 1781. His widow, Mary, died 1811, aged 77. Children:

1. JOHN, b. 1756; sergeant in Gen. Washington's life guard during the Revolutionary war; m. 1784, JENNET YOUNG, dau. of John Young. She d. 1823, aged 57. Ch.:
    1. George Y——, b. 1788; m. 1812, Bethiah (Lazell) Mitchell, dau. of Joseph Lazell and wid. of Asa Mitchell. Removed to Poughkeepsie, N. Y. Ch.:
        1. Abigail Ames, b. 1813.
        2. Asa Mitchell, b. 1815.

2. Jennet, b. 1790.
3. Marquis LaFayette, b. 1792.
4. Eunice Bass, b. 1797.
5. Robert, b. 1802.

2. MARY, b. 1758; m. JOSEPH WHITMAN.
3. THOMAS, b. 1760; m. 1783, MARTHA WHITMAN, dau. of Capt. Simeon Whitman; d. 1849, aged 89. Ch. :
    1. Thomas; went to Natick.
    2. Joanna Whitman; m. 1811, John Corthrell of Abington.
4. JOSEPH; m. and went to New York. Ch. :
    1. Willard, b. in Bridgewater, Dec. 19, 1784; grad. Harv. Coll., 1810; LL.D.; of Boston; judge of probate, author of several works on life insurance, patents, political economy, &c., &c.; d. 1873.
5. TURNER. (No. 77.)
6. DAVID; went to New York.

No. 77.

(V.) **Turner Phillips** (son of Thomas of E. Bridgewater : No. 76,) born at E. Bridgewater, Dec. 24, 1764; died at same place 1824. He married **Huldah Whitman**. Children :

1. LEUTHEL, b. Sept. 17, 1787.
2. JOSEPH, b. Mar. 21, 1790; removed to Windsor, Mass.; m. (1st) SARAH FREELOVE WHITMAN; (2d) SIBYL BATES. Ch., all b. in Windsor (by first marriage) :
    1. Joseph Watson, b. August 28, 1819; also several who d. in infancy.
    2. John Lemuel Thomas, b. Mar. 16, 1827; grad. at Williams Coll., 1847; principal of an academy in Spencertown, N. Y., from 1847 to 1849; teacher in Williston Sem., Easthampton, Mass., from 1849 to 1851. In 1851 he entered Andover Theolog. Sem. with the intention of fitting for the ministry, but after being there a little more than one year was compelled to relinquish his studies on account of failure of his eyesight. He was professor of Greek in Williams Coll. from 1857 to 1868, when the state of his eyes compelled him to retire. He removed to Ballston, N. Y., and took up farming, but returned to Williamstown in 1877 and held the position of college librarian till his death, April 4, 1879. Unmarried.
    "He accomplished vastly more than many educated men with no bodily infirmity."

3. Lucy Cornelia, b. Sept. 9, 1829; m. 1851, Isaac Newton Lincoln, b. in Plainfield, Sept. 16, 1825, son of Isaac King and Melinda (Stoddard) Lincoln. He was professor of Latin and French at Williams Coll. from 1853 to 1862. In 1853 he was ordained as an evangelist, and preached at South Williamstown and at other churches for some years. He d. Sept. 5, 1862.

3. ELECTE, b. Feb. 9, 1793.
4. HULDAH, b. March 31, 1802; m. JARED REED.

No. 78.

(IV.) **Mark Phillips** (son of Thomas of Marshfield: No. 75,) born 1736; married 1762, **Mercy Phillips,** dau. of Blaney Phillips of Hanson; died 1811, aged 75. She died 1816, aged 71. Children:

1. Chloe, b. 1764; m. 1784, ISAIAH WHITMAN.
2. MARK, b. 1768; m. 1789, CELIA, dau. of Job Chamberlin. Ch.:
   1. Lucinda, b. 1790; m. 1818, Melzar Hudson.
   2. Nathan, b. 1793.
   3. Nabby, b. 1798; m. 1821, Jonathan Pratt of Halifax.
   4. Wadsworth, b. 1800.
   5. Phebe, b. 1804; m. Benjamin H. Washburn.
   6. Celia, b. 1810; m. Nathaniel Porter.
3. MOLLY, b. 1770; m. 1791, BARZA KINGMAN.
4. SUSANNA, b. 1772; m. 1794, JACOB LOWDEN.
5. WADSWORTH, b. 1774. He and his brother Barzillai went West.
6. NABBY, b. 1777; d. 1807, unmarried.
7. BARZILLAI, b. 1779.
8. LUCY, b. 1783; m. 1807, SMARDUS SNELL.
9. MERCY, b. 1787; d. 1831, unmarried.

GENEALOGY OF
JOHN PHILLIPS
OF EASTON, MASS.

No. 79.

(I.) **Capt. John Phillips** of Easton, Mass., the first person in that town who received a captain's commission, was the ancestor of a large number of the Phillips name. His birthplace and origin have not been clearly shown.* He died in Easton, Nov. 14, 1760. Children :

1. THOMAS, b. in Easton, Jan. 25, 1712 ; of Ashfield. (No. 80.)
2. EXPERIENCE ; m. RICHARD ELLIS, an Irishman who was the first settler in Ashfield, Mass.†

---

* There are good reasons for believing that Capt. John Phillips may have been the oldest son, b. 1682, of Benjamin[2] and Sarah (Thomas) Phillips, of Marshfield, and grandson of John,[1] of Duxbury, 1638, and, if so, the brother of Thomas who sett. in E. Bridgewater about 1735. The coincidence of names and dates points directly to this source. In that case the number of his generation should be (III.) instead of (I.) and the number of each succeeding generation should be changed to coincide.

† For the following statements the compiler is indebted to Mr. Geo. Bassett of Ashfield, a descendant of Capt. John Phillips.

The town of Ashfield, called Huntstown prior to 1765, was granted to a company of soldiers for service in an expedition to Canada in 1690, commanded by Capt. Ephraim Hunt of Weymouth. There were three in that company by the name of Phillips. The first settler of Ashfield was Richard Ellis as stated above. The second was Thomas Phillips ; the third was Ebenezer Smith, whose wife was Richard Ellis's daughter. Thomas Phillips lived in Deerfield a while, " whether any more than a short time being afraid of the Indians, I do not know." In the above company there was John Phillips who drew lot No. 6 in the first division. John Phillips drew for Richard Phillips lot No. 13. Joshua Phillips, " who, I suppose, was my grandmother's brother." drew for Joshua Phillips lot No. 56. The proprietors of Huntstown met and chose John Phillips moderator, March, 1738, 1739 and 1740 ; " John Phillips committee to lay out lots, committee to build a corn mill 1743. Thomas Phillips was chosen on a committee to see that no one should carry white pine timber out of town ; Caleb Phillips and Thomas Phillips on a committee to settle the boundary between Huntstown and Deerfield ; Caleb Phillips to have the care of the corn mill ; Thomas Phillips to lay out 100 acre lots ; Philip Phillips collector, 1760." There was a Benjamin Phillips who had seven sons born from 1750 to 1767 : " I think," writes Mr. Bassett, " they were my grandmother Mercy Phillips's relatives."

No. 80.

(II.) **Thomas Phillips** (son of Capt. John of Easton:
No. 79,) born in Easton, Jan. 25, 1712; settled in Ashfield;
married **Elizabeth** ———. He is said to have married twice,
and whether this was his first or second wife does not appear
certain. He was prominent in town affairs and appears to have
been entrusted with discretionary charge of matters requiring
wise management. Child :

   1. PHILIP. (No. 81.)

No. 81.

(III.) **Capt. Philip Phillips** (son of Thomas of Ashfield : No. 80,) born in Ashfield, Feb. 3, 1738. His mother is
said to have died when he was a young babe, and a negress who
occupied the place of mother to him during his early infancy
was, with her husband, in return comfortably cared for by him
in their old age. He was justice of the peace, a member of the
Legislature one year, town tax collector, captain of a military
company in Ashfield, and had one platoon of his eleven sons at
the general muster, and these were ordered to parade before
the whole regiment. The youngest, aged fourteen, was the
drummer, and another was fifer. He died in Ashfield, Aug.
10, 1800. He married **Mercy Phillips*** of Dighton, Mass.
She had one brother, Richard Phillips, who formerly lived in
Ashfield and had children, and three brothers in Dighton,
Abiathar, Samuel and Joshua. She is said to have had two
sisters, one of whom married a Truesdell, the other a Dwelly.
She died in 1815, aged 78. Children :

   1. ELIJAH, b. Feb. 14, 1759 ; of West Virginia. (No. 82.)
   2. ABNER, b. March 25, 1760 ; res. in Ashfield.
   3. LEMUEL, b. Nov. 26, 1762 ; res. in Ashfield.
   4. PHILIP, b. July 29, 1764 : of Cassadaga, N. Y. (No. 85.)
   5. DAVID, b. Feb. 2, 1766 ; went to West Virginia.
   6. SIMEON, b. June 1, 1768 ; went to Conway, Mass.
   7. ISRAEL, b. May 23, 1770. (No. 87.)

---

* A recurrence of names with general connection of historical events leads us to
believe that she was a descendant of Dea. Nicholas Phillips of Weymouth, 1640.

8. JOSHUA, b. Nov. 30, 1771 ; res. in Ashfield.
9. ABIATHAR, b. Oct. 27, 1773 ; went to Cattaraugus, N. Y.
10. SAMUEL, b. Aug. 14, 1775. (No. 88.)
11. LISCOM, b. Mar. 23, 1777 ; of Adams. (No. 89.)
12. HANNAH, b. Feb. 5, 1779 ; m. HENRY BASSETT. Ch. :

    1. Susanna *Bassett*, b. March 17, 1801; m. Joseph F. Upton. She
        d. May 5, 1845.
    2. George *Bassett*, b. Apr. 2, 1803; residing in Ashfield in 1882.
    3. Mercy *Bassett*, b. June 4, 1805; m. Lorenzo Lilly; d. Feb. 21,
        1874.
    4. Philip *Bassett*, b. Sept. 19, 1807; d. June 17, 1874.
    5. Henry *Bassett*, b. Apr. 22, 1810.
    6. Hannah *Bassett*, b. July 21, 1813; d. Aug. 27, 1853.
    7. Anna *Bassett*, b. March 1, 1816.
    8. William *Bassett*, b. Nov. 1, 1819; d. Nov. 9, 1869.
    9. Mary *Bassett*, b. Nov. 7, 1822; d. July 17, 1827.

13. ANNA, b. Oct. 27, 1782 ; resided in Ashfield ; m. PHILIP*
    PORTER.

No. 82.

(IV.) **Elijah Phillips** (son of Philip of Ashfield: No.
81,) born Feb. 14, 1759. He and his brother David emigrated
to West Virginia, and their descendants lived at French Creek.
They were loyal men during the late war. One was a captain
in the Union army, having "some twelve or fourteen Phillipses
in his company." He married **Cynthia Goodwin** of Ashfield. He died in West Virginia. Children, in all seventeen :

1. ELIJAH ; of Buckland, Mass. (No. 83.)
2. MABEL.   5. MERCY.   8. CYNTHIA.   11. EDWIN.
3. ANSEL.   6. EUSEBRA.   9. SAMANTHA.   12. LYDIA.
4. ABIEZER.   7. LYMAN.   10. DELIA.   13. JONATHAN.

No. 83.

(V.) **Elijah Phillips** (son of Elijah: No. 82,) born in
Ashfield ; married **Fanny Rude**, and settled in Buckland,
Mass., where he died. Children :

1. CAROLINE, b. in Ashfield, Nov. 1, 1804 ; m. ALVIN RUDDOCK,
    and resided in Buckland ; not living, 1885.

---

* This name is probably wrong. "Porter Genealogy" by Jos. W. Porter, Burling-
ton, Me., says: Ebenezer Porter, son of John, b. 1780; m. Ann Phillips. Ch. b. in
Ashfield: 1. Philip Phillips Porter, b. Feb., 1804. Several other ch.

2. LEBBEUS RUDE, b. in Ashfield, Nov. 2, 1806. (No. 84.)
3. SIMEON, b. in Ashfield, Jan. 27, 1809; m. MYRA BEMENT; res. in New York City.
4. CALISTA, b. in Ashfield, Dec. 2, 1811; m. MERRICK SMITH, and moved to the West.
5. FANNY, b. in Ashfield, March 29, 1814; m. JONATHAN VINCENT, and moved to the West.
6. CATHARINE AMELIA, b. in Ashfield, June 6, 1816; d. unmarried.
7. ELIJAH BLISS, b. in Buckland, Aug. 26, 1818; m. ELIZABETH RUDE; living, 1885, in Illinois.
8. LYDIA MOULTON, b. in Buckland, Dec. 21, 1820; m. JOSHUA CRANSON.
9. AUGUSTIN WASHINGTON, b. in Hawley, March 22, 1823; m. (1st) HANNAH ROSINA MAYNARD, b. Jan. 3, 1826; she d. July 28, 1848; m. (2d) MARIA NUTTING, b. June 30, 1822. He was living, 1885, in Amherst, Mass. Ch., all by second marriage :

    1. Rosina Maria, b. in Buckland, Dec. 20, 1851; m. Edwin D. Davis of Mechanicsville, N. Y.
    2. Mary Ellis, b. in Amherst, June 27, 1853; m. Elijah Shaw of Hawley, Mass.
    3. Fannie Smith, b. in Amherst, Feb. 9, 1855; d. in Northampton, Aug. 1, 1856.
    4. Stanley Augustin, b. in Northampton, May 15, 1857; of Amherst; m. Martha E. Lamson.
    5. Harriet Whipple, b. in Buckland, Apr. 4, 1859; m. Frederic D. Kellogg of Hadley.
    6. Grace Humphrey, b. March 14, 1863.

10. MARIA, b. in Buckland, Apr. 17, 1827.

No. 84.

(VI.) **Rev. Lebbeus Rude Phillips** (son of Elijah of Buckland : No. 83,) born Nov. 2, 1806; grad. at Williams Coll., 1836; at East Windsor Theological Sem. He preached at Halifax, Vt., one year, and was ordained and installed, 1841, pastor of the Cong. Church and Society, Sharon, Mass. He was dismissed on account of failure of health in 1861, and soon after removed to Groton, Mass., where he resided some years, then removed to Newtonville, Mass., where he still lives, 1885.

He married, Aug., 1838, **Miss Susanna Heath Goddard** of Roxbury, Mass.   Children :

1. EDWARD GRIFFIN, b. in Roxbury, May 1, 1840 ; d. at three years of age.
2. CATHERINE AMELIA, b. 1842, in Sharon ; res. Newtonville ; m. ROBERT G. SHEDD, and has children.
3. HELEN ELIZABETH, b. in Sharon, May 24, 1844 ; d. in Brookline, Feb. 1, 1881 ; unmarried.
4. JOHN GODDARD, b. in Sharon, May 29, 1848 ; commission merchant ; res. Boston ; m. Oct. 8, 1874, MARY W. NIGHTINGALE. Ch. :
    1. Mary Nightingale, b. in Lexington, Oct. 17, 1875.
    2. John King, b. in Boston, Oct. 2, 1877 ; d. same place, Dec. 28, 1883.
    3. Anna Goddard, b. in Boston, Sept. 16, 1879.
    4. Nightingale, b. in Boston, Nov. 24, 1883.

No. 85.

(IV.) **Philip Phillips** (son of Philip of Ashfield : No. 81,) born July 29, 1764 ; resided in Ashfield a portion of his life, but afterwards emigrated to Cassadaga, Chautauqua Co., N. Y., where he died Dec. 16, 1847.   He married **Elizabeth Smith**, a descendant, in the ninth generation, of Rev. Henry Smith of England, and only daughter of Chilleab and Elizabeth (Sawyer) Smith of Ashfield.   Children :

1. SAWYER, b. 1791.   (No. 86.)
2. ELIZABETH ; m. JOHN ROBINSON ; d. about 1828. Ch. :
    1. Elescom.
3. ESTHER ; m. ISRAEL SMITH ; d. about 1830. No. ch.
4. PHILIP ; d. about 1808, aged eight.
5. JOSHUA ; d. 1836, aged twenty-eight ; unmarried.

No. 86.

(V.) **Sawyer Phillips** (son of Philip : No. 85,) born in Ashfield, Mass., 1791 ; died in Cassadaga, N. Y., 1872.   He married **Jane Parker** of New York, dau. of Benjamin Parker and granddau. of Thomas Parker of Washington Co., N. Y.

"A granddaughter of Elijah Phillips who emigrated from Ashfield to West Virginia, Miss Mabel Forbush, died recently at the hotel of Williston Phillips in Cassadaga, aged 68. She was a cousin of Sawyer Phillips, and came to reside in his family more than forty years ago. His wife dying soon after, in 1844, left a large family of children who thus came under the care and direction of this maiden relative. With the counsel of a mother as well as the affection and tenderness of a sister, she ever continued, till her death, to be a cherished member of each household of the family of Sawyer Phillips." Children, all appear to have been natives of Cassadaga :

1. ALONZO, b. 1821 ; d. when five years of age.
2. THOMAS DAVIS, b. 1822 ; a dentist; general agent for western New York, of the *Chicago Magnetic Shield Co.*, headquarters at Cassadaga ; m. SYBIL FISHER. Three children, all married.
3. WILLISTON, b. 1824 ; merchant and hotel keeper in Cassadaga ; m. (1st) MARY ELLIS ; (2d) ELIZA HATCH. Three children, one married.
4. ROSINA, b. 1825 ; d. 1836.
5. ALONZO PARKER, b. Dec. 28, 1826 ; a physician in Fredonia, N. Y. ; also dealer in fruit and ornamental trees ; m. FIDELIA WOODS. Ch. :
   1. Jennie F——, b. in Allegany, Cattaraugus Co., N. Y., Jan. 1, 1852; d. unmarried, aged 26.
   2. A—— Burton, b. in Allegany, Aug. 6, 1854 ; d. aged 25.
   3. Frank H——, b. in Cassadaga, July 14, 1860; d. in Fredonia, March 13, 1875.
6. WILLIAM WALLACE, b. Oct. 8, 1828 ; a farmer in Cassadaga ; m. CELESTINA ELEY. Four children.
7. CHARLES, b. 1830 (or 1829) ; res. in Cassadaga ;* m. EUNICE CUMMINGS. No children.

* Wednesday, Aug. 8, 1877, was the day set apart by this family for a reunion at the residence of Charles Phillips, Esq., who with his estimable wife and pleasant home made the occasion one long to be remembered by all.

The members of the family comprise eight brothers and one sister, and were all present with their wives and families except G. H. Phillips.

At a stated hour in the afternoon all assembled at the house of Esq. Phillips, and, grouped together in the beautiful maple arbor upon the lawn, were soon interchanging greetings with each other, and relating incidents regarding the history of the family from its earliest juvenile years down to the present. A special feature of the hour was an extensive collection of fine views of all the principal towns and cities and great men and buildings which had been carefully collected by Philip Phillips, the sweet singer, in his travels around the world upon his mission of Christian song, and with the classified arrangements which he was able to give them, made, as it were, panoramic pictures of the countries and places through which he had passed,

8. SAWYER, b. 1831 ; d. unmarried, 1854.

9. JOSHUA, b. 1833 ; d. unmarried, 1850.

and for an hour or two the company travelled in thought with him through the great cities and towns of the oriental lands and old country.

Immediately following this pictured journey, the friends gathered into the house and were pleasantly seated in the parlor, where all joined in singing—" And are we yet alive and see each other's face?" after which appropriate portions of the Scriptures were read in concert, and all again joined in singing—" Nearer my God to Thee." At the closing line of this beautiful hymn the host, Mr. Charles Phillips, arose and in a few very appropriate remarks, admirably suited to the occasion, spoke, with feelings at times too full for utterance, his gratitude to God for the opportunity of seeing and meeting his brothers and sisters upon this occasion, and expressed a desire that all would kneel and join with brother Philip in prayer, thanking God for his protecting care which had so tenderly followed them. Remarks were then made by Dr. T. D. Phillips, the oldest brother, with reference to the anticipated meeting they were then enjoying which he had been looking forward to during the past year; and, while much crowded the mind that he would like to speak of, he felt too much overcome with emotions of gratitude and love to speak them out. Williston Phillips, the next in years, followed with touching and feeling remarks appropriate to the hour, followed by Dr. A. P. Phillips, whose tender feelings were so touched by the hallowed influences of the hour, made touching mention of the present meeting and the bright hopes he had of a meeting above, where he felt was a member of his own family awaiting him, and the tender thread of life that was still holding together the living members of the same brought him into sweet sympathy with the associations of the hour and the thought of the Heaven beyond. Appropriate remarks were made by the uncle and aunt who had been so intimately known by the family from its earliest history, followed by the youngest brother, Z. Barney Phillips, who from his experiences during severe illness since the last meeting, spoke of the sweet faith which enabled him in the hours of near approach to the dark valley of death to penetrate its shadows and behold the beautiful sunlight beyond, with an earnest hope that all present might so live that when the final message should come all would have this sweet assurance and feel the presence of the dear Saviour in the last hour. Philip referred gratefully to the privileges he had and had improved of praying for each member of the family in every clime and country around the world, and felt the influences of his brothers' and sisters' prayers had helped him.

This closing the devotional exercises of the hour, the company, numbering thirty-seven adults and children, were escorted according to age to the pleasant office-rooms of Esq. Phillips adjoining the house, where were spread three tables with easy sittings for all, representing the three generations which were present. The rooms where these tables were so luxuriously spread were also most beautifully decorated with flowers and evergreens, and appropriate mottoes, the most beautiful and touching one being an excellent portrait of the father hanging entwined with evergreens and immortelles and just beneath these words, " We are all here." Being seated the blessing was sung, led by Philip Phillips, and was in the following beautiful words which all joined in singing :

> " Be present at our table, Lord,
> Be here and everywhere adored,
> These mercies bless, and grant that we
> May feast in Paradise with Thee."

The magnificent and ample repast was now partaken of ; and as the curtains of night began to draw their shadows about the beautiful hillsides and silvery lake the family separated, going to their homes and different fields of labor, but resolving to renew as often as possible these sweet reunions of earth.—*Fredonia Censor.*

10. PHILIP, b. 1834 ; author of and dealer in Church and Sunday
School music in New York City.   During the last ten years he
has travelled in America and other countries over 220,000
miles, and given his " Evenings of Sacred Song " as follows :
United States 1950 evenings, Canada 69, Great Britain 246,
Australia 141, Ceylon 16, India 32, Continent of Europe 29,
Oriental Countries 14.   Making in all 2497 services of song ;
dividing the proceeds with Christian objects, and conducting
the song service of forty-seven State Sunday School Conventions.   His sacred song books have sold in different countries
to the extent of over 2,500,000 copies.   He m. 1860, OLLIE
CLARK.   Two children.

11. ROSINA, b. 1836; m. 1862, MILTON E. BEEBE, architect, of
Buffalo, N. Y.   One child.

12. BENJAMIN CLARK, b. 1838 ; d. 1840.

13. ALPHONSO RESIGN, b. 1839 ; d. 1841.

14. GEORGE HARRISON, b. 1841 ; m. CAROLINE BAKER ; res. in
Springfield, Ohio.   Two children.

15. ZERAH BARNEY, b. 1843 ; a soldier in U. S. service through the
war of the Rebellion ; resided in Springfield, Ohio, where he
d. 1879.   He m. SALLIE SHARP.   Four children.

No. 87.

(IV.) **Israel Phillips** (son of Philip of Ashfield : No.
81,) born May 23, 1770 ; of Ashfield ; married **Mabel Beld-
ing** of same place.   Children, only one name given :

1. ISRAEL ; m. SABRINA WARD.   He d. at the age of sixty-four,
she at the age of seventy-five.   Ch., born in Ashfield :

    1. Emeline ; m. Henry Barrus.   She d. at the age of twenty,
    leaving one ch.

    2. John Ward, b. May 4, 1835 ; of Buckland ; a house painter ;
    m. in Ashfield, Dec. 24, 1875, Duverna Doloris Reniff, b. in
    Buckland, Jan. 30, 1858.   Ch., b. in Buckland :

        1. Fuella, b. Mar. 24, 1879.

        2. Winsor Lucius, b. Feb. 28, 1881.

        3. Eugene Millard, b. July 6, 1883.

    3. Alonzo ; farmer of Ashfield ; m. Eliza A. Green.   Three ch.

    4. Winsor ; accidentally shot and killed at thirty-seven years of
    age ; unmarried.

    5. Lois ; m. Henry Green.   No ch.

6. Mabel, b. June 3, 1840; m. May 17, 1860, Alonzo Payne. Ch. :
    1. Freddie Arthur *Payne*, b. in Conway, June 16, 1872.
    2. Della Emmeline *Payne*, b. in Charlemont, Feb. 6, 1877.
7. Edwin A———, b. Nov. 12, 1843; member of Co. K, 60th Reg.
    Mass. Vols. ; farmer of Ashfield ; m. June 9, 1869, Lizzie
    Ann Phillips. Ch. :
    1. Rosina A———, b. Aug. 12, 1870.
    2. Jane Evelyn, b. Apr. 4, 1872.
    3. Harlan Wesson, b. Feb. 16, 1874; d. Feb. 4, 1879.
    4. Harlan Winsor, b. Dec. 9, 1879.
8. Ann Eliza; m. Henry Bassett, Jr. No ch.
9. Ralph, b. Dec. 30, 1848; farmer; m. Mrs. Maria E. M. (Graves)
    Wilder. Ch. :
    1. Mattie S———, b. in Ashfield, Feb. 26, 1869.
    2. Asa, b. in A., Dec. 28, 1870.
    3. Hattie M———, b. in A., Aug. 20, 1872.
    4. Lena H———, b. in A., Dec. 31, 1873.
    5. Ralph Ernest, b. in Conway, June 25, 1876.
    6. Albert A———, b. in A., Jan. 28, 1878.
    7. Alice R———, b. in A., Oct. 1, 1881.
    8. Heman H———, b. in A., Apr. 8, 1883.

No. 88.

(IV.) **Samuel Phillips** (son of Philip of Ashfield : No.
81,) born Aug. 14, 1775 ; res. in Ashfield ; married and had
the following children :

1. SALLY, b. Dec., 1794 ; m. 1816, JOHN MANTOR MANSFIELD.
    She died July 21, 1853. Ch., all b. in Ashfield :
    1. Adolphus *Mansfield*, b. Oct. 31, 1820; d. July 21, 1836.
    2. Samuel *Mansfield*, b. Aug. 20, 1824; d. Apr. 18, 1849.
    3. Martha Ann *Mansfield*, b. Apr. 12, 1832; d. Oct 30, 1879.

2. RACHEL ; m. ANSEL ELMER.
3. EMILY ; m. ——— BASSETT.
4. FRANCIS, b. Apr. 27, 1796 ; of Florida, Mass. ; m. Dec. 4, 1823,
    ANN EDSON, b. Dec. 1, 1803. Ch. :
    1. Julia, b. Oct. 18, 1824.
    2. Francis R———, b. Sept. 27, 1826.
    3. John E———, b. Nov. 12, 1829 ; d. Apr. 7, 1879.
    4. Ansel Elmer, b. July 26, 1836 ; of Shelburne Falls.
    5. Eunice Lestina, b. Apr. 11, 1840.

5. ANSON ; m. ALVIRA DUNTON.

No. 89.

(IV.)   **Dr. Liscom Phillips** (son of Philip of Ashfield: No. 81,) born March 23, 1777 ; a physician in Adams, Mass. ; representative from Savoy during the war of 1812 ; died at South Adams in 1821.   He married **Nancy Padelford** of Taunton, Mass., daughter of Peleg Padelford, and twin to Dr. Alpheus Padelford.   Children :

1.   HENRY PADELFORD, b. in Savoy, Jan. 24, 1807 ; physician in North Adams ; living in Oct., 1880, but has since died.   He m. CECELIA H. TYLER, dau. of Dr. Wm. H. Tyler of Lanesboro, Mass.   Ch. :

> 1.   William H———, b. in Lanesboro, Jan., 1831 ; rec. degree from Williams Coll. about 1850 ; editor of *Holyoke News;* senator from northern Berkshire, 1874.   He m. Mellissa Gallup.
> 2.   Henry T———, b. in Lanesboro, 1835 ; physician in Cheshire, Mass.; m. Josephine Fowler.
> 3.   Harlan L———, b. in South Adams, 1837 ; book merchant of North Adams ; m. Emeline Hawley.
> 4.   Anna Gertrude, b. in North Adams, 1840.

2.   SARAH, now deceased, b. in Savoy, 1808 ; m. Dea. WILLIAM SMITH.

3.   ERASMUS DARWIN, b. in Savoy, 1810 ; resides in Geneva, Wis. ; m. CATHERINE BROWNING.

4.   CHARLES FOX, b. in Savoy, 1812 ; res. Blackwater; Wis. ; m. Miss FARNUM of Wisconsin.

5.   WILLIAM, b. in South Adams ; d. when eleven years of age.

6.   JULIA ANN DEAN, b. in Savoy, 1815.

7.   BENJAMIN FRANKLIN, b. in South Adams, 1817 ; woollen manufacturer, of Adams ; representative one year ; m. (1st) Miss MORAN, (2d) Miss MARIA O'NEIL.

8.   ALBERT LISCOM, b. at South Adams, 1821 ; wool dealer of Racine, Wis. ; representative from Racine some years since ; recently nominated for Senator from his district.   He m. Miss MARY GREEN.

No. 90.

Oliver Phillips (supposed by his descendants to have been son of Joshua Phillips of Easton, but his connection with John, No. 79, is uncertain,) was born in Easton, Nov. 22, 1751,* moved from Easton to Marlborough, Vt., and died in

---

* One record says 1750.

Newfane, Vt., October 5, 1836. He married **Bathsheba Howard.** Children :

1. EDSELL, b. Dec. 30, 1770 ; d. May 14, 1802.
2. BETTY, b. Oct. 13, 1772.
3. SILENCE, b. Sept. 7, 1774 ; d. June 13, 1803.
4. OLIVER, b. Nov. 12, 1776 ; d. May 26, 1832.
5. SIMEON, b. Nov. 17, 1778.
6. BATHSHEBA, b. Feb. 11, 1781 ; d. July 21, 1802.
7. JOSHUA, b. July 8, 1783 ; d. in battle, Sept. 17, 1814.
8. MOSES HAYWOOD (twin), b. July 8, 1783 ; d. Nov. 13, 1803.
9. NATHAN, b. April 1, 1787 ; m. HANNAH MORSE, and d. in Newfane, March 4, 1844. Ch., all born in Newfane :
    1. Bathsheba, b. March 1, 1811; m. Rev. D. M. Crane.
    2. Sidney, b. Aug. 23, 1813; m. Abby Atwood, in Boston. Ch. :
        1. Sidney Atwood; grad. Dartmouth Coll., 1869; lawyer of South Framingham.
        2. Mary S———.
    3. Adin M———, b. Feb. 6, 1816; resides in Bridgeport, Conn. ; m. Rebecca Sanborn. Ch. :
        1. Ebenezer S———, b. in Newfane, Jan. 13, 1842.
    4. Aurelia, b. Jan. 11, 1818; m. Warren Lazelle.
    5. Nathan O———, b. Oct. 20, 1822; m. in Boston, 1849, Mary A. Philbrook. Ch. :
        1. Eugenie, b. in Boston, Feb. 23, 1850; m. in Minneapolis, Thomas Downing.
        2. Herbert N———, b. in Minnesota, Nov. 12, 1853; d. same place, June 7, 1872.
        3. Proctor H———, b. in Minnesota, Nov. 15, 1859.
        4. Edith M———, b. in Minnesota, Nov. 1, 1874; d. same place, Aug. 16, 1876.
    6. Mary H———, b. March 6, 1827; m. Edwin F. Sherman, and d. in Vt., March 11, 1848.
10. DANIEL, b. Nov. 1, 1789 ; drowned in Mississippi River, May 12, 1818.

GENEALOGY

OF THE

FAMILY OF JAMES PHILLIPS,

OF IPSWICH, MASS.

No. 91.

(I.) **James Phillips,** born in England. Early in life he left his native land, and seeking a new home, emigrated to America and landed at Ipswich, Mass. He followed the occupation of ship carpenter, lived in Ipswich, Haverhill and Bradford, and died in the latter place. Neither the time of his birth nor of his death appears to be known, nor the length of time he lived in either of the above places ; but he was probably born about the year 1700. His descendants have scattered over New England and to the far West. Some of them have evinced uncommon ability in the development and successful management of extensive business operations ; while some have distinguished themselves by heroic loyalty to their country in its times of peril. He married **Molly Lord** of Ipswich. Children :

1. JAMES ; of Rowley. (No. 92.)
2. JOHN ; of North Andover. (No. 98.)
3. MOLLY ; went with a family from Ipswich to Newfoundland, " and made her grave there."
4. KATHARINE ; m. ――― EDGERLY, and settled in Gilmanton, N. H.
5. ELEANOR ; m. ――― SMITH, and settled in N. H.

No. 92.

(II.) **James Phillips** (son of James of Ipswich : No. 91,) born, probably in Ipswich, Feb., 1729 ; resided in Rowley

and died there, Feb. 28, 1787.   He married **Judith Platts.**
Children, all born in Rowley :

1. MERCY, b. Sept. 21, 1754 ; m. WILLIAM DICKINSON ; resided in
   Rowley, and d. Feb. 21, 1833.
2. MARY, b. March 29, 1757 ; d. March 17, 1779.
3. JAMES, b. Aug. 8, 1759 ; m. SARAH PICKARD ; supposed to have
   been lost at sea.
4. JOHN, b. Aug. 20, 1761 ; of Portland, Me.   (No. 93.)
5. DAVID, b. Jan. 17, 1765 ; d. Feb. 2, 1815.
6. NATHAN, b. Feb. 6, 1768 ; of Rowley.   (No. 94.)
7. JUDITH, b. April 9, 1771 ; d. Oct. 8, 1775.
8. PLATTS, b. March 12, 1774 ; d. Oct. 8, 1775.
9. SETH, b. July 27, 1777 ; shoe dealer in Portland, Maine ; d.
   July 14, 1815.   Unmarried.

No. 93.

(III.) **John Phillips** (son of James of Rowley : No. 92,)
born Aug. 20, 1761.   His business was commerce and naviga-
tion ; residence, Portland, Me. ;   died April 19, 1826.   He m.
1789, **Margaret Spear** of North Yarmouth, Me., born 1771.
She died Oct. 9, 1856.   Children :

1. PAMELIA PLATTS, b. July 12, 1794 ; d. Oct. 26, 1879 ; m. twice.
   Her first husband, a native of Fryeburg, Me., was editor and
   proprietor of the *Portland Gazette.*   Her second husband,
   JAMES ALDEN, was a shipmaster.
2. MARY D———, b. Feb. 2, 1797 ; m. CHARLES MOODY, a merchant of Portland, who d. in 1870.   She d. March 10, 1876.
   Ch. :

1. Daniel *Moody.*	3. Emma *Moody.*
2. Frank *Moody.*	4. Edward *Moody.*

3. MARGARET, b. April 7, 1800 ; d. Feb. 10, 1864 ; unmarried.
4. ELIZA, b. Aug. 11, 1802 ; d. April 19, 1873.   She m. ELIAS
   SHAW, merchant of Portland, who d. in California.   Ch. :

   1. Frederic E. *Shaw;* pastor of a church in East Machias.
   2. John P. *Shaw;* d. in 1870.
   3. Margaret *Shaw;* m. A. J. Swett ; res. Brooklyn, N. Y.
   4. Octavia J. P. *Shaw;* m. S. C. Strout, lawyer in Portland.

5. HARRIETT J———, b. June 7, 1808 ; m. June 24, 1829, CHARLES

O. EMERSON. He graduated at Harvard College, 1818 ; counsellor-at-law, in York, Me. ; d. June 22, 1863. Ch. :

  1. Edward O. *Emerson;* served through the war of the Rebellion
as an officer; merchant, of Titusville, Penn. Four children.

  2. Frank P. *Emerson;* shipmaster, of York.

  3. Andrew L. *Emerson;* served through the war of the Rebellion
as an officer; shipmaster, of York.

  4. Abbie C. *Emerson;* m. Jere McIntire of York.

6. DEBORAH T———, b. Sept. 30, 1810 ; m. MOSES LUNT, M. D.
He is not living. Two children ; one daughter, unmarried,
survives.

7. JOHN EDWARD, b. Jan. 29, 1813 ; d. Feb. 22, 1851. Ch. :

  1. Walstein, b. June 11, 1837 ; captain in the Maine Cavalry; was
shot and killed in the advance while leading on his men at
the battle of the Wilderness, June 24, 1864.

  2. Edward; of Skowhegan, Me.

  3. ———, daughter, name not given.

8-12. ———, four sons and one daughter, who died in infancy.

No. 94.

(III.) **Nathan Phillips** (son of James of Rowley : No.
92,) born Feb. 6, 1768 ; a farmer in Rowley ; died June 30,
1849. He married **Lydia Pingree,** daughter of John and
Elizabeth Pingree of Rowley. Children, all born in Rowley :

1. ELIZABETH, b. June 9, 1800 ; m. Dec. 30, 1824, BENJAMIN
SCOTT, a farmer of North Beverly, where she still resides
(1880). He d. in that place, Jan. 3, 1877. Ch. :

  1. Sylvester *Scott,* b. Sept. 19, 1825 ; for several years principal of
young ladies' Seminary in Alexandria, Va., but left on the
breaking out of the war and came to Boston, where he was
associated with Dr. Dio Lewis in his gymnasium until his
death June 18, 1865. He m. Dec. 25, 1854, Lydia N. Mosely
of Westfield, Mass. Ch. :

    1. Lucy Eva *Scott,* b. July 13, 1856 ; d. Aug. 28, 1873.

    2. Benjamin Sylvester *Scott,* b. Oct. 21, 1859 ; student in
a medical School in Cincinnati, Ohio.

  2. Benjamin *Scott,* b. March 3, 1834 ; machinist by trade ; d. Sept.
16, 1874.

2. JULIA THERESE, b. Jan. 23, 1802. (No. 95.)

3. ALONZO PLATTS, b. May 2, 1804. (No. 96.)

4. LYDIA, b. Feb. 6, 1806 ; res. 1885, in North Beverly.

5. CYNTHIA, b. July 29, 1808 ; res. 1885, in North Beverly.
6. JOHN MILTON, b. Sept. 26, 1810 ; d. July 17, 1818.
7. HANNAH MARIA, b. April 26, 1813 ; d. June 27, 1818.
8. REBECCA, b. Jan. 30, 1816 ; m. Oct. 10, 1838, WALTER R.
    WEBSTER, a farmer of Bridgewater, N. H. He d. in Bridge-
    water, Nov. 26, 1873. Ch. :

> 1. Mary Amanda *Webster*, b. July 2, 1839.
> 2. Alonso Phillips *Webster*, b. Nov. 17, 1840; drowned July 23, 1854.
> 3. Lydia Angeline *Webster*, b. Feb. 25, 1844; principal of the High School in Council Bluffs, Iowa.
> 4. William Pingree *Webster*, b. July 10, 1847; a civil engineer on the frontier.
> 5. Adelaide Rebecca *Webster*, b. April 13, 1858; a student in Wellesley College.

9. JOHN MILTON, b. March 15, 1820 ; merchant in Council Bluffs,
    in wholesale and retail boot and shoe business, having his two
    sons, Nathan and J. M., Jr., as partners. He m. Dec. 4, 1845,
    OLIVE NELSON CRESSEY of Rowley, Mass. She d. March 13,
    1878. Ch. :

> 1. David Milton, b. Nov. 3, 1846 ; d. March 19, 1854.
> 2. Nathan, b. Dec. 21, 1852; merchant, of Council Bluffs.
> 3. Mary Olive, b. Dec. 14, 1855.
> 4. John Milton, b. Oct. 21, 1857; merchant, of Council Bluffs.
> 5. Cynthia Emma, b. June 4, 1862.
> 6. Ruth Maria, b. March 9, 1864.
> 7. Grenville Dodge, b. Feb. 15, 1867.

No. 95.

(IV.) **Julia Theresa Phillips** (No. 94 : 2.) married
Sylvanus Dodge, postmaster and merchant in South Dan-
vers, Mass. They removed to Nebraska in 1855, and to
Council Bluffs, Iowa, in 1858. He died in the latter place,
Dec. 23, 1871. Their son, N. P. Dodge, writes :

" My mother left a comfortable home in Danvers, Mass., after
she was fifty years old, went with her husband and children to
the frontier of Nebraska and settled in Dodge Co., among the
Pawnee Indians, the farthest white settlement at that time west
of the Missouri river—no white settlement beyond until you
reached Salt Lake City, one thousand miles. That was in

G M Dodge

1855. It seems like a dream, so wonderful and rapid have been the changes since then in the country west of us." Ch. :

1. GRENVILLE MELLEN DODGE, b. in Danvers, Sept. 23, 1829, d. Oct. 6, 1829.
2. GRENVILLE MELLEN DODGE, b. in Danvers, April 12, 1831 ;

civil engineer. The following brief outline of his eventful and remarkable career, with the letter of commendation from Gen. Sherman, the compiler is enabled to give through the kindness of N. P. Dodge, his brother.

His advantages for early education were quite limited, having only the benefits of common schools during the winters. Between the ages of ten and seventeen he worked summers at gardening and farming, and as a clerk in a general mercantile store. He occupied his leisure hours during these years in fitting himself for college, and in 1844 entered the Norwich Military University of Vermont. In 1851 he emigrated to the West and settled in Peru, Ill., as civil engineer. His settlement here was followed for two years by his participation in the locating and construction of several of the most important railroad lines of that region. He afterwards moved to Iowa City. In 1853 he made a reconnoisance west of the Missouri river, with a view of determining the location of the great Pacific Railroad of the future. Nov. 11, 1854, he removed to Council Bluffs, Iowa, where he was subsequently engaged in banking, real estate and mercantile business, and also organized the "Council Bluffs Guards."

At the breaking out of the war in 1861, after being sent by the government of Iowa to Washington, to arrange for the arming and equipment of Iowa troops, he raised the 4th Iowa Infantry regiment, of which he was commissioned Colonel, and also the 2d Iowa (Dodge's) Battery. In July, 1861, he marched with his command into Missouri, and was successful in operating against the Confederate forces which were then occupying that State. He reported with his regiment and battery in August, 1861, to General Frémont at St. Louis, and was soon after assigned to the command of the fourth brigade, and led the advance in the capture of Springfield, Mo. He took a prominent part in the celebrated battle of Pea Ridge, had three horses killed under him, and was seriously wounded. He was made Brigadier General for his gallant conduct in this battle. After recovering from his wounds he was designated to command the district of Columbus, Ky., and while holding the command, defeated several forces of the enemy, capturing Gen. Faulkner, near Island No. 10, and taking many prisoners. Late in 1862, having previously been given the command of the 2d division of the Army of the Tennessee, he was assigned to the command of the district of Corinth, Miss. He opened the campaign of 1863 by defeating the confederate forces under Forrest, Roddy, Fergueson and others. July 5th, 1863, he was assigned to the command of the left wing of the 16th Army Corps, with headquarters at Corinth, Miss. His forces made a raid on Grenada, Miss., in connection with a movement from Vicksburg, which resulted in driving the enemy south of that place, and capturing fifty-five locomotives and a thousand cars.

While at the head of the 16th Army Corps, he joined Gen. Sherman in his march to Chattanooga, and in the Spring of 1864, was entrusted with the advance of the Army of the Tennessee. His corps took part in all the battles of Gen. Sherman's forces in the march from Chattanooga to Atlanta. In recognition of his services in this campaign, he was made Major General by the General Government. During the siege of Atlanta, his energetic and well timed action in moving his forces against the enemy under Hood, resulted in saving the stores and transportation of the Army of the Tennessee, and the army from a threatened condition. A few weeks after the battle of Atlanta, the army still besieging that city, Gen. Dodge received a gunshot wound in the forehead while standing in a rifle pit, on the skirmish line, superintending an advance. This was on the 19th of August, 1864. He soon after reported to Gen. Sherman for duty, but, owing to his physical condition, was ordered to the district of Vicksburg, and immediately transferred to the department of the Missouri by the President of the United States, relieving Gen. Rosecranz.

Missouri was overrun by Guerillas, and the national troops were in bad condition. He soon brought the army into good standing, effectually quelled the general Indian outbreak which just then threatened the whole frontier, and a vigorous fight was made against the Guerillas of Missouri, Arkansas and the Indian Territory. He received the surrender of 4000 of Kirby Smith's army in Missouri, and of the confederate general, Jeff. Thompson, with 8000 officers and men in Arkansas. At the close of the war, Gen. Dodge's command was made to include the whole Indian country of the West and North-west.

At his urgent request he was relieved of his command in June, 1866, and, on retiring from the army, was appointed Chief Engineer of the Union Pacific Railroad. He was nominated for Congress by the Republicans of the 5th Iowa district in 1866, and elected by a majority 2000 higher than had ever been given in that district. He declined a renomination and returned to push forward the construction of the Union Pacific Railroad. To this great work he bent all his energies. As chief engineer of the road, he made the plans for the great iron bridge which spans the Missouri River between Council Bluffs and Omaha, having charge of its construction till the time of his leaving the road as chief engineer. He supervised the relations of the road with the government, saw that the law was adhered to and the work conscientiously done, having no interest in the Construction Company, its contracts or profits.

In 1868 the Union Pacific Railroad was completed, and very soon afterwards Gen. Dodge became Chief Engineer of the Southern Pacific, now the Texas and Pacific Railroad, where he took control of the surveys and construction, and from July, 1872, to December, 1873, he completed the surveys along the thirty-second parallel of latitude from Sherman, Texas to the Pacific Ocean at San Diego, a distance of 1900 miles, and also put under construction 500 miles of the road. Since 1873 he has been engaged in the management of the Union Pacific and other western railroads.

General Dodge is a member of the Odd Fellows, and takes an interest in whatever develops his State, American society and the country at large. His characteristics are,—great energy, industry, and persistency in any work he undertakes. His honor and integrity are unimpeachable.

11

When contemplating a visit to Europe with his family, in the season of 1877, he received the following letter :

"HEADQUARTERS ARMY OF THE UNITED STATES,
WASHINGTON, D. C., April 20, 1877.

To U. S. CONSULS, Abroad :

I have just learned that General G. M. Dodge is about going to Europe, where he may leave his children to school whilst he returns to America, where he is actively employed in railroad construction and management.

I take great pleasure in commending Genl. Dodge and family to the courtesy and politeness of all Americans, especially such as occupy official positions, because Genl. Dodge is one of the Generals who actually fought throughout the Civil War, with great honor and great skill, commanding a regiment, brigade, division, and finally a *corps d'armée*, the highest rank command to which any officer can attain.

He was with me in the West, especially in the Atlanta campaign where he was severely wounded, close to Atlanta, and I therefore think that he and especially his children, should experience the attention of all officers of a Government that might have perished had it not been for the blood of just such men as General Dodge.

With great respect, &c.,

W. T. SHERMAN,
General."

General Dodge m. in Salem, Mass., May 29, 1854, Miss ANNIE BROWN of Peru, Ill. Ch. :

1. Lettie *Dodge*, b. June 17, 1855; m. Nov. 25, 1874, Robert E. Montgomery, a lawyer of Council Bluffs. Two children.
2. Ella *Dodge*, b. Dec. 12, 1858; m. May 5, 1880, Frank Scott Pusey of Council Bluffs.
3. Annie *Dodge*, b. March 7, 1866.

3. NATHAN PHILLIPS DODGE, b. in South Danvers (now Peabody), Mass., Aug. 20, 1837 ; a real estate agent in Council Bluffs ; president of the Council Bluffs Savings Bank ; m. Sept. 22, 1864, SUSANNA C. LOCKWOOD of Council Bluffs. Ch. :

1. Carrie Louise *Dodge*, b. March 25, 1866.
2. John Lockwood *Dodge*, b. Dec. 10, 1867.
3. Phillips *Dodge*, b. March 24, 1872.
4. Ellen Lockwood *Dodge*, b. Jan. 14, 1875.
5. —— a son, b. Aug. 31, 1880.

4. JULIA MARY DODGE, b. in Danvers, Mass., Jan. 14, 1843 ; m.
   Sept. 29, 1868, JAMES B. BEARD of Council Bluffs.   Ch. :
   1. Edwin Spencer *Beard*, b. July 8, 1870.
   2. Grenville Mellen Dodge *Beard*, b. Aug. 24, 1872.

No. 96.

(IV.) **Alonzo Platts Phillips** (son of Nathan of Rowley : No. 94,) born May 2, 1804 ; a shoe manufacturer in
Peabody, Mass., previously to 1870.   He also established, and
was connected with, a wholesale and retail boot and shoe store
in Council Bluffs, Iowa, the same business now successively
carried on in that place by the firm of J. M. Phillips & Sons.
He was a member of the Legislature in 1856.   In 1870 he
removed to Medway, where he still resides, 1885.   In 1880
his daughter wrote : "My father is unusually vigorous, physi-
cally and mentally, so that in his seventy-seventh year he
regularly does laborious work upon his land, and keeps up, as
always, a lively interest in the public questions of the day."
He married (1st) April 15, 1830, **Louisana Dodge**, who
died Sept. 28, 1863, dau. of Phineas and Mercy Dodge of
Rowley ; (2d) Oct. 12, 1865, **Mrs. Irene F. Proctor**,
living, 1880, widow of Aaron C. Proctor, and dau. of Elisha
C. and Irene F. Upton of Peabody.   Children :

1. OSCAR, b. July 27, 1833.   (No. 97.)
2. ELIZABETH MERCY, b. in Danvers (now Peabody), June 12,
   1837 ; d. in Medway, Dec. 17, 1881 ; unmarried.   Her death
   was regarded as a great loss to the family, the church and
   community.   "To a mind naturally clear and vigorous, she
   had brought attainments by culture and refinement which
   qualified for much usefulness.   Deeply impressed with a sense
   of the great need of Christian work in every department of
   society, she actively sought to do good and to promote the
   personal comfort and spiritual well being of all whom she could
   reach.   Self-denying and conscientious, but kind and courteous
   in her intercourse with all, she endeared herself to a circle of
   warm friends."   She was in her usual place at the religious
   meeting of the Wednesday evening preceding her death, and
   again on Thursday with the ladies of the Benevolent Society,

after which she was suddenly siezed with some affection of the brain, and alternating between delirium and consciousness, suddenly died Saturday noon. " She left as a precious legacy to her family and a large circle of friends, the fragrance of a pure and well-spent life in the service of the dear Master who has called her to his blessed home."

3. LYDIA MARIA, b. same place, Sept. 6, 1839 ; d. Aug. 29, 1840.
4. LYDIA MARIA, b. same place, Jan. 3, 1842 ; d. May 24, 1883, unmarried.
5. LUCY DODGE, b. same place, Oct. 6, 1844 ; d. Apr. 11, 1871.

No. 97.

(V.) **Oscar Phillips** (son of Alonzo Platts : No. 96,) born July 27, 1833 ; treasurer of the Heywood Boot and Shoe Co., Worcester, Mass. He married, Sept. 18, 1855, **Irene Trask,** dau. of Edward D. and Hannah L. Trask of Peabody. Children :

1. IRENE, b. Sept. 27, 1856 ; attended Wellesley College three years, but left without graduating to engage in teaching in the Michigan Female Seminary at Kalamazoo. She m. Dec. 13, 1881, Charles A. Huse, M. D., of Worcester. He d. July 3, 1884. Ch. :

    1. Charles Phillips *Huse*, b. Mar. 3, 1883.

2. MARIA, b. Oct. 1, 1858 ; entered Smith College, but left on account of ill health.
3. OSCAR, b. June 15, 1861 ; d. June 30, 1863.
4. LOUISANA DODGE, b. Feb. 5, 1865.
5. HANNAH BROWN, b. March 18, 1867.
6. HENRY LUCIEN, b. Aug. 20, 1871.

No. 98.

(II.) **John Phillips** (son of James of Ipswich : No. 91,) a farmer in North Andover, where he owned a good farm. His brother's granddaughter, now eighty years of age, recalls visiting him with her father, when she was ten years old, and remembers him as a noble looking, genial old man of eighty,

and living in comfort.   He married **Elizabeth Haggatt.**
Children :

1. TIMOTHY ; settled in Bradford.   Ch. :
    1. Alonzo; a clergyman, now deceased; m. Rebecca Kimball.
    2. Rufus; living, 1880, in Chester.

2. SAMUEL ; m. HITTY HAGGATT, and lived in Bradford.   Ch. :
    1. Hitty.   2. Betsey.   3. Leonard.   4. Ruby.
    5. Samuel.   6. Mary.   7. Daniel.   8. Hiram.
    9. James.   10. Charles.

3. JAMES.   After his father's death, he with two sisters, all unmarried, lived on the homestead farm.

4. ELIZABETH.

5. MARY.

6. ——— name not given.

GENEALOGY

OF THE

FAMILY OF WALTER PHILLIPS,

OF DAMARISCOTTA, ME., 1661.

No. 99.

(I.) **Walter Phillips,** who was one of the John Mason colony that settled the "Sheepscott Plantation" about 1630, first appears in the early records in 1661, when he bought by deed of the Indians land at Damariscotta, Me.* In 1665 he was appointed clerk and recorder of a land commission for that part of Maine.

In 1680 the village of "Sheepscott Plantation" was burnt by the Indians, and Walter Phillips and others fled to Charlestown, Mass. In 1689 he was appointed by the General Court a tavern-keeper at Salem village, now Peabody.

In 1693, John Phillips and his brother Walter, Senr., bought about 500 acres of land of Daniel King, in the eastern part of Swampscott, Mass., then called "Linn."

In 1694, John Phillips died, and Walter, Senr., was appointed guardian of his three children, John, Jacob and Hannah, all under fourteen years when their father died.

Nov. 10, 1702, Walter Phillips sold his Damariscotta land to C. Tappan of Newbury. His will is dated Oct. 13, 1704, and that of his wife **Margaret,** Nov. 8, 1708. Children :

1. MARGARET.	3. JANE.	5. WALTER. (No. 100.)
2. SARAH.	4. JAMES.	6. JOHN.

---

* The brief records of this family were furnished by Mr. Geo. H. Phillips of Holliston, and the items relating to Walter Phillips, Sr., are from information gathered from Mass. Historical rooms, State House Library, History of Salem, Salem Registry of Deeds, and Salem Registry of Wills.

No. 100.

(II.)   **Walter Phillips** (son of Walter of Damariscotta :
No. 99,) signed Quakers' list "Lynn 22th 4mo., 1703 ; " died
in 1733.   His wife's name was **Ruth.**   Children* :

1. WALTER.   His posterity are to be found in Lynn and Swampscott at the present time.
2. RICHARD.   3. RUTH.   4. JONATHAN.   (No. 101.)

No. 101.

(III.)   **Jonathan Phillips** (son of Walter of Lynn : No.
100,) died 1757 ; his wife **Mary** a few years later.   Children :

1. WALTER.   (No. 102.)
2. GIDEON ; had several children, but only a few of the Phillips
   name are known to be of his posterity.
3. JAMES.   His descendants are numerous in Swampscott.
4. JONATHAN.   5. HANNAH.   6. SARAH.   7. MARY.
   8. PATIENCE.   9. RUTH.   10. ABIGAIL.

No. 102.

(IV.)   **Walter Phillips** (son of Jonathan : No. 101,)
born Sept. 18, 1726 ; a Quaker, and a few of his descendants
were of the same faith ; died March 18, 1800.   He m. Sept.
26, 1752, **Content Hood,** born Sept. 4, 1732 ; she died
Aug. 11, 1805.   Children :

1. HANNAH, b. 1755 ; d. 1805.   She m. ——— Dow of N. H.
2. BENJAMIN, b. 1757 ; d. 1809.   Had ten children, but only one
   grandson of the Phillips name is now of his descendants.
   Descendants of his daughters live in Mass. and Va.
3. JONATHAN, b. 1759 ; d. 1800.   No descendants.
4. JOHN, b. Dec. 30, 1760 ; d. Nov. 19, 1835.   He m. 1788,
   JUDITH Dow, b. Jan. 7, 1766 ; she d. Oct. 8, 1850.   Ch. : †
     1. John, b. 1789; d. 1859.
     2. Jonathan D———, b. 1791; d. 1864.
     3. Stephen, b. 1792; d. 1817.   No. family.

---

* Salem records.

† Of these children, John, Jonathan D., Walter, Hannah and Louisa, have
descendants in Me., N. H., and Mass.

4. Ann D———, b. 1794; living in Maynard, 1884. No family.
5. Walter, b. 1796; d. 1875.
6. Judith, b. 1798; d. 1835. She m. ——— Pond of Salem. No children.
7. Hannah, b. 1799; d. 1859. She m. ——— Hood of Nahant.
8. Mary, b. 1803; d. 1841. No family.
9. George, b. Feb. 27, 1805; d. April 3, 1857. He m. May 31, 1840, Elizabeth Silsbee, b. Feb. 27, 1811; d. Oct. 14, 1877. Ch. :

    1. George H———, b. Mar. 13, 1841; resides in Holliston; m. Aug. 31, 1870, Abbie G. Hawes. Ch. :

        1. Walter E——— H———, b. Jan. 14, 1874.

    2. Edward N———, b. Feb. 17, 1844; d. Dec. 25, 1846.
    3. Edward, b. Feb. 5, 1848; d. Sept. 5, 1848.
    4. Arthur J———, b. Jan. 18, 1852; m. Oct. 20, 1881, Anna R. Pease. Child :

        1. Edward I———, b. Sept. 27, 1882.

10. Henry (twin), b. and d. Feb. 27, 1805.
11. Louisa, b. 1807; d. 1865. She m. ——— Hoag of N. H.

5. ELIZABETH, b. 1763 ; d. 1831. She m. ——— READE ; in Iowa.
6. SARAH, b. 1764 ; d. 1834. She. m. ——— SILSBEE ; of Lynn.
7. WALTER. b. 1766 ; d. 1852. His descendants are living in Lynn and Swampscott.
8. ABIGAIL, b. 1768 ; d. 1831. She m. ——— Dow ; of N. H.

GENEALOGY

OF THE

FAMILY OF ANDREW PHILLIPS,

OF KITTERY, ME., 1700.

No. 103.

(I.) **Andrew Phillips** emigrated from England about the year 1700, in company with Sir Wm. Pepperell, his mother's brother, and located in Kittery, Me. Two brothers of Andrew located farther east. He m. Jan. 1, 1727, **Miriam Mitchell.** Children :

1. SUSANNA, b. Feb. 26, 1732.
2. SARAH, b. Aug. 13, 1734.
3. ABIGAIL, b. June 19, 1736.
4. JANE, b. Oct. 9, 1737.
5. MIRIAM, b. May 19, 1739.   (?)
6. ELIZABETH, b. June 22, 1742.
7. AGNES, b. Dec. 1, 1743.
8. ANDREW.   (No. 104.)

No. 104.

(II.) **Andrew Phillips** (son of Andrew, of Kittery : No. 103,) born Feb. 24, 1748; resided in Kittery; occupation marine; died July 10, 1830 (aged 84 according to copy furnished, but if so, was probably b. 1746). He m. Mar. 19, 1771, **Lettuce Fernald.** Children :

1. ANDREW, b. Jan. 16, 1773; went to Isleboro, Me.; was tide waiter in the war of 1812, and lost while cruising in his boat. He m. THANKFUL AMES.   Ch. :
   1. Sarah, b. Feb. 14, 1797.
   2. Lydia, b. May 11, 1799.

3. Luther, b. May 3, 1801; m. in Orland, Me., Feb. 28, 1823, Elsa Trott. He carried on the fishing business; deacon of the Baptist Church; has held many offices of trust in the town; was representative; residing, 1880, in East Hancock, Me.

2. LETTUCE, b. Sept. 10, 1776.
3. JOHN, b. Jan. 31, 1779; m. (1st) MARY CHAMBERS; (2d) HANNAH SEAWARD. Ch., all by first marriage :
  1. Mary Ann, b. Feb. 27, 1800; d. Feb. 2, 1876.
  2. John, b. July 4, 1802; d.
  3. William, b. Dec. 12, 1803.
  4. Abbie S——, b. 1805.
  5. Alfred S——, b. Oct. 23, 1807.
  6. Joseph S——, b. July 23, 1809; residing, 1880, at Kittery Point; m. Nov. 29, 1831, Joanna D. Woodman. She d. Jan. 13, 1880. Ch. :
    1. Charles W——, b. April 7, 1833; d. July 21, 1850.
    2. Georgeana, b. Sept. 12, 1834.
    3. John J——, b. Feb. 15, 1836; d. Sept. 3, 1868.
    4. Sabra O——, b. Jan. 22, 1838.
    5. Manning, b. July 27, 1840.
    6. Lucy J—— Toby, b. Oct. 24, 1841; d. July 15, 1868.
    7. Carrie M——, b. Sept. 14, 1843; d. June 22, 1875.
    8. Sarah A——, b. April 21, 1846.
  7. Salome H——, b. Aug. 9, 1811.
  8. Nancy D——, b. July 2, 1813.
  9. Augusta H——, b. July 7, 1815.
  10. Eliza L——, b. Dec. 6, 1819.
  11. Eliza L——, b. June 3, 1822.

4. THOMAS, b. March 5, 1781; d. 1835. He m. Jan. 23, 1802, MAY WEEKS, b. Mar 3, 1784; she d. Sept. 8, 1870. Ch. :
  1. Thomas F——, b. July 20, 1803; d. Nov. 26, 1846.
  2. Samuel W——, b. Dec. 23, 1804; d. Oct. 28, 1850.
  3. Nancy, b. Oct. 21, 1807; d. Nov. 13, 1861.
  4. Josiah, b. March 3, 1810; d. Dec. 19, 1830.
  5. Andrew, b. Sept. 13, 1812; d. Nov. 4, 1836.
  6. May E——, b. June 20, 1815; d. Oct. 18, 1842.
  7. Manning, b. Oct. 25, 1817; d. May 30, 1833.
  8. John, b. June 8, 1821; d. June 18, 1821.
  9. Isaac D—— (twin), b. June 8, 1821; resident of Kittery, where he was town clerk four years; m. Sept. 12, 1843, Mary B. Gerrish of Portsmouth, N. H. Ch. :
    1. George H——, b. Nov. 22, 1844.
    2. Isaac Andrew, b. Jan. 5, 1846.
    3. Laura I——, b. Dec. 10, 1848.
    4. Alice C——, b. July 15, 1851; d. Jan. 7, 1874.
    5. Mary E——, b. Sept. 10, 1855.
    6. Adah M——, b. Sept. 8, 1857.

5. JOSIAH, b. Sept. 7, 1783; d. April 26, 1846. He m. LYDIA
BILLINGS, b. Mar. 12, 1792; she d. Sept. 29, 1846. Ch.:

    1. Josiah, b. Oct. 19, 1813; d. July 1, 1841.
    2. Lydia, b. Jan. 17, 1816.
    3. Irene, b. Aug. 6, 1818.
    4. Oliver, b. Sept. 7, 1821; d. Aug., 1861.
    5. Ivory L———, b. Dec. 27, 1824; d.
    6. Edwin F-———, b. June 8, 1831; d. Apr. 16, 1851.

6. WILLIAM, b. Sept. 16, 1786.
7. HANNAH, b. Dec. 4, 1771. [? 1791].

GENEALOGIES

OF THE

PHILLIPS FAMILIES

OF RHODE ISLAND.

The inhabitants of this name in Rhode Island have nearly all been farmers; and although not many of them have held high stations in public life or accumulated great wealth, yet they have usually been very respectable people.

No. 105.

(I.)   **Michael Phillips** (parentage not given,) died in Smithfield, R. I., Jan. 1, 1776, aged 84.

No. 106.

(II.)   **Elijah Phillips** (son of Michael: No. 105,) died in Mansfield, Conn., 1829, aged 80.

No. 107.

(III.)   **Rev. Asa Phillips** (son of Elijah: No. 106,) born May 8, 1769; resided in Marcellus, N. Y., where he died Sept. 17, 1813. He m. Dec., 1791, **Ann Works,** born 1771; she died Aug. 24, 1848.   Children:

1.   MICHAEL, b. Aug. 1, 1792; a physician; d. Sept. 21, 1847.
2.   ASA, b. Jan. 12, 1794; d. Oct. 2, 1865.
3.   ELIJAH, b. Dec. 28, 1795; res. in Hinmansville, Oswego Co., N. Y., where he d. July 5, 1874.   He m. LUCY EASTMAN, April 13, 1817.   Ch.:

>   1.   Asa, b. in Marcellus, Feb. 2, 1818; m. Sept. 13, 1840, Mary Ann Dier; res. Violet, Ontario.   Children, all born in Loughboro Ontario:

>>   1.   William H——— H———, b. July 25, 1841; grad. at Wesleyan University, 1865, and at Heidelberg, Germany, 1868; teacher at Wilbraham Academy.   He m. Carrie Houghton.   Ch.:

>>>   1.   Edward C.

2. Robert E——, b. June 6, 1843; m. (1st) Sarah
   Parker, who d. April 14, 1873; (2d) Lucy Lasher;
   residence, Fulton, N. Y.
3. Ordelia, b. Mar. 25, 1847; m. George E. Carscallen;
   res. Napanee, Ont.
4. Ann Amelia, b. May 29, 1850; m. Thomas R. Wilde;
   res. Napanee.
5. Rachel C——, b. Feb. 5, 1854; res. Violet, Ont.
6. H—— Bradway, b. June 29, 1856; m. Mary Augusta
   Phillips; res. Fulton, N. Y.
7. Josephine, b. April 26, 1863; d. in Loughboro, May 12,
   1866.

2. Hester Ann, b. in Marcellus, Feb. 5, 1820; m. Hiram Bradway.
   She d. Sept. 16, 1865.
3. Samantha, b. in Marcellus, Feb. 22, 1822; d. July 26, 1823.
4. Mary, b. in Granby, N. Y., Oct 6, 1824; m. Joseph Wright;
   residence, Plainfield, Mich.
5. James S——, b. in Granby, Oct. 22, 1826; residence, Plainfield, Mich.
6. Elijah, b. in Granby, Jan. 1, 1829; d. July 13, 1829.
7. George, b. in Granby, July 15, 1830; res. Michigan.
8. Henry Orlando, b. in Granby, Oct. 24, 1832; d. Sept. 5, 1833.

4. ANNA, b. Jan. 17, 1797; d. 1827.
5. PETER, b. May 25, 1799; d. 1800.
6. GEORGE, b. Sept. 9, 1801; died.
7. MARY, b. Sept. 17, 1804; m. —— BUNDY; resides, Syracuse,
   Kansas.
8. CYRUS, b. Sept. 9, 1807; living, 1878, in Fulton, N. Y.
9. JOHN, b. Feb. 4, 1810; died.
10. RHODA, b. March 25, 1813; m. Dr. MORRELL; living, 1878, in
    Elmira, N. Y.

No. 108.

(I.) Richard Phillips (parentage not given). Child:

No. 109.

(II.) John Phillips (son of Richard: No. 108,) lived
and died in Scituate, R. I. He married —— Brown.
Children:

1. JACOB.   2. NATHANIEL.   3. DAVID.
   4. EZEKIEL. (No. 110.)
   5. JOHN. Also several daughters.

No. 110.

(III.) **Ezekiel Phillips** (son of John of Scituate: No. 109,) born in Smithfield, R. I., Feb. 14, 1730; residence, Foster, R. I., where he died Nov. 30, 1804. He held military commissions, said to be still in possession of one of his grandsons, dated 1758 and 1759, and signed by Stephen Hopkins, Gov. of R. I. He married **Susanna Whitman,** born in Smithfield, 1751; died in Foster, May 26, 1816. Children:

1. Augustus; of Foster and Natick, R. I. (No. 111.)
2. Sarah, b. in Foster, May 27, 1773; m. Ezra Goodspeed; resided in Foster and had a family of children.
3. Charles, b. in Foster, May 31, 1776; d. in Foster, June 3, 1797.
4. Ezekiel, b. in Foster, Feb. 20, 1779; d. in Foster, May 15, 1797.
5. Rhoda, b. Sept. 2, 1781; m. Abram Phillips; resided in Foster and had a family of children, one of whom, Ezekiel Phillips, resided in Blackstone, Mass.
6. Valentine, b. in Foster, Sept. 21, 1785; d. same place, Jan. 27, 1797.

No. 111.

(IV.) **Augustus Phillips** (son of Ezekiel of Foster: No. 110,) born in Scituate or Foster, June 28, 1771; died at Natick, R. I., June 30, 1843. He married **Sally Davis,** born in Foster, May 10, 1778; died at Natick, April 10, 1843. Children, all born in Foster:

1. Orpha, b. Nov. 16, 1797; d. June 27, 1801.
2. Darius, b. Jan. 25, 1800; d. May 31, 1817.
3. Jervis, b. May 9, 1802; m. Betsey Tucker, and had a family of children; d. in Smithfield, Jan. 20, 1845.
4. Charles, b. May 2, 1805; resides, Central Village, Plainfield, Conn.; m. at Foster, Mar. 13, 1825, Hannah Gorton Hill, b. Jan. 25, 1810. Ch.:

    1. Perley Hill, b. in Foster, 1825; d. same place, June 18, 1842.
    2. Susan Ann, b. in Foster, March 8, 1827; m. Jonathan Gorton of Central Village, where she d. Mar. 8, 1851.

12

3. Hiram Jilson, b. in Foster, Aug. 8, 1828; m. Maria B. Davis;
    residence, Hartford, Conn. Ch. :
    1. Hannah R——, b. Oct. 27, 1864.
    2. Charles O——, b. Dec. 12, 1865.
4. Charles, b. in Foster, Aug. 22, 1830; m. Eveline E. Hunt; res.
    Dakota City, Neb.
5. Phebe Maria, b. in Foster, June 27, 1832; m. William Maffatt;
    res. Central Village, Conn.
6. Sarah Davis, b. in Foster, April 30, 1834; d. same place, Sept.
    24, 1837.
7. Henry Allen, b. Jan. 10, 1836; m. Lavinda Tanner; res. Provi-
    dence. R. I.
8. Sarah Davis, b. in Killingly, Conn., Jan. 10, 1840; d. in Moosup,
    Conn., June 26, 1842.
9. Perley Hill, b. in Moosup, Apr. 13, 1842; m. Josephine Chap-
    pell; res. North Windham, Conn.
10. Eliza, b. in Moosup, Apr. 11, 1844; m. George W. Miller; res.
    Hartford, Conn.
11. Mary Frances, b. in Central Village, June 2, 1846; m. Joseph
    W. Carter; res. Central Village.
12. George Albert, b. in Central Village, March 7, 1848; res. same
    place.
13. Darius, b. in Central Village, May 28, 1851; m. Anna E. Bowen;
    res. Thurlow Station, Del. Co., Penn.
14. John, b. and d. in Central Village, Feb. 22, 1854.
15. Byron Augustus, b. in Central Village, Apr. 7, 1855; d. same
    place, Jan. 10, 1861.

5. **Perley**, b. Aug. 14, 1807; d. at Blackstone, Mass., Feb. 26,
    1823.

6. **Henry Augustus**, b. June 17, 1809; d. at Natick, R. I., April
    12, 1832.

7. **Ira Davis**, b. Jan. 21, 1814; m. **Sarah Ann Sherman**, b.
    in Exeter, May 12, 1818; residence, Lonsdale, R. I. Ch. :
    1. Ann Elizabeth, b. in Natick, Mar. 28, 1838; d. Oct. 6, 1838.
    2. Sarah E——, b. in Providence, Nov. 22, 1839; m. Ezra Bliss
        of Pawtucket. Two sons and two daughters.
    3. Hannah F——, b. in Warwick, R. I., May 15, 1842; d. same
        place, March 27, 1844.
    4. Hannah F——, b. in Warwick, July 14, 1845; m. George F.
        Sheldon of Pawtucket. Two daughters.
    5. Arthur R——, b. in Pawtucket, Jan. 14, 1848; d. same place,
        Sept. 3, 1849.
    6. Arthur R——, b. in Pawtucket, Feb. 26, 1850.
    7. Ellie A——, b. same place, July 31, 1853.
    8. Ida I——, b. same place, July 6, 1857.

8. **Sarah Ann**, b. Nov. 20, 1816; d. in Natick, July 4, 1833.

9. DARIUS, b. June 7, 1819; m. SARAH RISLEY; resided in Col-
    chester, Conn., and Stoughton, Mass.

No. 112.

John Phillips (parentage not given,) removed from Smithfield, R. I., to Somers, Conn., about 1780.   Children:

1. MARY; m. BENJAMIN BALLOU of Smithfield.
2. MERCY; m. JOHN COE of Smithfield.
3. AMY; m. ——— FULLER, and settled in Conn.
4. ANNA; unmarried.
5. GIDEON.   (No. 113.)
6. JONATHAN; removed to Somers, Conn.
7. ELIJAH; m. ——— OLNEY, and removed to Somers.
8. JOHN; removed to Somers.
9. SALLY; m. RUFUS SMITH, and lived in Smithfield.
10. ASA.
    One record has SARAH, perhaps identical with Sally.

No. 113.

Gideon Phillips (son of John of Smithfield: No. 112,)
born in Smithfield, R. I., June 15, 1760; resided in Smithfield,
and Mansfield and Somers, Conn., and died in Ellington,
Conn., Nov. 6, 1833.   He was a soldier in the war of the
Revolution.   He married (1st) in Smithfield, May 26, 1782,
Hannah Appleby; (2d) Barbara Arnold; (3d) Anna
Mitchell.   Children (by first marriage):

1. MARTIN, b. in Smithfield, Mar. 22, 1784; a soldier in the war
    of 1812; m. at Mansfield, Conn., Mar. 21, 1814, MARY L.
    WOODWORTH.   She was living, 1878, in Hartford, Conn.   Ch.:
    1. ———, a son, b. and d. April 5, 1815.
    2. Mary H———, b. June 5, 1816; d. Dec. 9, 1835.
    3. Albert, b. July 19, 1819; m. Dec. 12, 1842, Elizabeth Stowell of
        Middlebury, Vt.   Ch., all born at Rockville, Conn.:
        1. Susan, b. May 10, 1845; m. Gilbert Dawson.
        2. Frank Leroy, b. April 10, 1851; d. Oct. 11, 1852.
        3. Albert Wallace, b. Mar. 30, 1856; editor, 1878, of the
            Tolland County Gleaner.
    4. Caroline Lord, b. Oct. 4, 1822; m. June 25, 1849, C. A. Atkins
        of New Haven.

5. Ellsworth W——, b. Aug. 13, 1826; a soldier in the war of
   the Rebellion; m. in New York, Dec. 27, 1858, Louisa P.
   Hassack. Ch. :

    1. Louisa P——, b. May 4, 1860; d. July 25, same year.
    2. Carrie.   3. Eugene.

6. ——, a son, b. Nov. 10, 1828; d, Nov. 11, following.
7. ——, a daughter, b. May 15, 1831; d. May 23, following.
8. Esther, b. May 29, 1834; d. Oct. 6, 1835.
9. Sarah Louisa, b. Apr. 12, 1836; d. Oct. 3, 1841.

2. ESTHER, b. in Smithfield, March 31, 1786; m. SILAS SMITH of
   Smithfield, where she d. Dec. 22, 1856.
3. MERCY, b. Sept. 3, 1787; m. GEORGE ANDREWS of Woonsocket,
   where she d. Sept. 18, 1877. Ch. :

    1. Hannah L. *Andrews*, b. Jan. 5, 1813; m. Albert G. Wilber.
    2. Esther Sayles *Andrews*, b. Apr. 23, 1818.

(By second marriage) :

4. WILLIAM, b. 1796; m. in R. I. Ch. :

    1. Addison.   2. George.   3. Oliver.   4. Mary.

5. NANCY, b. 1800; d. in Providence; unmarried.

No. 114.

(I.) **Joshua Phillips** (parentage not given, said to be of
Scotch descent,) was with his wife **Freelove** and seven
children of Smithfield, R. I., in 1764. He bought land that year
in Hubbardston, Mass., where he afterwards lived, having first,
it is said, removed to Rutland, Mass. Four of his sons, Joshua,
Richard, Paine and Gideon served in the Revolutionary War.
Children :

1. FREELOVE, b. 1749; m. NATHAN STONE.
2. JOSHUA, } b. about 1750.
3. JAMES ; } m. SARAH NOURSE of Rutland, Dec. 4, 1767. Ch. :

    1. Relief, b. Sept. 6, 1768.

4. ESECK, b. 1752 ; d. June, 1777 (killed at the raising of a frame).
5. RICHARD, b. Sept. 4, 1754 ; of Dublin, N. H. (No. 115.)
6. PAINE, } b. Nov. 7, 1763.
7. GIDEON ; } of Roxbury, N. H. (No. 116.) ·

No. 115.

(II.) **Richard Phillips** (son of Joshua : No. 114,) from Smithfield, R. I., born Sept. 4, 1754; Revolutionary soldier and pensioner; settled in Dublin, N. H., 1781, on lot 12, range 5; died Nov. 18, 1834. He "accompanied Com. Whipple on his famous expedition to France with dispatches from Congress to that Government. The daring displayed in running the blockade in Narragansett Bay, and their narrow escape from capture near Newfoundland on their return, are reported as incidents of this expedition." He married in Rutland, Mass., 1778,* **Olive Evans**, born Mar. 7, 1755, died Apr. 10, 1850, dau. of David Evans of Hopkinton, Mass. Children :

1. RICHARD, b. March 25, 1779 ; d. Aug. 25, 1788.
2. JAMES, b. May 13, 1781 ; d. Sept. 4, 1788.
3. GEORGE WASHINGTON, b. March 2, 1783 ; m. Oct. 7, 1804, LUCINDA BEMIS of Marlborough, N. H. He d. in the army during the war with Great Britain. Ch. :
    1. Freelove P——, b. June 10, 1805; d. in Worcester, July 28, 1853. She m. Otis Phillips, and had children.
    2. Lucinda W——, b. Mar. 21, 1807; d. Apr. 15, 1847; m. June 8, 1831, Wm. Wilson, Jr., of Keene.
    3. Elvira, b. May 10, 1809; d. July 30, 1827; m. June 1, 1825, Gilman Grimes of Hancock.
    4. George W—— A——, b. June 16, 1811; m. Oct. 15, 1830.
4. OLIVE, b. Jan. 12, 1788: m. (1st) Oct. 7, 1803, EBENEZER BULLARD, who d. Jan. 11, 1811 ; m. (2d) June 28, 1826, RICHARD PHILLIPS of Roxbury, N. H. Ch. (by first marriage) :
    1. Richard *Bullard*, b. June 21, 1808; d. Apr. 9, 1810.
    2. James *Bullard*, b. May 11, 1810; of Boston; m. (1st) Sept. 15, 1836, Rebecca Souther, who d. March 10, 1847; had ch.; m. (2d) Jan. 25, 1849, Levina Ford of Marshfield, Mass.

    (By second marriage) :
    3. Freelove, b. Feb. 5, 1827; m. Aug. 30, 1846, Isaiah Souther of Boston.
    4. Andrew, b. June 10, 1828; d. Sept. 19, 1828.
    5. Rebecca, b. July 13; d. July 14, 1829.
    6. William, b. Sept. 25, 1831. †

---

* One account says July 11, 1779.

† History of Dublin, N. H., 1855.

No. 116.

(II.) **Gideon Phillips** (son of Joshua: No. 114;)
married **Chloe Shattuck**, May 5, 1786, and removed to
Roxbury, N. H., where he is said to have died.   Children :

1. ISABEL, b. Feb. 28, 1787 ; m. REUBEN ALDEN, who d. Nov. 24,
   1856, aged 69. She d. Feb. 28, 1870. Ch. :
   1. George *Alden ;* m., had three ch. :
      1. Isabella.   2. Nellie.   8. Willie.
   2. Sarah *Alden ;* m. Benjamin Clark.
   3. Cornelia *Alden ;* m. Samuel Roberts.
   4. Fidelia *Alden ;* m. Edward Haskell.
   5. Pauline *Alden.*
   6. Luna [?] *Alden.*
   7. Eunice *Alden.*
2. REUBEN, b. March 24, 1788 ; m. and res. in Roxbury, N. H.
3. BARBARA, b. March 19, 1793 ; m. and res. in Nelson, N. H.
4. RUFUS, b. Nov. 25, 1795 ; d. in the army.
5. ANNA, b. April 13, 1799 ; m. SAMUEL WARREN, and res. in
   Hubbardston. Ch. :
   1. Chloe *Warren,* b. Aug 11, 1816 ; res. Boston.
   2. Abigail *Warren,* b. Aug. 7, 1817 ; d. Feb. 15, 1819.
   3. Abigail H. *Warren ;* m. Dec. 6, 1842, Charles Conant of Barre.
   4. Phebe A——— *Warren ;* m. (1st) Addison Ellenwood; (2d)
      Hammet Billings of Boston.
   5. Rufus *Warren ;* res. Brookfield.
   6. Reuben *Warren,* b. Apr. 14, 1832 ; removed.
6. RICHARD, b. Apr. 13, 1801 ; m., it appears, his cousin, OLIVE
   PHILLIPS, and lived in Dublin, N. H.
7. JOSHUA, b. Nov. 28, 1802 ; res. in Hubbardston ; m. Aug. 4,
   1825, JULIA STONE of Rutland ; he d. Nov. 25, 1859. Ch. :
   1. Martha, b. Mar. 26, 1827 ; d. Apr. 7, 1831.
   2. Elizabeth, b. Mar. 3, 1833 ; d. Sept. 2, 1844.
   3. George Whitefield, b. July 5, 1836 ; grad. Amherst Coll., 1861 ;
      Andover Theological Seminary, 1864 ; was ordained and
      installed Oct. 12, same year, at Haydenville, Mass., where he
      preached about four years, then settled over the First Cong.
      Church. Columbus, Ohio, where he preached till 1871, when
      he became pastor of the Plymouth Church, Worcester, Mass.,
      which position he still holds. He m. Sept. 14, 1864, Sarah
      Ball of Amherst, Mass., dau. of Rev. Mason Ball.
   4. David Everett, b. July 26, 1842 ; of Columbus, Ohio ; m. June
      23, 1868, Nellie E. Armington of Rutland, Mass. She d. in
      Columbus, Sept. 23, 1879.

8. GIDEON, b. Mar. 15, 1807.
9. JAMES, b. Mar. 15, 1809 ; m. REBECCA LOVEWELL, June 26, 1831 ; she d. Mar. 28, 1876. Ch. :

> 1. Benjamin Franklin, b. in Hubbardston, Feb. 20, 1836; m. Nov., 1865, Mary L. Whitney of Gardner; res. South Gardner, Mass. Ch. :
>
>> 1. Stella S———, b. at South Gardner, Sept. 11, 1866.
>> 2. Eva L———, b. at South Gardner, Dec. 26, 1875.
>
> 2. Delia Ann, b. Mar., 1837; d. Sept. 3, 1851.
> 3. Savira, b. in Princeton, Mass., Nov. 13, 1843; m. Moses Bennett.
> 4. Louisa, b. in Princeton, Oct. 3, 1848 ; m. May 17, 1866, Jacob Shaffer.

No. 117.

Jeremy Phillips (parentage not given,) farmer, of Gloucester, R. I., where he died about 1822, aged about 70 or 75 years. He was buried on the homestead farm by the side of old graves, the occupants of which are unknown. The farm is the same occupied of late by Wm. Angell. Children— there were two daughters whose names are not given :

1. ROBERT. He was associated for a time with his two brothers, David and Bani, in the manufacture of cotton goods, at Wallum Pond, in Burrillville. He had six sons, all of whom died of consumption and were buried in Douglas, Mass.
2. STEPHEN.
3. DAVID, b. in Gloucester. (No. 118.)
4. BANI ; after engaging for a time with his two brothers, in the manufacture of cotton goods, he left the business and engaged in keeping a store in Johnston, R. I. There he m. (1st) ——— OLVERSON. She died leaving two children. He m. (2d) OLIVE COMSTOCK of Thompson, Conn., and moved to the homestead farm and had five more children, two of whom were living in 1878. He died about 1835, and was buried in Johnston. It was his misfortune to become addicted to the frequent use of stimulants in early life, which occasioned discomfort and separation in the family, but he was regarded by all who knew him as a man of talent, of general intelligence,

naturally kind-hearted, and of a thoroughly business turn of mind. Ch. (by first marriage) :

    1. Bani.   2. Mary Ann.

(By second marriage) :

    3. Sally.   4. Jeremiah.   5. Daniel; of East Douglas.
    6. Sarah.   7. Maria.

No. 118.

David Phillips (son of Jeremy of Gloucester : No. 117,) born in Gloucester, Nov. 10, 1769 ; married **Amey Smith**, and resided in North Scituate, where he died Aug. 9, 1847. Children :

1. HARLEY, b. Nov. 11, 1792.
2. BETSEY, b. March 28, 1795.
3. OSTRANDER, b. Aug. 11, 1796 ; d. Feb. 2, 1822.
4. STEPHEN, b. March 17, 1798.
5. SARAH ANN, b. June 2, 1800.
6. AMEY, b. Feb. 18, 1802. All the preceding d. previously to 1878.
7. DAVID, b. July 10, 1804 ; resided at North Scituate. Ch. :
    1. Emeline Rhodes, b. Aug. 25, 1827.
    2. Abby Fenner, b. Aug. 4, 1829; d. Jan. 26, 1832.
    3. Ostrander, b. Nov. 1, 1831; d. Jan. 15, 1873.
    4. Elizabeth Braman, b. Jan. 9, 1834.
    5. Abby P——, b. March 9, 1837.
    6. Herbert, b. March 12, 1839; sergeant in Co. C, 11th Reg. R. I. Vols.
    7. Alice Arnold, b. Oct. 4, 1841.
    8. Eugene Francis, b. Nov. 10, 1843; corporal in Co. A, 10th Reg. R. I. Vols.; manufacturer in Providence of patent finished insulated telegraph wire, patent electric cordage, patent rubber covered wire, patent lead encased wire, magnet wire, &c., &c. Ch. :
        1. Eugene Rowland, b. Jan. 17, 1871.
        2. Edith Josephine, b. Dec. 2, 1872.
        3. Frank Nichols, b. July 6, 1874.
    9. Charles Field, b. Oct. 27, 1846; d. Oct. 1, 1847.
8. ELMIRAH, b. July 11, 1806.
9. MARIA, b. Nov. 1, 1808 ; d.
10. LOUISA, b. Oct. 9, 1810.
11. ALBERT B——, b. Nov. 3, 1813.
12. CHARLOTTE, b. Oct. 3, 1816.

No. 119.

Jeremiah Phillips (parentage not given,) born in Newport, R. I., May 18, 1733 ; died in Griswold, Conn., May, 1818. He married (1st) Elizabeth Brown of Newport; married (2d) May 11, 1777, Margaret Stanton, born Oct. 25, 1748 ; she died in Griswold, 1798. Children (by first marriage) :

1. WILLIAM, b. Sept. 19, 1758.
2. SARAH, b. Nov. 6, 1759.
3. MARY, b. Dec. 17, 1760.
4. PENELOPE, b. April 11, 1762.
5. ELIZABETH, b. Jan. 19, 1764 ; m. STEPHEN CHURCH of Fall River.
6. MARY, b. Sept. 2, 1765.
7. JOHN, b. May 22, 1767.
8. CATHERINE, b. May 13, 1769 ; d. in Newport, 1841.
9. SAMUEL, b. Jan. 7, 1771 ; d. in Norwich, Conn., Dec. 9, 1844. He m. MARY PARKS.

(By second marriage) :

10. JEREMIAH, b. in Preston, Conn., Feb. 29, 1779 ; m. Ch. :
    1. Sarah Packard, b. at Jewett City, Conn., March 20, 1802; a school teacher for fifty years; unmarried; residing, 1878, in Providence.
    2. Stephen Abbott, b. at Jewett City, Jan. 14, 1804; m. (1st) Betsey Brown; (2d) Rebecca Rickard, both deceased.
    3. James J———; d. in infancy.
    4. James J———; d. in infancy.
    5. William J———, b. at Jewett City, Mar. 27, 1809; d. 1875. He m. Cerena Lee, now deceased.
    6. Benjamin C———, b. at Jewett City, Jan. 25, 1811; d. in Cincinnati, Ohio, 1849. He m. Maria Richards, now deceased.
    7. Mary; d. in infancy.
    8. Emily, b. April 15, 1815 , m. Theophilus Salisbury of Providence, where they reside.
11. BARBARA, b. March 24, 1780 ; m. STEPHEN BENJAMIN, and d. in Colchester, Conn., 1846.
12. JOHN, b. in Griswold, Jan. 30, 1782 ; res. in Lisbon, Conn., where he d. Feb. 3, 1862. He m. CHLOE KINGSLEY, who d. in Lisbon, 1852. Ch. :
    1. John Francis; d. in 1827.
    2. Gurdon B———; living in Conn., 1878.

3. Henry B——; d. 1870.
4. George A——; living in Conn., 1878.
5. Elizabeth K——; d. 1871.
6. Olive A——; living 1878.
7. Joseph H——; a local preacher, in Conn.   Ch. :
    1. Ellen Victory, b. in Lisbon, July 19, 1840; m. Asa P. Burdick; res. Providence.
    2. John Hamlet, b. in Lisbon, Nov. 9, 1841; d. 1862.
    3. Daniel Alliston, b. in Norwich, March 17, 1845; m. Sarah Chandler; d. 1878.
    4. Martha Jane, b. in Lisbon, July 31, 1850; d. July 26, 1866.
    5. Lydia Adelaid, b. in Norwich, Nov. 8, 1852; res. Providence.
    6. Joseph Norton, b. in Lisbon, Oct. 13, 1854; res. Norwich.
    7. Grace Maria, b. in Griswold, June 29, 1859; d. Aug. 30, 1860.
    8. Grace Annabell, b. in Griswold, Aug. 23, 1861; res. Norwich.
8. Jerusha B——; living, 1878.
9. Charles; d. in infancy.
10. Charles F——; d. in infancy.

13. ELIJAH, b. Feb. 13, 1784.
14. WILLIAM, b. Aug. 12, 1785.
15. STANTON, b. Aug. 31, 1787; d. in Lisbon, Oct., 1867. He m. Feb. 21, 1816, ABBY KAZER, living, 1878, in Norwich.
16. ESTHER, b. Nov. 13, 1789; d. in Norwich, Dec. 29, 1862. She m. 1807, THOMAS JACKSON, who d. 1853.

No. 120.

Bartholomew Phillips (parentage not given,) born Nov. 10, 1734, is said to have settled in Rhode Island during the Revolutionary War. He died Sept. 4, 1778. He married **Elizabeth Ellery,** who was born Sept. 17, 1734, and died Aug. 8, 1791. Children :

1. ABIGAIL, b. Sept. 17, 1756; m. Apr. 17, 1776, PHILIP POTTER. Ch. :
    1. Bartholomew *Potter*, b. Aug. 23, 1778.
    2. Abigail *Potter*, b. May 10, 1780.
    3. Philip *Potter*, b. Feb. 14, 1782.
    4. David *Potter*, b. Dec. 29, 1785.

> 5. Elizabeth *Potter*, b. June 6, 1788; m. Apr. 14, 1808, Daniel Whitney. Their dau., Elizabeth *Whitney*, b. in Ashford, Conn., Feb. 21, 1809; m. Mar. 28, 1832, James Chamberlain, and res., 1878, in Bath, N. H.

2. JERUSHA, b. Oct. 4, 1758.
3. CHLOE, b. Dec. 17, 1760.
4. WILLIAM ELLERY, b. Jan. 7, 1766.

OTHER FAMILIES OR BRANCHES OF THE NAME.

Except when so stated it is not known that there is any connection between the following branches, or that any of them are connected with the main branches of this work.

No. 121.

Reuel Phillips, born at East Granby, Conn. ; when about five years of age he removed to Albany Co., N. Y., and lost all trace of his family connections. He married in Berne, N. Y., **Sarah Landers.** Later in life he removed to Northfield, Cook Co., Ill., where he died Feb. 7, 1857, aged 77 years, 6 mos. Children :

1. ELIZA.
2. JOSEPH. Ch. :

> 1. Oscar, b. in Albany, N. Y., Dec. 9, 1829; entered the U. S. army Feb. 17, 1847, and served through the Mexican War. At the close of the war he went with his regiment, 5th U. S. Mounted Infantry, in which he acted as bugler, to Texas, and was stationed at San Antonio, Corpus Christi and elsewhere, and employed to keep the Comanches, Apaches and others in check, and was discharged Feb. 17, 1852, having served five years. In 1852 he carried the mail in Texas and Indian Territory from Fort Washita, Chickasaw Nation, to Fort Belknap, on the Brazos River. Aug. 7, 1861, he enlisted in California, in the 4th U. S. Infantry, was ordered to Washington, and participated in many of the principal battles of the late war. At the close of his term he was honorably discharged. He m. July 28, 1868, Angie L. Ellsworth of Bennington, Vt.; residing, 1878, Cohoes, N. Y. Child :
>> 1. Grace Angie, b. in North Adams, Mass., July 11, 1871.
> 2. George W——, b. 1831.
> 3. Adalaide M——, b. 1833; m. —— Van Dyck of Schenectady.

3. REUEL, b. in Berne, Nov. 17, 1808; m. ELIZA A. ALLEN, b. Oct. 19, 1810; residence, West Northfield, Ill. Ch. :

    1. Catharine Adelia; m. Alonzo Kennecott.
    2. Ann Judson; deceased.
    3. A—— W——, b. June 10, 1834; served three years as Union soldier in the late war, and was in about twenty battles, among which were Malvern Hill, Fredericksburg, Chancellorsville and Gettysburg.

4. ——; d. more than 60 years ago.
5. ——; also d. young.
6. HARRIET.   7. JOHN MILTON.   8. SARAH M——.
    9. WILLIAM.   10. DANIEL.   11. SETH S——.

One record includes others, and mentions ELMINA and CATHARINE.

No. 122.

Elihu Phillips married **Elizabeth Spear,** and resided in Rupert, Vt., to which place he is supposed, by his grandson, Josiah S. Phillips, to have removed from Connecticut, and to the latter State from Mass. He d. in Rupert. Children :

1. ELIHU.   2. HORACE.
3. ELAM, b. April 7, 1791; d. in Tilly, Ill., May 12, 1876; m. CHLOE MOREHOUSE. Ch. (by first marriage) :

    1. Josiah Sherman, b. in Sandgate, Vt., Nov. 16, 1814; m. Maria F. Griffin; res. Lowell, Mass.
    2. Huldah Maria, b. in Rupert; m. Hon. John Kimball of Concord, N. H.
    3. Squire Morehouse; d. 1843.
    4. Moses Spear; d. 1846.

      (By second marriage) :

    5. Rheuma Curtis; m. Dalhousie Priestly.

      (By third marriage) :

    6. Silas N——. He and is three younger brothers were in the late Southern War.
    7. Pamelia; m. —— Symonds.
    8. James E——.   9. George.   10. Myron.

4. ELIZABETH ; m. SEELEY SHERMAN.
5. SQUIRE ; m. CATHARINE MOREHOUSE.
6. MOSES ; m. CHARLOTTE RANSOM.
7. THANKFUL ; m. IRA WEED.
8. CYNTHIA ; m. WILLIAM WEED.

These children were born in Rupert, Vt., and resided there and in Salem, N. Y. for some years. One or two of them went to New York and the West in the later years of their lives.

No. 123.

Peter Phillips of Oxford, Mass.; married 1766, **Hannah Nichols** of same place. This may have been the "Peter Philips" mentioned in Worcester Co. Probate Records, who, May 8, 1748, "aged about 14 years, son of John Philips, late of Roxbury, County of Suffolk, appointed Benjamin Newell of Dudley, guardian;" or he may have come from the vicinity of Smithfield, R. I., whence so many of the name first make their appearance. There is a tradition among his descendants that they are of Irish descent. Children :

1. HANNAH, b. Sept. 18, 1767. Hannah Phillips and Joseph Buckminster Jones, both of Oxford, were published May 21, 1784.
2. EDWARD, b. June 10, 1772; res. in Charlton, Mass.; d. prior to July 6, 1819. He m. in Oxford, May 21, 1795, RUTH ATWOOD, formerly of Dedham. She d. June 26, 1824. Ch.:
    1. Hannah; m. Alvin Wood of Webster.
    2. William; m. Polly Baker, who was b. Mar. 19, 1794, dau. of Jos. Capen Baker. She d. Sept. 17, 1861. Ch.:
        1. Albigence Waldo, b. June 7, 1821. He volunteered to serve in the war of the Rebellion, but was refused and afterwards drafted into service, taken prisoner at the South, and never heard from again.
        2. Susan, b. Sept. 11, 1823; m. T. F. Eddy; went to Morris, Ill.
        3. Levina, b. June 22, 1824; m. Wm. A. White, a native of Paisley, Scotland; res. Grafton.
        4. William Eaton, b. Oct. 23, 1825; m. and went to San Francisco, Cal.
        5. John, b. Oct. 19, 1827; m. —— Baker; went to Millington, Ill.
        6. Ruth, b. Apr. 6, 1829; d. Sept. 16, 1830.
        7. Ruth Ann, b. Sept. 2, 1831; m. Henry S. Dealing, who d. Aug. 13. 1866, aged 36 years, 11 m., 19 d., and she m. (2d) John A. Ward of Charlton.
        8. Rufus, b. Aug. 12, 1833; went to Silver City, Idaho.
    3. Nancy; m. Rufus Mixer, a justice of the peace and highly esteemed citizen of Charlton. She was living, 1878, in Leicester.
    4. John; went to Pennsylvania.

No. 124.

Dr. William Phillips, born Dec. 14, 1741 ; wife's name, **Huldah ;** resided in Candia, N. H., where he died May 9, 1813. Had fourteen children, only one name given :

1. JAMES MASON, b. April 7, 1801 ; m. LYDIA WHITTEMORE ; d. in West Cambridge, Mass., Apr. 9, 1839. Ch. :

   1. Lydia A———, b. Aug 3, 1828; d. Apr. 6, 1854.
   2. William Mason, b. in Arlington, Mass., May 15, 1831; m. Mary Ruth Brown; residence, Reading, Mass. Ch., all born in Reading :

      1. Mary Alice, b. Jan. 6, 1853; d. Aug. 9, 1870.
      2. Carrie Williamine, b. March 11, 1855.
      3. Fred Mason, b. Feb. 8, 1859; in 1878 with John P. Squire & Co., Faneuil Hall Market, Boston.
      4. Fannie Louise, b. Sept. 16, 1869.
      5. William Stanwood, b. Sept. 12, 1873.
   3. Samuel W———, b. Feb. 19, 1832, in Dedham, Mass. ; residence, Lynnfield, Mass.
   4. Henry Lee, b. in Dedham, Apr. 23, 1834; d. in Danvers, July, 1875.
   5. Susan Jane, b. June 25, 1836; m. Stilman J. Poole; resides in Rockland, Mass.
   6. Aaron Whittemore, b. Nov. 15, 1838; d. Aug., 1866.

No. 125.

Samuel Phillips, born in Mass. ; died 1796, aged about 80. Children :

1. SEBA, b. in Conn. ; when about twenty years of age he went to Vermont; d. Feb. 5, 1861, aged 76. His wife, FLAVILLA, d. July 4, 1868. Ch. :

   1. Nelson L———, b. 1811 or 1812. Ch. :

      1. Julia.   3. Charles N.
      2. Andrew J.   4. Willie E.

   2. Jason A——— ; m. in Wentworth, Vt., April 20, 1844, Adeline Bean. Ch. :

      1. Arabel Grace, b. Apr. 6, 1845, in Fairlee, Vt.
      2. Joseph Henry, b. Oct. 9, 1846.
      3. Fred M———, b. in Wentworth, Vt., Feb. 4, 1849.
      4. Frank G———, b. in Wentworth, Oct. 8, 1851.
      5. Angie Bean, b. in Wentworth, July 22, 1859.

   3. Corodon O.   4. Alson R.
   5. Flavilla C——— ; d. Oct. 6, 1851.

2. AMI, b. in New York City.

No. 126.

Samuel Phillips, born May 24, 1750; married in 1772, **Elizabeth Clemons;** resided in Berkley, Mass., and died March 18, 1809.* Children:

1. SAMUEL; m. POLLY PIERCE.
2. REUBEN C———, b. in Berkley, Feb. 13, 1782; m. NANCY SIMMONS; res. in Berkley, and d. May 19, 1869. Ch.:
    1. Edwin, b. in Berkley, Nov. 29, 1806; m. Sally Cornell; d. May 19, 1869. Ch.:
        1. Charles.   2. James
           One of them residing in Arlington, Mass.
    2. Nancy, b. in Berkley, June 22, 1810; m. E. F. Bugbee; res. Taunton.
    3. Baalis, b. in Dighton, Oct. 31, 1812; res Taunton; m. (1st) Sally P. Bugbee; m. (2d) Abbie Bugbee. Ch.:
        1. Baalis F———, b. in Berkley, Aug. 15, 1838; m. Eliza Staples of Taunton, where he resides.
        2. Sarah F———, b. in Berkley, May 24, 1841; m. G. H. Norcutt of Taunton.
        3. William O———, b. in Taunton. July 19, 1848; m. Ella I. Goff; res. Taunton.
        4. Mary Emma, b. in Taunton, May 12, 1858.
    4. Mary Ann, b. June 22, 1818; m. Dean Westgate.
    5. Samuel; soldier in the late Southern war.
    6. Betsey, b. June, 1821; m. Benj. Norcutt.
    7. Elias.   8. Shepherd, b. June, 1830.   9. Franklin.
    10. Harriet, b. Jan. 31, 1831; m. Otis P. Bugbee.
3. BETSEY.   6. REBECCA.
4. CHARITY.   7. REBY; m. ELISHA PIERCE.
5. ELIZABETH.   8. HANNAH.

No. 127.

(I.) **Thomas Phillips,** born on the ocean in 1717. His parents located in Pennsylvania.

No. 128.

(II.) **Jenkin Phillips** (son of Thomas: No. 127,) born in Virginia; married **Miss Hannah Butcher;** res. in Virginia and Kentucky, and died in Kentucky.

---

* Samuel had two brothers, Nathaniel and Isaac. Isaac went privateering, and that was the last heard of him.

No. 129.

(III.) **Thomas Phillips** (son of Jenkin : No. 128,) born in Virginia, 1761 ; married **Sallie Botts**; died in Jefferson Co., Va. Children :

1. DAVID BOTTS ; m. Mrs. ANN LEWIS HARDING, Aug., 1829. Ch. :
    1. Sallie, b. Aug. 22, 1830; m. June 22, 1852, Dr. J. M. Keller of Alabama.
    2. Mary E———, b. Aug. 23, 1832; m. Richard Christmas.
    3. Thomas J———, b. Oct. 6, 1834; m. 1865, Jane Miller. Child :
        1. Ewell D.
2. SAMUEL.   3. JENKIN.   4. JEFFERSON.   5. RICHARD.
6. NANCY.   7. HENRY.   8. MURRAY.

No. 130.

George Phillips was born in Birmingham, England ; married **Miss Jones**; emigrated to Boston, Mass., in 1818 or about that time, and died in Boston. He was the son of George Phillips of Birmingham, who married Miss Colton or Cotton, and grandson of George Phillips of Aston, near Birmingham. Prior to the year 1818 this family resided at Aston and Birmingham for a great many years. Children, all born in Birmingham, England :

1. GEORGE.   3. ANN.   5. EDWIN.
2. LAVINIA.   4. JOHN.   6. LOUISA.
7. WILLIAM ; m. ANN MARIA STOW, dau. of Edward Stow of Boston. Ch. :
    1. William C ———, b. in Dedham, Mass.
    2. George, b. in Boston.
    3. John, b. in Boston; lawyer in New York City; resides in Brooklyn, N. Y.
    4. Ann B———, b. in Boston.
    5. Mary, b. in Brooklyn, N. Y.
    6. Edith, b. in Brooklyn, N. Y.
    7. Norah, b. in Brooklyn, N. Y.
8. MARY.   9. MARGARET.   10. MARTHA.
11. FRANCES.   12. HENRY.

No. 131.

Thomas Phillips, born in Manchester, Eng., 1800; died in Providence, R. I., 1871; was the son of George Phillips, born 1764 and died 1815, and grandson of John Phillips, born 1740 and died 1800.   Children:

1. THOMAS, b. in Manchester, Eng.
2. WILLIAM H———, b. in New York City.
3. GEORGE R———, b. in Providence, R. I.
4–8. Five daughters, b. in Providence.

No. 132.

Rev. Daniel Phillips, born in Swansea, Wales; came to America in 1848; preached in the Welsh language in Pittsburg, Pa., till 1851, and the next year entered Amherst Coll.; grad. 1856; grad. from Andover Theo. Sem., 1859; since 1860 has preached as Congregationalist in English, mostly in Mass.; lately of North Chelmsford.   He was the son of Daniel Phillips, who was born in Ponteberem in 1799, and became a master builder; married Miss Ann Grier, and removed to Swansea, where he did business on a large scale.   "His mind was quick and comprehensive, with great business capacity.   Although he died when only 26 years old, he had accumulated considerable property."   He, Daniel, Sr., had a brother David, who came to America about 1817.   They were sons of John Phillips, a man of strong natural powers and considerable means, who was born in Ponteberem, Wales; lived and died in same town. This branch originated from Carmarthenshire and Pembrokeshire, and from there has spread over England and Wales, and elsewhere.

The Rev. Daniel Phillips married, 1860, **Miss Elizabeth Ruth Wheelock** * of Amherst, Mass.   Children:

1. ANNA KEYES, b. in Orange, Mass., Dec. 15, 1853.
2. PAUL CRYSOSTOM, b. in Ayer, Mass., Dec. 20, 1865.
3. JOHN GRIER, b. in Ayer, May 27, 1867; d. Sept. 10, 1867.
4. ELIZABETH RUTH, b. in Ayer, July 12, 1868.
5. MARY CHARLOTTE, b. in Ayer, Sept. 12, 1870.

* See No. 22.
13

No. 133.

James Phillips, born in Wales, G. B., 1781. The exact locality of his birth is not known, but is thought to have been Pembrokeshire. He emigrated to America in the summer of 1801, and settled in Whitestown, N. Y. In 1840 he removed to Homer, N. Y.; died June 12, 1852: "a kind husband, an affectionate father and a very industrious man." He married in New York city, March 12, 1803, Miss Sarah Evans, who died Nov. 10, 1843, aged 63. Children:

1. BENJAMIN, b. Oct. 21, 1805; minister of the M. E. Church, connected with the Black River Conference; m. (1st) June 18, 1833, Miss CAROLINE FLETCHER of Lansingville, N. Y. She d. and he m. (2d) about 1853, Miss SARAH OSBORN of Herkimer. He d. in Cortlandville, Feb. 17, 1863. One child, R. M. Phillips, b. June 22, 1837; enlisted in Co. F, 10th N. Y. Cav.; d. in Warrenton, Va., Mar. 31, 1864.
2. MARY, b. Aug. 24, 1807; m. (1st) SYLVANUS REES of Utica. He d. and she m. (2d) MICHAEL SPENCER of Cortlandville. where she d. April 2, 1868.
3. JOHN, b. Dec. 29, 1808; paper manufacturer; m. twice; d. in Avon, N. Y., July 4, 1868. One child, John H.; res. Rochester; conductor.
4. DAVID, b. Nov. 29, 1810; wholesale and retail paper dealer, with firm of Jos. Haywood & Co., N. Y. city; unmarried.
5. RACHEL, b. July 24, 1812; d. Aug. 27, 1827.
6. HENRY D., b. Dec. 17, 1814; sail manufacturer, Williamsburg; d. Oct. 24, 1848. One son, Albert H.; provision merchant in Brooklyn; m. Emma Linston.
7. SARAH, b. Nov. 13, 1818; d. Mar. 3, 1842.
8. JAMES, b. Oct. 16, 1820; farmer, living at the West; m. twice.
9. ANN H., b. Dec. 23, 1823; d. June 21, 1846.

No. 134.

William Phillips, born in Marblehead, son of William Phillips, of Marblehead, who married ——— Bartlett. He married Jane Adams; res. in Boston, and was drowned in Boston Harbor. Children, all born in Marblehead:

1. DAVID ADAMS, b. 1796; m. ELIZABETH BROWN. Ch.:
    1. Charles S———, b. July 1, 1833, in Boston; of West Newton; house and sign painter. Ch.:
        1. Charles Gorham, b. at Auburndale, Mass , Oct. 25, 1859.
        2. Carrie L———, b. at West Newton, Apr. 19, 1866.
    2. John, b. in Boston, 1836; d.
    3. William, b. in Boston, 1838; d.
2. WILLIAM; m. DEBORAH CROCKER; of Lynn.
3. JOHN ADAMS, b. 1806; m. CAROLINE LOVELL.
4. ELIZABETH; d. prior to 1878; m. JOSEPH BARBER.
5. MARGARET; d.
6. HANNAH J———; m. CHARLES BURLINGAME; of Charlestown.
7. SARAH ANN; m. FRANK KEMP; of Boston Highlands.
8. JOHANNAH; m. JOHN MUNROE; both d. prior to 1878.
9. JANE; 'd. prior to 1878; m. GEORGE GREEN.

No. 135.

Luther Phillips married **Lydia H. Adams.** He appears to have been son of Thomas[3] (of the family of Thomas,[2] Thomas,[1] No. 70,) and Abigail (Chandler) Phillips. She was born Jan. 26, 1786, and died May 22, 1851, dau. of Francis and Mercy (Adams) Adams, and gr.dau. of Francis and Keziah (Atwood) Adams. Children :

1. CAROLINE, b. Oct. 8, 1807; m. ARBA PRATT of Bridgewater.
2. ABIGAIL, b. July 6, 1809; m. NOAH CHANDLER.
3. MARY ANN, b. Aug. 18, 1811; m. JOHN OLDHAM of Pembroke.
4. LUTHER, b. Feb. 22, 1814; m. DINAH MOREHEAD of Duxbury. Ch.:
    1. George L———, b. 1840.
    2. Ellen T———, b. 1842.
    3. Sally, b. 1848.
5. AUGUSTUS, b. June 18, 1815; m. JERUSHA B. BARTON of Duxbury. Ch.:
    1. Mary A———, b. 1850.
    2. Louisa D———, b. 1852.
    3. Henry C———, b. 1854.
    4. Wendell, b. 1857.
    5. Augustus H———; d. young.
6. JUDITH, b. June 3, 1816; d. Sept. 19, following.—Gen. of the Adams Family of Kingston, Mass.

EARLY FAMILIES IN THE VICINITY OF BOSTON.

Some of the first of the name in New England after Rev. George Phillips of Watertown, were John of Dorchester, Nicholas of Weymouth, Henry of Dedham, and William of Boston or Charlestown, all as early as 1640. There were two by the name of Nicholas, a little later in Boston, who had families, but how related to Nicholas of Weymouth, does not appear. They multiplied rapidly, and within fifty years after the settlement of the Massachusetts Colony, there were a large number of this name living in Boston and the neighboring towns.*

136. JOHN PHILLIPS ; of Dorchester ; came, probably in the *Mary and John*, 1630 ; admitted freeman, Aug. 7, 1632 ; constable of the town, 1636 ; said to have removed to Boston ; one of the ♦founders and deacon of the Second Church with which he united, June 5, 1650. His first wife, Joanna, d. Oct. 22, 1675, and he m. (2d) widow SARAH MINOR. He d. Dec. 16, 1682, aged 77. Ch. :

    1. Mary, b. April, 1633; d. young.
    2. John, b. April, 1635.
    3. Mary, b. 1636.
    4. Israel, b. 1642. All died before maturity except Mary 2d, who m. (1st) George Munjoy of Falmouth ; and (2d) Robert Lawrence of same place.

137. NICHOLAS PHILLIPS, deacon ; of Weymouth, 1640 ; freeman, May 13, 1640 ; d. Sept., 1672. In his will, proved Oct. 3, 1672, he makes his oldest son, Richard, executor. Ch. :

    1. Richard ; living, 1679. (See No. 147.)
    2. Experience, b. May 8, 1641 ; m. ——— King, and was living, 1679.
    3. Caleb, b. Jan. 22, 1644 ; one copy says " 22 (11) 1638."
    4. Joshua ; in Capt. Turner's Company on Conn. River, 1676 ; d. April, 1679, leaving no family.
    5. Benjamin. (No. 148.)
    6. Alice or Elizabeth ; m. ——— Shaw, and was living, 1671.
    7. Hannah ; m. ——— White, and was living, 1679.
    8. Abigail.

138. HENRY PHILLIPS ; butcher ; of Dedham and Boston ; said to have gone first from Watertown to Dedham ; chosen ensign of Dedham, Oct. 27, 1648 ; was of Boston, 1664. He was evidently brother

---

* Savage's Genealogical Dictionary, Vol. 3: Wyman's Charlestown Genealogies: Genealogical and Historical Register: Collection of C. J. F. Binney : Mass. Colony Records.

of Dea. Nicholas Phillips of Weymouth, and may have been bro. of John of Dorchester, or, possibly bro. of John of Charlestown ; d. 1686, buried Feb. 3.   He m. (1st) ELIZABETH BROCK, who d. Aug. 1, 1640 ; (2d) ANNE HUNTING, May 1, 1641, at Dedham ; (3d) MARY DWIGHT.   Ch. :

    1. Mary ; d. 1640.
    2. Anne ; d. young.
    3. Abigail, b. Oct. 20, 1645.
    4. Nathaniel; bap. Apr. 3, 1653 ; d. prior to 1685.
    5. Eleazer, b. Oct. 8, 1654. (No. 139.)
    6. Timothy, b. Sept 15 (bap. 19), 1658. (No. 143.)
    7. Mary, b. Nov. 28, 1660.
    8. Elisha, b. May 12 (bap. 15), 1665.
    9. Jonathan, b. Sept. 12, 1666.
    10. John, b. July 9 (bap. 10), 1670; of Boston; m. at Charlestown, Mary Gross of Boston, June 25, 1797 ; d. prior to 1705.
    11. Joseph, b. Feb. 19 (bap. 28), 1674–5.

139. ELEAZER PHILLIPS, Capt. (son of Henry, 138) ; m. (1st) ANN FOSTER, who d., and he m. (2d) SARAH CUTLER, and after she d., he m. (3d) ELIZABETH BILL. He d. Apr., 1709. Ch. (bap. at Charlestown Church) :

    1. Eleazer, b. Apr. 23, 1682. (No. 140.).
    2. Anna ; bap. (with Eleazer) Oct. 12, 1684.
    3. Nathaniel, b. 1688 ; d. young.
    4. Isaac, b. July 7, 1689.
    5. Joseph, b. July 17 (bap. 20), 1690. (No. 142.)
    6. Elizabeth; bap. Oct 23, 1692.
    7. Jonathan, b. Nov. 19 (bap. 24), 1695 ; m. Sarah Lynde; d. of small-pox. Jan. 2, 1721–2, aged 26.

140. ELEAZER PHILLIPS (son of Eleazer, 139) ; admitted to the Church, Charlestown, May 13, 1733 ; m. (1st) LYDIA WAITE, who d. Apr. 4, 1738, aged 47 ; m. (2d) ELIZABETH LANGTON. Ch., all by first marriage :

    1. Lydia ; bap. Sept. 28, 1707.
    2. Eleazer, b. in Boston, Sept. 25, 1710.
    3. Timothy, b. Oct. 4 (bap. 10), 1714.
    4. Richard, b. Feb 2, 1716–17. (No. 141.)
    5. Nathaniel; bap. Apr. 19. 1719 ; d. Jan. 25, following.
    6. Samuel; bap. Oct. 29, 1721.

141. RICHARD PHILLIPS (son of Eleazer, 140) ; merchant ; m. ELIZABETH HENDLEY. Ch. :

    1. Eleazer ; bap. Jan. 15, 1748–9.
    2. Jonathan ; bap. Jan. 13, 1751.
    3. Richard ; d. young.

142. JOSEPH PHILLIPS (son of Eleazer, 139) ; buys of Blaney five and one-half acres of land, 1710 ; town clerk, 1727 ; m. ELIZABETH GIBSON, Oct. 4, 1711. She was admitted to the First Church, Charlestown, 1719. He d. Jan. 16, 1755, aged 64. Ch. :

    1. Joseph; bap. July 20, 1712.
    2. Elizabeth; bap. Jan. 30, 1714–15.
    3. Joseph; bap. Oct 4, 1719.

143. TIMOTHY PHILLIPS, Capt. (son of Henry, 138) ; probably admitted to First Church, Charlestown, 1687, and freeman, 1689–90 ; m. (1st) in Boston, ———— ; (2d) MARY SMITH. He d. at the age of 53. Ch. :

    1. Henry, b. June 16, 1682.
    2. Timothy, b. Dec. 24, 1686–7 ; d. at 26 years of age.
    3. Sarah; bap. Aug. 30, 1691.
    4. John, b. July 14 (bap. 15), 1694. (No. 144.)

144. JOHN PHILLIPS (son of Timothy, 143) ; admitted to church Mar. 24, 1727–8 ; m. (1st) FRANCES GARLAND, in Boston, Apr. 15, 1717, who d. aged 25 ; m. (2d) ALICE (BRIGDEN) PHILLIPS, widow of Benjamin, who was grandson of Dea. Nicholas Phillips of Weymouth. Ch. :

    1. Sarah; bap. Apr. 10, 1720, Charlestown Church.
    2. Henry; also bap. Apr. 10, 1720.
    3. John, b. Dec. 29, 1724. (No. 145.)
    4. Timothy (by 2d m.), bap. Apr. 20, 1728.
    5. Nathaniel, b. Jan. 1 (bap. 5), 1734–5 ; mason ; admitted to Charlestown Church, Jan. 1, 1758 ; removed to Marlboro ; m. Anne Chamberlain, June 21, 1757, who d. in Barre, Aug., 1815, aged 82 : one ch. d. in Charlestown.
    6. Samuel; bap. Sept. 11, 1737; d. 1750.

145. JOHN PHILLIPS (son of John, 144) ; m. Aug. 1, 1746, ANN HUGO. Ch. :

    1. John; bap. Apr. 19, 1747; St. Johns, N. F.
    2. Henry; bap. Apr. 25, 1756.
    3. Timothy; bap. Apr. 11, 1762.

146. SAMUEL PHILLIPS (stated by *Wyman* to be son of Henry, of Dedham, 138) ; of Boston ; stationer ; m. HANNAH GILLAM. Ch. :

    1. Gillam, who was bro.-in-law to Peter Faneuil.
    2. Henry, who was in a duel on Boston Common, 1728.

147. RICHARD PHILLIPS (son, probably, of Nicholas, 137) ; of Weymouth ; wife, MARY. Ch. :

    1. Mary, b. May 21, 1660; d. young.
    2. Mary, b. May 24, 1661.

3. Joshua, b. May 10, 1662; Amy, b. Oct. 10, 1687, and Joshua, b. Apr. 19, 1689, recorded as ch. of Joshua and Amy Phillips of Weymouth, appear to have been his.
4. Nicholas, b. Mar. 30, 1664. (See No. 150.)
5. Elizabeth, b. Nov. 27, 1665.
6. Richard, b. Oct. 20, 1667.
7. Samuel, b. May 7, 1670.

148. BENJAMIN PHILLIPS (son of Nicholas, 137), ship carpenter; admitted to First Church, Charlestown, Apr. 3, 1681: m. ANNE ———. He d. Feb. 13, 1687, in middle age; inventory Mar. 11, 1689. Ch.:

1. Benjamin, b. Oct. 2, 1680. (No. 149.)
2. Joshua, b. Apr. 14 (bap. 19), 1685.

149. BENJAMIN PHILLIPS (son of Benj., 148); appears to have m. (1st) LUCY BOYLSTON, Mar. 10, 1702, who d., and he m. (2d) ALICE BRIGDEN. He d. Feb. 3, 1721–2. His widow m. John Phillips (144). Ch., all by first m., except possibly the last; bap. at Charlestown Church:

1. Lucy; bap. Mar. 25, 1704.
2. Benjamin, b. April 11 (bap. 13), 1707.
3. Hannah; bap. July 17, 1708.
4. Johannah; bap. June 8, 1712.
5. Mary; bap. Oct. 9, 1715.
6. Joshua; bap. Feb. 9, 1717–18; m. (1st) Apr. 19, 1739, Mary Mallet; m. (2d) Abigail Goodwin; son Joshua d. in Cambridge, July, 1764.
7. Spencer; bap. Oct. 1, 1721.

150. NICHOLAS PHILLIPS (probably son of Richard, 147, but possibly son of one of the two following); of Weymouth; m. MARY ———. Ch.:

1. Mary, b. Nov. 29, 1690; died.
2. Mary, b. Aug. 24, 1692.
3. Nicholas, b. May 23, 1697; d. Aug. 21, 1744.
4. Hannah, b. May 23, 1697.

151. NICHOLAS PHILLIPS; of Boston; seems to have been a shopkeeper; probably came from England; m. Dec. 4, 1651, HANNAH SALTER. He d. prior to Apr. 24, 1670. Ch.:

1. Elizabeth, b. Feb. 24, 1653.
2. Hannah, b. Nov. 25, 1654.
3. Nicholas, b. Feb. 26, 1657; d. Aug. following.
4. Nicholas, b. May 12, 1660.
5. Abigail, b. Feb. 20, 1662.
6. Sarah, b. Apr. 13, 1665.
7. Thomas, b. Oct. 19, 1667.

152. NICHOLAS PHILLIPS (origin unknown) ; of Boston ; butcher ;
m. PHILIPPA ———. Ch. :

 1. Nicholas, b. Nov. 30, 1665.
 2. John, b. May 3, 1667 ; d. soon.
 3. John, b. June 21, 1669.
 4. Joseph, b. May 14, 1671.
 5. Benjamin, b. May 14, 1671.
 6. Mary, b. June 23, 1674.

153. JOHN PHILLIPS, Col. ; "nephew of Thos. Parker of Arrow-
sick, the mate of the first ship at Plymouth from England;" of
Charlestown ; master mariner ; admitted to church, June 11, 1676 ;
freeman, 1677 ; treasurer of the Province and judge of the County
Court; d. March 20, 1726, aged 93 yrs., 9 mos. He m. (1st) July
19, 1655, CATHARINE, dau. of John Anderson. She d. Feb. 24,
1698–9, and he m. (2d) SARAH GRAVES, 1701. Ch. :

 1. Catharine, b. Aug. 30, 1662 ; d. young.
 2. Samuel, b. Feb. 16, 1664 ; d. young.
 3. Mehitable, b. July 1, 1668.
 4. Abigail, b. June 19, 1670 ; m. Cotton Mather, May 4, 1686, and
  d. Nov. 28, 1702.
 5. Catharine, b. June 23, 1672.
 6. John, b. Mar. 8, 1673; said to have d. at two yrs., but if so,
  there must have been another of this name, for John and
  Henry, sons of late Col. John were living in Charlestown in
  1726.
 7. Mary ; bap. Mar. 14, 1675.
 8. Anderson, b. July 11, 1680.
 9. Henry ; bap. Dec. 4, 1681 ; merchant ; m. May 27, 1708, Joanna
  Everton ; d. Dec. 14, 1729 ; no ch.

154. JOHN PHILLIPS (son of John,* 153) ; sea-capt. ; m. (1st)
Aug. 15, 1694, MARY HAYMAN, who d. ; m. (2d) Sept. 11, 1702,
ANNE, widow of Isaac Greenwood, and dau. of Col. John Lynde of
Charlestown. He d. Nov. 4, 1756, in his 82d year. Ch. :

 1. Samuel ; bap. Nov. 24, 1695 ; d.
 2. John, b. Jan. 15 (bap. 17), 1697 ; shipwright ; living, 1722 ; m.
  Elizabeth ———.
 3. Samuel, b. Dec. 26 (bap. 31), 1699 ; absent with army in Spain ;
  inherited estate from S. Hayman.
 4. Anne, b. 1702.

---

* Genealogies and Estates of Charlestown. T. B. Wyman; p. 741. Savage in his
Genealogical Dictionary, Vol. 3, p. 413, gives the nine children of Col. John Phillips,
but does not mention the second John, whose birth appears to have been in the first
part of the year 1675, so he may have been a twin with Mary unless there is an error
in the date of her birth.

5. Catharine; bap, in Charlestown Church, March 12, 1709.
6. Sarah; bap. March 11, 1710.
7. Anderson. b. Feb. 5 (bap. 6), 1715. (No. 155.)

155. ANDERSON PHILLIPS (son of John, 154) ; seaman or capt. ;
m. Mar. 19, 1741, DORCAS BINNEY of Hull, who d. Jan. 9, 1763,
in her 43d year. He d. 1792. Ch., some of them born in Hull :

1. John, b. Dec. 13, 1741; d.
2. John, b. May 9, 1743.
3. Anna, b. Feb. 26, 1744.
4. Dorcas, b. Sept. 9, 1748.
5. Henry, b. July 3, 1751; d. 1752.
6. Sarah; b. Apr. 18, 1753; died.
7. Sarah, b. May 3, 1754.
8. Anderson, b. Apr. 12, 1758; mariner; drowned at Boston, Jan.
   21, 1808; will proved Jan. 22, devised all to wife Mary.
9. Abigail; b. Dec. 18, 1762; d. 1763.
10. Mary; unmarried.

156. ANDREW PHILLIPS (origin unknown) ; m. ELIZABETH ———.
Ch. :

1. Ephraim, b. March, 1659.
2. Andrew, bap. in Charlestown. 1687, aged 25. (No. 157.)

157. ANDREW PHILLIPS (son of Andrew, 156) ; m. SARAH SMITH,
Nov. 11, 1683 ; d. Dec. 10, 1717. Ch. :

1. Andrew, b. July 23, 1687. (No. 158.)
2. Ebenezer, b. Aug. 17, 1695; m. Mary Smith, and had son John,
   b. Sept. 11, 1722.
3. Joanna, b. Sept. 8, 1697.
4. Samuel, single man, admr. to bro. Ebenezer, 28. July 11, 1723.

158. ANDREW PHILLIPS (son of Andrew, 157) ; cordwainer ; Killingly ; m. MARY COVILL, Aug. 17, 1706. Ch. :

1. Andrew,* b. Apr. 22, 1707.
2. John, b. Apr. 30, 1709.
3. Elizabeth, b. July 24, 1711.

159. WILLIAM PHILLIPS, Major ; of Boston ; innholder ; probably
the same one made freeman, May 13, 1640 ; also licensed by General
Court to sell wine to the Indians, all others forbidden under penalty
of 20s. Wm. and Mary Phillips adm. to First Church, Charlestown,
Sept. 23, 1639. Appears to have been in Saco, Me., 1663 and 1665.
He m. (1st) MARY ———, who d. May 1, 1646 ; (2d) SUSANNA
STANLEY ; her will, dated Sept. 10, 1650, mentions sons Wm. and

* Andrew Phillips of Killingly, m. Elizabeth[4] Lamb, (Abial[3] and Hannah " Taylor," Abial,[2] Thomas[1] of Roxbury. 1630), who was b. in Oxford, Mass., July 21, 1716.

Nathaniel, daus. Elizabeth and Phebe;   (3d) BRIDGET SANFORD, who
was living, a widow, 1689.   Ch. :

1. William; mariner; of Boston.
2. Elizabeth.
3. Phebe, b. Apr. 7, 1640.
4. Nathaniel, b. Feb. 5, 1642; no heirs.
5. Mary, b. Feb. 17, 1644.
6. John, b. Sept. 18, 1656.
7. Samuel, b. Mar. 16, 1658, had wife Sarah and son William, Apr.
   1, 1688.
8. William, b. Jan. 28, 1660.

160.   WILLIAM PHILLIPS (son of Wm., Jr. and grandson of Wm.,
159) ; of Boston ; he and wife, Ann, in 1738, deed land on the west
side of Kennebec River, which was sold by Ferdinando Gorges to
his grandfather, Maj. Wm. Phillips, and wife Bridget of Saco, and
by them to his father, Wm. Phillips.

161.   JOHN PHILLIPS, Capt. ; merchant, of Boston ; will proved
Jan., 1759.   He m. ANN, b. 1715, dau. of Dea. Wm. Engs. [? Eng-
lish] whose grandfather came to Boston, 1635.   Ch. :

1. John; Capt. in the British Army; m. Miss Levi, a Jewess, of
   N. Y., and lived in Canada; had four ch.
2. Samuel.
3. Nancy; m. ——— Payson.
4. Penelope; m. ——— Rowe.
5. Polly; m. ——— Finley.
6. Jenny; m. ——— Scott.
7. Thomas; Capt.; living, 1784, and had three ch. living.
8. Sally.

FRAGMENTARY RECORDS.

The following records are nearly all of dates prior to the present century, and but few of them show any connection with the foregoing genealogies. Where only the christian name is given, the surname, Phillips, is of course to be understood.

ALEXANDER PHILLIPS, soldier in King Philip's war, 1675 ; m. MARY FIELD.—*Charlestown Gen.*

ALEXANDER, admitted to Charlestown Church, 1699, Mar. 17.

ANDREW, SARAH, wife of, admitted to First Church, Charlestown, 1686.

ASA, of Milford, Mass., m. RHODA, dau. of Abner Hazeltine of Wardsborough, Vt. He was b. Nov. 5, 1731.

ANDREW and ELIZABETH, Reuben, son of ; d. Oct. 1, 1740.—*Oxford town records.*

AMOS, of Hollis, N. H., Nov., 1740.

ANN, m. JOHN FAULKNER, Oct. 20, 1758.—*N. Y. Marriages.*

ASA, son of Jonathan and Sarah, b. Apr. 3, 1761.—*Oxford town records.*

ANDREW of Kittery, Me., Agnes, dau. of ; m. Thomas Edgerly, 1767 or 1768. Jenny, dau. of same ; m. James Edgerly, and d. 1772.

ANN, m. ARTHUR LOUGHARNE, July 22, 1773.—*N. Y. Marriages.*

ABRAHAM, m. CATHARINE COONY, Nov. 17, 1779.—*Id.*

ASA, of Auburn, Mass., and Polly White of Worcester, published Apr. 5, 1782.

BENJAMIN, in King Philip's war, 1675 ; also William, Nathaniel, Zachary and Henry.

BENJAMIN, of Marshfield, admitted freeman, June, 1689.

BENJAMIN, son of Benjamin, bap. May 22, 1747 ; also Nathan, son of Benjamin, Feb. 4, 1749 ; also Joseph, son of Jeremiah, Apr. 27, 1750.—*Milton church records.*

BENJAMIN, in Capt. Hatch's company (10th) Louisburg soldiers.

BENJAMIN, of American troops, among the prisoners at Quebec, Dec. 31, 1775.

CHARLES, ch. of ; David, b. Mar. 17, 1656 ; d. Aug. 16, 1656. Abigail, b. Oct. 29, 1655 [?]. John, b. Aug. 15, 1658 ; d. Nov., 1661. George, b. Dec. 20, 1663. John, b. June 27, 1667.— Genealogical Items Relative to Lynn, Mass.

CALEB, m. in Boston, Dec. 31, 1730, to ELIZABETH WENTWORTH.

CHRISTOPHER, justice of the peace, North Kingstown, R. I., May 15, 1736.

DAVID, son of Philip and Rachel, b. Mar. 1, 1659–60.—*Hist. and Gen. Reg.*, vol. 14.

DANIEL, in Capt. Gallop's company for the expedition to Canada, 1690.

DAVID, m. LYDIA HATCH, Nov. 6, 1758.—*Pembroke Marriages.*

DAVID, will dated 1786.—*N. Y. Surrogate Records.*

ELMER, living in Virginia, at West and Sherlow Hundred, about 1623. —*List of Emigrants to America.*

ELEAZER, ticket granted to, in the *Providence*, for Boston, June 28, 1679.—*Id.*

EPHRAIM, and Mary his pretended wife, of Taunton, 1680.—*Plym. Col. Records*, vol. 6.

EPHRAIM, petitions that he might live in Norwich one year, 1692.

ELEAZER, of Charlestown, admitted freeman, Mar. 22, 1689–90.

ELEAZER, admitted to Charlestown Church, Nov. 25, 1705.

EDWARD PHILLIPS and MARY JONES, m. July 12, 1714.—*Portsmouth, N. H., Marriages.*

EPHRAIM, m. ANN FENWICK, June 30, 1719, in Boston.

ELIZA, member of First Church, Marblehead, 1746.

ELIZA, member of First Church, Marblehead, 1762.

EBENEZER, m. ABIGAIL PRATT, and had Ebenezer, b. Aug. 12, 1766. —*Barry's Hist. of Framingham.*

EBENEZER, m. HANNAH BROWN, Apr. 8. 1773.—*Holliston town records.*

EBENEZER, m. LYDIA DUNTON, Oct. 28, 1773.—*Southboro town records.*

EBENEZER, in Revolutionary war, from Waltham.

ERASMUS JOHN, Capt. in his Majesty's 35th Reg. Will proved July 15, 1777.—*N. Y. Co. Surrogate Records.*

ELSE, m. MOSES SMITH, Dec. 9, 1782.—*N. Y. Marriages.*

EDWARD, of Lancaster, est. of, administered Apr. 13, 1784 ; £273, 15s.—*Worcester Co. Probate Records.*

GEORGE, inhabitant of Norwich, Conn., 1726.

GEORGE, will dated 1741.—*N. Y. Co. Surrogate Records.*

GEORGE, Capt., and HOPE his wife, had dau. Margaret (Hamlin), who d. Sept. 6, 1748, in her 36th year.—Old burying-ground, Middletown, Conn.

GEORGE, had son Peter who was in Rev. war. Had two other sons, George, and Louis. Peter had eleven ch. The youngest, David, b. Nov. 16, 1836 ; m. Amelia Miron, and had five ch., all b. in Plattsburg, N. Y. ; in 1878 he was of Springfield, Mass.

GEORGE, of Harwich, Mass. ; m. (1st) Jan. 3, 1797, JEMIMA WEEKES ; m. (2d) April 25, 1802, her cousin, DOROTHY WEEKES.

GEORGE, of Harwich, Mass. ; m. about 1816, DORCAS. dau. of David and Mehitable (Weeks) Clark.

HENRY, living at " Warwick Squeake," Va., about 1623. — *List of Emigrants to America.*

HENRY, Ensign, of Hadley, chosen assistant at Boston, May 15, 1672 ; of Hadley, Nov. 7, 1683.

HEPZIBAH, mem. of First Church, Marblehead, 1718.

HEZEKIAH, land granted to, in Scarboro, Me., 1720 ; was of Scarboro, 1722.

HENRY, Esq., moderator of town meeting in Framingham, Mass., June 12, 1728.—Barry's Hist.

HANNAH PHILLIPS, wife of Dr. AMOS PUTNAM ; d. Oct. 2, 1758, aged about 33.—Danvers Inscriptions.

HANNAH m. July, 1820, LEVI STEARNS of Goshen, Mass. ; she d. in Oak Creek, Wis.

HENRY PHILLIPS, of England ; m. Nov. 5, 1782, MARY DRIFFIELD, dau. of Rev. ———— Driffield, Rector of Chelsworth, Co. Suffolk, 1754. Henry was of a family of six brothers, all said to have been in the Royal Army, and one of these, an ensign, fell at Bunker Hill in the service of the king.

Philip John, son of Henry, bap. Nov. 5, 1785 ; educated at Christ's Hospital, " a Blue Coat Boy ; " d. in Windsor, Eng., July 27, 1825 ; m. Jan. 16, 1816, Elizabeth Hammond, b. in London, Jan. 4, 1793 ; she d. at Hatley, Stanstead Co., Canada, Feb. 8. 1862, dau. of George Hammond, of the Royal Navy. Three ch. :

Charles, second ch. of Philip John, b. Apr. 17, 182) ; of Boston, Mass. ; m. Elizabeth Hall. Ch. :

1. Charles Henry, b. in Roxbury, Mass., Mar. 18, 1853 ; m. Emma Rawley, of Me.
2. Walter Hall, b. in Barnston, Canada, Dec. 1, 1863.
3. Annie Grace, b. in same place, Aug. 24, 1865.

HUGH, m. ELIZABETH LINDSAY, Oct. 4, 1763.—*N. Y. Marriages.*

HEZEKIAH, wounded at Quebec, Dec. 31, 1775.

ISAAC, of Groton, Dec. 31, 1746.

ISRAEL, July 2, 1781, aged 16, son of Israel Phillips, late of Uxbridge, deceased; P. Darling of Mendon, appointed guardian. — *Worcester Co. Pro. Rec.*

JOHN, Mass., 1630, styled servant; went to Plymouth, 1631.

JAMES, to Virginia in the *Transport*, 1635.

JOHN, to Virginia in the *Merchant's Hope*, 1635.

JOHN PHILLIPS and JAMES LINDELL " are graunted eich of them a garden place vpon Stony Brooke in Duxborrow by Phillip Delanoyes, and to be layd forth for them by Mr. Collyer, Jonathan Brewster & Willm Bassett." — Plymouth Colony Records, vol. 1, p. 145.

JOHN PHILLIPS and six others " of Duxborrow are graunted four acres a peace of vpland abutting vpon the Stony Brooke in Duxborrow, by the milne, and to rang south and north in lengh and east & west in breadth," 1640.—*Id.*, vol. 1, p. 153.

JOHN PHILLIPS granted twenty acres of land in " Duxborrow," 1640. —*Id.*, p. 165.

JOHN, in list of those able to bear arms in " Duxborrow," 1643.— *Id.*, vol. 8, p. 189.

JOHN, 1653, had a case in Plymouth Court.—*Id.*, vol. 3, p. 39.

JOHN, propounded " to take up his freedom," 1659.—*Id.*, vol. 3, p. 163.

JOHN : Sixteen acres of land " which had been given out to John Phillips joined land of Roger Chaundler of Duxborrow," Feb., 1644.—*Id.*, vol. 12, p. 109.

JOHN : July 6, 1638, " William Renolds of Duxborrow," acknowledged the sale of half of his black heifer to John Phillips.— *Id.*, vol. 12, p. 31.

JOHN, June 19, 1648, signed an agreement by making his mark.—*Id.*, vol. 12, p. 163.

JOHN, and MARY ; Mary, dau. of, b. July 13, 1652.—Early rec. of Boston.

JOHN, m. RUTH, dau. of Robert Burdick, who was of Newport, R. I., May 22, 1655.

JOHN, admitted freeman, July 13, 1658 ; of inhabitants about Casco Bay.

JOHN, of Saco, Aug. 3, 1664.—Mass. Records.

JAMES, of Taunton, took the freeman's oath, 1657.

JAMES, nephew and legatee of Wm. Parker of Taunton, whose will was dated March 15, 1659.

JAMES, of Taunton, ch. of; James, b. Jan. 1, 1661; Nathaniel, b. March 25, 1664; Sara, b. March 17, 1667; William, b. Aug. 21, 1669; Seth, b. Aug. 14, 1671; Daniel, b. May 9, 1673; Ebenezer, b. Jan. 16, 1674.—*Hist. and Gen. Reg.*, vol. 16, p. 325.

JAMES, on jury warned by constable of Taunton, Sept. 20, 1672.

JOHN and BENJAMIN, Oct. 27, 1685, own land in Marshfield, which had been given by the town to John Phillips.

JAMES, m. ABIGAIL HATHAWAY, in Taunton, Dec. 9, 1685.

JACOB, d. Sept. 19, 1688.—*Danvers church records.*

JACOB, d. of sm.-pox at Salem Village, Sept. 19, 1691.

JOHN and ELIZABETH, of Weymouth, ch. of; John, b. Feb. 18, 1692; Richard, b. Nov. 25, 1693.—*Hist. and Gen. Reg.*, vol. 3, pp. 60, 171.

JOHN and ELIZABETH of Easton. Mass., ch. of; Experience, Samuel, Jothan, Caleb, Joan, Thomas, Richard.

    Elizabeth, wife of Capt. John Phillips, d. June 24, 1748. Bridget, wife of Capt. John Phillips, "deceased and departed this life for a beter March 17, 1764." "Capten John Phillips" d. Nov. 14, 1760, "he being the first Capten that ever bore a Commish in the town of Easton."—*Easton town records.**

JOSEPH, MICHAEL, JOHN, BRIDGET, and SUSANNAH PHILLIPS; ch. of Joseph, all bap. in Bristol, R. I., church, 1723.

JOANNA, widow, of Boston, 1742.

JOHN, Capt., of N. Bridgewater; m. Apr. 19, 1749.

JOHN, of Bellingham, Mass.,; m. May 25, 1768, SARAH, dau. of Ezra Pond, b. Nov. 13, 1750.—Pond Genealogy.

JOHN, m. LYDIA MORTON, Oct. 18, 1752. Plymouth Records.

JOHN [probably third son of Ebenezer, Sr., of Southboro], whose wife was HANNAH, had Joanna, b. Aug. 24, 1755, Martha, b. Aug. 20, 1757, Elizabeth, b. June 15, 1764.—Ward's Hist. of Shrewsbury, p. 410.

JOHN, Capt., buried Nov. 7, 1756; Eleazer, buried Feb. 18, 1763; Col. Phillips d. Apr. 17 (buried 23), 1763.—Diary of Robert Calley, Charlestown.

---

* The record from Easton was received after the genealogy of Capt. John Phillips, No. 79, had been printed, and does not confirm the supposition then expressed, that he was son of Benjamin and Sarah (Thomas) Phillips of Marshfield. It now appears probable that he was from Weymouth.

JONATHAN, of Oxford; m. SARAH PARKER of Worcester, pub. in Oxford, Feb. 9, 1760. Ch.: Asa, b. Apr. 3, 1761; Reuben, b. July 5, 1763; Sarah, b. Mar. 27, 1765; Jonathan, b. Mar. 26, 1768; d. Dec. 1, 1768; also dau. Sarah d. same day.—*Oxford, Mass., town records.*

JOHN, m. AMY BLINDBOROUGH, Dec. 15, 1762.—*N. Y. Marriages.*

JOHN, of Lancaster, inventory dated March 24, 1763; £318, 6s. 2d. Rebecca Phillips, admin'x.

JOSHUA lived in Hubbardston at the organization of the town, 1767. —Hist. of Worcester Co., vol. 1, p. 586.

JEDEDIAH, of American troops, among the prisoners at Quebec, Dec. 31, 1775.

JOHN, m. ELIZABETH MORRELL, Mar. 17, 1778; JACOB, m. CATHARINE OOSTRANDER, Nov. 27, 1772.—*N. Y. Marriages.*

JOHN, of Lancaster, d., inventory taken Aug. 29, 1785; £417, 7s. 5d. — *Wor. Co. Probate records.*

JONATHAN, of Templeton, d., inventory taken Aug. 14, 1826.

LAVINIA, of Gloucester [R. I.] and Elias Kingsbury of Oxford, published June 18, 1791.

MARTINE, of Medfield, 1664.

MARY, of Taunton, fined 3s. 4d., June 4th, 1668; also June, 1670, fined 3s. 4d.—*Plym. Col. Rec.*, vol. 8, pp. 126, 130.

MARY, petition of, to sell wood lots, answered May 11, 1681.—*Mass. Rec.*, vol. 5, p. 316.

Mr. PHILLIPS, of Sherborn, Jan. 11, 1717–18.

MARY, of Little Compton, R. I., m. Oct. 7, 1734, EPHRAIM DAVENPORT, b. Dec. 25, 1708.

MARY, native of Ipswich, m. Feb. 21, 1739–40, CHARLES RUNDLET of Stratham.

MARGARET PHILIPS, m. WM. SOULE, Apr. 26, 1758. — *N. Y. Marriages.*

MOSES, m. SARAH WISNER, Jan. 22, 1768.—*Id.*

MARGARET PHILIPS, m. JOHN OGILVIE, Apr. 15, 1769.—*Id.*

MAXWELL ADDISON PHILLIPS, Lieut. in 3d Cherokee Indian Reg. Vols., U. S. A., 1862; Capt., 1863–5; of Salina, Kan., 1866; non-grad. Mich. Univ., 1870; grad. Lane Theol. Sem., 1872, May 16, and ord. (Pres.) same day; went a missionary to Mexico; preached in City of Mexico till Oct., 1873; preached in Zacatecas four years, and was joint editor of " *La Antorcha Evangelica;* " removed, 1877 to Mérida, Yucatan; returned to Mexico City, 1879, to preach and aid in organizing a Theol.

Sem. ; teaching Greek in this Sem., 1880, and preparing a " *Spanish-Greek Text Book* " for the use of students in Bible study.—*Mich. Univ. Catalogue.*

NICHOLAS, commissioner for Weymouth, May 10, 1643.

NATHANIEL, in York Co., Me., 1665.

NEAL PHILLIPS of Weymouth, in Dorsetshire, G. B. ; m. Oct. 21, 1725, ELIZABETH SHAW, widow, of Portsmouth. *Marriages in Portsmouth, N. H.*

NEHEMIAH, son of Samuel and Abigail (Frost) Phillips, b. in Groton, Feb. 28, 1744, m. PATIENCE ———, and removed to Shirley, Apr. 3, 1774, with four ch., Moses, Patience, Mary and Abigail.—Chandler's Hist. of Shirley, Mass., p. 603.

NICHOLAS, of Weymouth ; m. in Hull, June 12, 1781, widow MARY GREENLEAF, b. 1748. She was dau. of Jos. Gould and wife Hannah, dau. of Dea. John and Hannah (Paine) Binney of Hull.

2d Lieut. Nichs. Phillips of 2d Artillery, of Castle Island, stationed at Hull, 1779.

Nicholas, by wife Mary, had in Hull, Nicholas, b. Mar. 15, 1782, Zeruiah, July 3, 1783.

Nicholas was of Hull, 1786.

Widow Phillips, of Hull, 1791. — *Collection of C. J. F. Binney.*

NATHANIEL, WILLIAM, and NATHANIEL, Jr., in Capt. Haskins's company of militia, 1773.

" PHILLIP PHILLIPP," aged 15, serv. to John Cooper, in the *Hopewell*, of London ; vrs. New England ; Apr. 1, 1635.

PHILLIP and RACHEL, dau. of ; d. Aug. 15, 1656 ; son David, b. Mar. 1, 1659.

PETER, May 8, 1748, aged about 14, son of John " Philips," late of Roxbury, Suffolk Co., appointed Benj. Newell of Dudley, guardian.—*Prob. rec.*

PETER, of Dudley, and Susanna Gleason, of Charlton, published May 10, 1760.

PETER and SUSANNA, Sabra, dau. of, b. Apr. 6, 1763. — *Sturbridge town rec.*

POLLY, of Auburn, m. ZIBA FISKE of Sutton, Nov. 30, 1806.

RICHARD, aged 20 ; among the passengers to Virginia, May 28, 1635.

RICHARD, aged 14 ; among the passengers to Virginia, Aug. 21, 1635.

RICHARD, of Weymouth, took freeman's oath, May 8, 1678.

REUBEN, m. Oct. 4, 1781, SARAH RICE ; both of Auburn, Mass.

14

SAMUEL, of Taunton ; m. wid. MARY COBB, May 15, 1676.
 Mehitable, dau. of Samuel, Jan 9, 1676-7.
 Samuel, son of Samuel, Aug. 29, 1678.
SAMUEL, of Taunton, propounded for freeman, 1686.
SARAH, b. July 27, 1762 ; m. HOSEA MERRILL.   He was living in
 Pittsfield, Mass., Nov. 18, 1850, but she d. previously.
SARAH, m. Feb. 8, 1783, MUNGO NOBLE.—*N. Y. Marriages.*
SARAH, m. Dec. 30, 1773, DAVID ROE.—*Id.*
THOMAS, aged 26, in the *William and Thomas,* 1618.—*List of
 emigrants* [*to Virginia.*]
THOMAS, "living at the plantation over against James City," Feb.
 16, 1623.—*Id.*
THOMAS, living at Chaplain's Choice, Va., Feb. 16, 1623.—*Id.*
THOMAS, in the *Assurance,* 1635.—*Id.*
THOMAS, ——— "Court gave way to the Governor to free his servant
 Thom : Philips," about 1640.—*Mass. Rec.*
THOMAS, of Yarmouth, had wife Annis or Agnesse, 1653.—*Plym.
 Col. Rec.*
THOMAS, another Thos. and William, took the freeman's oath at a
 Court at Pemaquid, July 22, 1674.—*Hist. and Gen. Register,*
 vol. 3, p. 243.
THOMAS and WILLIAM, took the freeman's oath, Oct. 7, 1674.—*Mass.
 Rec.,* vol. 5, p. 18.
THOMAS PHELLPS *alias* Phillips, d. ; inventory Oct. 27, 1674.
THOMAS, m. 1722, ABIGAIL RIDER.—*Plym. Col. Rec.*
THOMSON, of Jamaica, m. 1725, [?] "Mrs." HANNAH COTTON.
 Ch. : Hannah, b. July 20, 1728.—*Id.*
THOMAS, m. SARAH BLOODGOOD, Sept. 21, 1763.—*N. Y. Marriages.*
TIMOTHY, m. Oct., 1787, DEBORAH BUSWELL, both of Bradford.
WILLIAM, of Taunton, in list of those able to bear arms, 1643.
WILLIAM, son of William, Jr. and Martha, b. Jan. 13, 1651-2.
 Martha, dau. of Wm., mariner, and Martha, b. Mar. 10, 1653.
 —Early records of Boston.—*H. and G. Reg.,* vol. 9.
WILLIAM, mentioned in Jno. Robinson's will, June 2, 1653.   Early
 Suffolk wills.
WILLIAM, of Saco, 1665.—*Mass. Rec.*
WILLIAM, soldier from Dedham, Oct. 9, 1675.
WILLIAM, Major, mentioned in will of Brian Pendleton, Aug. 9, 1677.
WALTER, Sr., of Salem Village, admitted freeman, Apr. 18, 1690.
WILLIAM, son of Wm. and Botley Phillips, of Weymouth, b. Mar. 8,
 1696.

W<small>ALTER</small>, and Walter, Jr., signed Quaker's list, "Lynn, 22th 4mo., 1703."—*H. and G. Reg.*, vol. 2.

W<small>ILLIAM</small>, aged 35, d. June 12, 1705 ; Hannah, wife of Wm., d. June 6, 1705. Old Colony Inscriptions, Lakeville, Nov. 14, 1853. —*Id.*, vol. 8, p. 286.

W<small>ILLIAM</small>, will dated 1759.—*N. Y. Co. Surrogate Records.*

W<small>ILLIAM</small> " P<small>HILIPS</small>," will dated only 1759, proved July 14, 1759 ; mentions wife, sons David, William, Thomas, daus. Elizabeth Williams, and ———— Lawrence.—*Id.*

W<small>ILLIAM</small>, will dated 1769.—*Id.*

W<small>ILLIAM</small>, will dated 1778.—*Id.*

W<small>ILLIAM</small>, will dated 1781.—*Id.*

W<small>ILLIAM</small> W<small>IRT</small> P<small>HILLIPS</small>, b. in Montgomery Co., N. Y., Sept. 23, 1796 ; grad. Union Coll., 1815 ; prominent Presbyterian preacher in New York city from 1818 till his death, March 20, 1865.

Z<small>ACHARY</small>, petition of, answered by Court, Oct. 16, 1650.—*Mass. Records.*

Z<small>ACHARY</small>, witnessed will of Philip Long, of Boston, Oct. 27, 1658.

Z<small>ECHARIAH</small>, son of Zechariah and Elizabeth, b. Mar. 5, 1656–7. *Boston Records.*

Z<small>ECHARIAH</small> and wife E<small>LIZABETH</small>, had Elizabeth, b. June 29, 1661.

See also fragmentary records on page 125.

GRADUATES OF THIS NAME FROM SOME OF THE PRINCIPAL AMERICAN COLLEGES.

HARVARD COLLEGE.

Samuel,	1650 ; d. 1696.	Stephen Clarendon,	1819 ; d. 1857.
George,	1686 ; d. 1739.	John Charles,	1826 ; d. 1878.
Samuel,	1708 ; d. 1771.	William,	1828 ; d. 1829.
Samuel,	1712 ; d. 1717.	George William,	1829 ; d. 1880.
Henry,	1724 ; d. 1729.	Wendell,	1831 ; d. 1884.
Samuel,	1734 ; d. 1790.	Grenville Tudor,	1836 ; d. 1863.
John,	1735 ; d. 1795.	William,	1839 ; d. 1873.
John,	1736 ; d. 1787.	Stephen Henry,	1842.
John,	1745 ; d. ?	Edward Bromfield,	1845 ; d. 1848.
Samuel,	1771 ; d. 1802.	George William,	1847.
John,	1788 ; d. 1823.	Willard Quincy,	1855.
John,	1795 ; d. 1820.	John Charles,	1858 ; d. 1885.
Willard,	1810 ; d. 1873.	Charles Appleton,	1860 ; d. 1877.
Thomas Walley,	1814 ; d. 1859.	Edward Emerson,	1878.
Samuel,	1819 ; d. 1877.	William Magruder,	1878.
	John Sanburn,	1885.	

YALE.

George, 1769.   Horace, 1868.   Smith Franklin, 1880.

WILLIAMS.

John Evertson,	1825.	Benjamin Franklin,	1852.
Lebbeus Rude,	1836.	Edgar,	1859.
John Lemuel Thomas,	1847.	Duane Seneca,	1850.

AMHERST.

Daniel,   1856.   George Whitefield,   1861.

DARTMOUTH.

Burroughs, 1849.   Harvey Thomas, 1849.   Sidney Atwood, 1869.

BOWDOIN.

William Edwards,	1842.		James Liddell,	1860.
John Wyman,	1858.		George Washington,	1878.

PRINCETON, N. J.

John,	1774.	William Wilson Latta,	1848.
John,	1808.	John F.,	1849.
Lewis William Randolph,	1808.	Alfred,	1850.
Jonathan Dickinson,	1831.	Alexander Hamilton,	1851.
William R.,	1841.	Samuel Lewis,	1858.
Benjamin Thomas,	1842.	James Richard,	1867.

BROWN.

William,	1826.	Daniel William,	1837.
Joseph F.,	1827.	William Brown,	1858.

COLBY.

Andrew Croswell,	1849.

COLUMBIA.

John W.,	1808.

UNION.

William Wirt,	1815.	Alexander H.,	1825.

HAMILTON.

Albert,	1865.	Albert Cossit,	1871.

MICHIGAN.

Horace,	1871.

INDEX I.

CHRISTIAN NAMES OF PHILLIPSES.

The first number in the parenthesis is that of the "family," and then follows the number in each succeeding generation under which the name may be found.

The names given under the head of Fragmentary Records, page 195, being arranged alphabetically will not be found in this index.

The term "Ear. Fam." refers to the Early Families beginning on page 188.

Betty, (71:9), 127
Betty, (90:2), 145
Blaney, Pembroke, Mass., (71), 126
Blaney, Fitchburg, Mass.. (71:2), 127
Blaney, Pembroke, Mass., (72:7), 127
Burroughs, 204
Byron A., Plainfield, Conn.,
(111:4:15), 170
Caleb, Bridgewater, Mass., 125
Caleb, 135
Caleb (Ear. Fam.), 188
Calista, (58:3), 110
Calista, Ashfield, Mass., (83:4), 138
Calvin T., S. Hanover, Mass.,
(73:1:1), 128
Caroline, Andover, Mass., (8:10), 25
Caroline, Sturbridge, Mass., (25:1), 59
Caroline, Buckland, Mass., (83:1), 137
Caroline, Mass., (135:1), 187
Caroline Crowninshield, (13:6:7), 32
Caroline E., Greenfield, Mass.,
(33:10), 76
Caroline H., Northmoreland, Pa.,
(32:6), 70
Caroline Lord, (113:1:4), 171
Caroline S., Salem, Mass., (8:2:1:1), 24
Carrie, Laurens, N. Y., (37:1:1), 79
Carrie, College Springs, Iowa,
(64a:1:1), 114
Carrie, (113:1:5:2), 172
Carrie B., Greenfield, Mass., (36:9:3), 78
Carrie L., West Newton, Mass.,
(134:1:1:2), 187
Carrie M., Kittery, Me., (104:3:6:7), 164
Carrie W., Reading, Mass.,
(124:1:2:2), 182
Catharine, Grafton, Mass., (65:1), 115
Catharine (Ear. Fam.), 192, 193
Catharine Adelia, (121:3:1), 180
Catharine A., Ashfield, Mass., (83:6), 138
Catherine, Salem, Mass., (18:1:11), 42
Catherine, Medway, Mass., (48:8), 100
Catherine, Rutland, N. Y.. (57:5), 109
Catherine, Champion, N. Y., (58:7), 110
Catherine, Hanson, Mass., (73:1:2) 128
Catherine, Newport, R. I., (119:8), 177
Catherine A., Nat. Bridge, N. Y.,
(58:27), 110
Catherine A., Newtonville, Mass.,
(84:2), 139
Catherine A., Nat. Bridge, N. Y.,
(62:2), 112
Catherine Fiske, Worcester, Mass.,
(44:1), 92
Celia, (78:2:6), 133
Celia F., Spencer, Mass., (26:6:1), 61
Chandler, (70:2:4:5), 126
Chapin, Chicago, Ill., (32:2:3), 70
Charity, Berkley, Mass., (126:4), 183
Charles, Chicago, Ill., (29:3:5), 67
Charles, Searsmont, Me., (74:3:1), 128
Charles, Cassadaga, N. Y., (86:7), 140
Charles, Bradford, Mass., (98:2:10) 157
Charles, Foster, R. I., (110:3), 169
Charles, Plainfield, Conn., (111:4), 169
Charles, Dakota City, Neb., (111:4:4), 170
Charles, Lisbon, Conn., (119:12:9), 178
Charles, Mass., (126:2:1:1), 183
Charles, Boston, Mass., 197
15

Charles, West Newton, Mass.,
(134:1:1), 187
Charles A., Winhall, Vt., (54:8:5), 105
Charles A., Salem, Mass.,
(18:1:9), 42, 204
Charles C., Greenfield, Mass., (33:5), 74
Charles E., Lombard, Ill., (64a:3), 114
Charles F., Lisbon, Conn.,
(119:12:10), 178
Charles F., N. Scituate, R. I.,
(118:7:9), 176
Charles F., Hanson, Mass., (73:1:4), 128
Charles Follinsby, Greece, N. Y.,
(30:3:2:3), 68
Charles Fox, Blackwater, Wis.,
(89:4), 144
Charles Gorham, Auburndale, Mass.,
(134:1:1:1), 187
Charles H., Penn., (39:1), 82
Charles H.. Lake Mills, Wis., (28:4), 64
Charles H., Roxbury, Mass., 197
Charles Heywood, Kan., (65:2:6), 115
Charles L., Washington, Ohio,
(63:1:3), 112
Charles Noble, Greenfield, Mass.,
(36:9), 78
Charles N., (125:1:1:3), 182
Charles O., Brattleboro, Vt., (38:3), 81
Charles O., Hartford, Conn.,
(111:4:3:2), 170
Charles Raymond, New Haven, Conn.,
(33:8:6), 75
Charles W., Hartford, Conn., (43:5), 89
Charles W.. Kittery, Me.,
(104:3:6:1), 164
Charlotte, Spencer, Mass., (26:3), 61
Charlotte, N. Scituate, R. I., (118:12), 176
Charlotte F., Brookline, Mass.,
(44:5:2), 93
Charlotte H., Brookline, Mass., (44:4), 92
Charlotte L.. Chicago, Ill., (37:3:1), 79
Chester Herbert, Fitzwilliam, N. H.,
(53:10:4), 105
Chloe, E. Bridgewater, Mass., (78:1), 133
Chloe, (120:3), 179
Christian, Duxbury, Mass., (71:4), 127
Christian W., Pembroke, Mass.,
(72:6), 127
Christopher, Rainham, England, 9
Clara Jane, Nat. Bridge, N. Y.,
(58:2:6), 110
Clara May, W. Springfield, Mass.,
(33:11:2), 76
Clara W., Auburn, Mass., (45:1:1), 94
Clarendon, Rutland, N. Y., (58), 109
Clarissa, Dudley, Mass.. (41:2), 83
Clarissa, Chesterfield, N. H., (51:3), 102
Clarissa, Washington, D. C..
(57:2), 109, 112
Clarissa C., Pittsfield, Mass., (33:7), 75
Clarissa M., Charlton, Mass., (42:3), 87
Clark J., (61:3), 111
Clement C., Portland, Oregon, (36:4), 77
Clesson B., Philadelphia, Pa., (40:2), 82
Cora Frances, (28:1:1), 64
Corah C. C., Washington, Ohio,
(63:1:3:1), 112
Corodon O., Vt., (125:1:3), 182
Curtis, Charlton, Mass., (42), 86

16

John,	(102:4:1), 160
John, Kittery, Me.,	(104:3), 164
John,	(104:3:2), 164
John, Kittery, Me.,	(104:4:8), 164
John, Marcellus, N. Y.,	(107:9), 168
John, Scituate, R. I.,	(109), 168
John, Scituate, R. I.,	(109:5), 168
John, Plainfield, Conn.,	(111:4:14), 170
John, Somers, Conn.,	(112), 171
John, Somers, Conn.,	(112:8), 171
John, Lisbon, Conn.,	(119:12), 177
John, Millington, Ill.,	(123:2:2:5), 181
John, Pa.,	(123:2:4), 181
John,	(130:4), 184
John, Brooklyn, N. Y.,	(130:7:3), 184
John, Ponteberem, Wales,	185
John, England,	185
John, Avon, N. Y.,	(133:3), 186
John, Boston, Mass.,	(134:1:2), 187
John, Dorchester. Mass.,	(136), 188
John [? Charlestown], Mass.,	(144), 190
John [? Charlestown], Mass.,	(145), 190
John, Charlestown, Mass.,	(153), 192
John [? Charlestown], Mass.,	(154), 192
John, Boston, Mass.,	(161) 194
John (Ear. Fam.),	188, 189, 190, 192, 193, 194
John Adams, Boston, Mass.,	(134:3), 187
John Charles, Boston, Mass.,	(13:6), 32
John C., Boston, Mass.,	(13:6:2), 32
John Evertson,	37
John E., Grafton, Mass.,	(65:2:3), 115
John E.,	(88:4:3), 143
John Edward, Portland, Me.,	(93:7), 149
John F., Lake Mills. Wis.,	(28:1), 63
John F., Hartwick, N. Y.,	(87:1:3), 79
John Franklin, Chicago, Ill.,	(37:3), 79
John F., Brookline, Mass.,	(44:3), 92
John F., Lisbon, Conn.,	(119:12:1), 177
John G., Westminster. Vt.,	(53:6:5), 104
John Gale, Quidnick, R. I.,	(65:2), 115
John Goddard, Boston, Mass.,	(84:4), 139
John Grier, Ayer, Mass.,	(132:3), 185
John Hancock, Springfield, Mass.,	(33:6), 74
John Hamlet, Lisbon, Conn.,	(119:12:7:2), 178
John H., Rochester, N. Y.,	(133:3:1), 186
John J., Kittery, Me.,	(104:3:6:8), 164
John King, Boston, Mass.,	(84:4:2), 139
John Lane. Champion, N. Y.,	(59:1), 110
John L. T., Williamstown, Mass.,	(77:2:2), 132
John M., Council Bluffs, Iowa,	(94:9), 150
John M., Council Bluffs, Iowa,	(94:9:4), 150
John Milton,	(121:7), 180
John Sanburn,	204
John Towne, Laurens, N. Y.,	(34), 76
John W.,	205
John W., Buckland, Mass.,	(87:1:2), 142
John Wyman,	205
Jonas, Morristown, N. J.,	(14:1:4), 37
Jonas Allen, Athol, Mass.,	(54:9), 106
Jonathan, Southboro, Mass.,	(46:3:2), 96
Jonathan, W. Va.,	(82:13), 137
Jonathan, Lynn, Mass.,	(101), 160
Jonathan,	(101:4), 160

Jonathan,	(102:3), 160
Jonathan, Somers, Conn.,	(112:6), 171
Jonathan, Boston, Mass.,	(10:3), 28
Jonathan, Watertown, Mass.,	(15), 39
Jonathan, Marblehead, Mass.,	(16), 40
Jonathan, Watertown, Mass.,	(19:7), 43
Jonathan, Sturbridge, Mass.,	(21), 47
Jonathan, Sturbridge, Mass.,	(21:8), 48
Jonathan (Ear. Fam.),	189
Jonathan D.,	(102:4:2), 160
Jonathan Mason, Boston, Mass.,	(10:3:2), 28
Jonathan P., Lake Mills, Wis.,	(28), 62
Joseph, Boston, Mass.,	(11:7), 30
Joseph, Brookhaven, N. Y.,	38
Joseph, Oxford, Mass.,	(20), 44
Joseph, Oxford, Mass.,	(20:2), 45
Joseph, Oxford, Mass.,	(20:2:3), 46
Joseph, Marshfield, Mass.,	(68:5), 124
Joseph, Marshfield, Mass.,	(69:2), 124
Joseph, [? Duxbury], Mass.,	125
Joseph, New York..	(76:4), 132
Joseph, Windsor, Mass.,	(77:2), 132
Joseph,	(121:2), 179
Joseph, [? Charlestown], Mass.,	(142), 190
Joseph (Ear. Fam.),	189, 190, 192
Joseph F.,	205
Joseph H., Lisbon, Conn.,	(119:12:7), 178
Joseph Henry, Vt.,	(125:1:2:2), 182
Joseph N., Norwich, Conn.,	(119:12:7:6), 178
Joseph S., Kittery, Me.,	(104:3:6), 164
Joseph W., Windsor, Mass.,	(77:2:1), 132
Josephine, Loughboro, Ont.,	(107:3:1:7), 168
Joshua,	135
Joshua, Dighton, Mass.,	136
Joshua, Ashfield, Mass.,	(81:8), 137
Joshua,	(85:5), 139
Joshua, Cassadaga, N. Y.,	(86:9), 141
Joshua,	(90:7), 145
Joshua, Hubbardston, Mass.,	(114), 172
Joshua, Smithfield, R. I.,	(114:2), 172
Joshua, Hubbardston, Mass.,	(116:7), 174
Joshua (Ear. Fam.),	188, 191
Josiah, Brookhaven, N. Y.,	38
Josiah, Southboro, Mass.,	(47:8), 99
Josiah, Medway, Mass.,	(50), 101
Josiah, Rutland, N. Y.,	(60), 111
Josiah, Watertown, N. Y.,	(64), 113
Josiah, Kittery. Me.,	(104:4:4), 164
Josiah, Kittery, Me.,	(104:5), 165
Josiah, Kittery, Me.,	(104:5:1), 165
Josiah E., Medway, Mass.,	(50:2), 101
Josiah S., Lowell, Mass.,	(122:3:1), 180
Jotham, Lancaster, Mass.,	43
Judith, Rowley, Mass.,	(92:7), 148
Judith, Salem, Mass.,	(102:4:6), 161
Judith, Mass.,	(135:6), 187
Julia, Andover, Mass.,	(8:11), 25
Julia,	(88:4:1), 143
Julia,	(125:1:1:1), 182
Julia A., Allston, Mass.,	(53:6:1), 103
Julia A., Oak Park, Ill.,	(64a:7), 114
Julia Ann D., Savoy, Mass.,	(89:6), 144
Julia T., Council Bluffs, Iowa,	(95), 150
Kate M., Providence, R. I.,	(66:2), 116
Katharine, Gilmanton, N. H.,	(91:4), 147
Laura I., Kittery, Me.,	(104:4:9:3), 164

Mary, Weston, Mass., (19:2:5:2), 43
Mary, Watertown, Mass., (19:4), 43
Mary, Watertown. Mass., (19:8:4), 43
Mary, Sturbridge, Mass., (21:1), 48
Mary, Sturbridge, Mass., (24:7), 57
Mary, Spencer, Mass., (26:2), 61
Mary, Southboro, Mass., (46:4), 98
Mary, Athol, Mass., (47:10), 99
Mary, Medway, Mass., (48:2), 100
Mary, Windsor, Vt., (53:4:3), 103
Mary, Holliston, Mass.. (55:3), 107
Mary, Grafton, Mass., (56:6), 198
Mary, [? Bridgewater], Mass., 125
Mary, (70:2:1), 126
Mary, (70:2:4:4), 126
Mary, (71:2:5), 127
Mary, E. Bridgewater, Mass., (76:2), 132
Mary, Rowley, Mass., (92:2), 148
Mary, Bradford, Mass., (98:2:6), 157
Mary, N. Andover. Mass., (98:5), 157
Mary, (101:7), 160
Mary, (102:4:8), 161
Mary, Plainfield, Mich., (107:3:4), 168
Mary, Syracuse, N. Y., (107:7), 168
Mary, Smithfield, R. I., (112:1), 171
Mary, (113:4:4), 172
Mary, (119:3), 177
Mary, (119:10:7), 177
Mary, Brooklyn, N. Y., (130:7:5), 184
Mary, (130:8), 184
Mary, Utica, N. Y., (133:2), 186
Mary (Ear. Fam.).
188, 189, 190, 191, 192, 193, 194
Mary Ann, Andover, Mass., (8:8), 25
Mary Ann, Boston, Mass., (11:6), 30
Mary Ann, Sturbridge. Mass.,
(25:3), 60
Mary A., Waterloo, Wis., (28:6), 65
Mary A., Greenfield, Mass., (33:2), 73
Mary Ann, Athol, Mass., (38:5), 81
Mary Ann, Me., (104:3:1), 164
Mary Augusta, Fulton, N. Y., 168
Mary A., Gloucester, R. I., (117:4:2), 176
Mary Alice, Reading, Mass.,
(124:1:2:1), 182
Mary Ann, Berkley, Mass., (126:2:4), 183
Mary A., Pembroke, Mass., (135:3), 187
Mary A., Mass., (135:5:1), 187
Mary B., Salem, Mass., (18:1:2:3), 42
Mary B., Laurens, N. Y., (37:1:2), 79
Mary Charlotte, Ayer, Mass., (132:5), 185
Mary D., Portland, Me., (93:2), 148
Mary E., Amherst, Mass., (88:9:2), 138
Mary E., Kittery, Me., (104:4:9:5), 164
Mary Emma, Taunton, Mass.,
(126:2:3:4), 183
Mary E., (129:1:2), 184
Mary F., Medway, Mass., (49:5:2), 101
Mary Frances, Plainfield, Conn.,
(111:4:11), 170
Mary H., Westboro, Mass., (43:1), 89
Mary H., Newfane, Vt., (90:9:6), 145
Mary H., (113:1:2), 171
Mary J., Champion, N. Y.. (57:9), 109
Mary J., Nat. Bridge, N. Y., (62:4), 112
Mary Jane, Nugent, Iowa, (64:2), 113
Mary Louise, New Haven, Conn.,
(33:8:3:2), 75
Mary Lucy, Charlton, Mass., (42:2), 87

Mary Louise, Forest Grove, Oregon,
(64a:6:2), 114
Mary M., Laurens, N. Y., (34:2), 76
Mary M., (61:7), 111
Mary N., Lexington, Mass., (84:4:1), 139
Mary Olive, Council Bluffs, Iowa,
(94:9:3), 150
Mary R., Oak Park, Ill., (64a:2), 114
Mary S., Northmoreland, Pa., (32:1), 70
Mary S., (90:9:2:2), 145
Martha, Auburn, Mass., (30:2), 67
Martha, Chesterfield, N. H., (47:3:1), 99
Martha, Chesterfield, N. H., (51:7), 102
Martha, Fitzwilliam, N. H., (52:7), 102
Martha, Hubbardston, Mass.,
(116:7:1), 174
Martha, (130:10), 184
Martha A., Milford, Mass., (50:3), 101
Martha J., Winhall, Vt., (54:8:6), 105
Martha Jane, Lisbon, Conn.,
(119:12:7:4), 178
Martha L., Greece, N. Y., (30:3:2:2), 68
Martha S., Boston, Mass., (10:3:1), 28
Mattie S., Ashfield, Mass.,
(87:1:9:1), 143
Maud Adelaide, W. Thompson, Conn.,
(36:7:4), 78
Maxwell Addison, 197
May E., Kittery, Me., (104:4:6), 164
Mehitable, Pembroke, Mass., (72:5), 127
Mehitable (Ear. Fam.), 192
Mehitable Allen, Hanson, Mass.,
(73:2), 128
Melinda, Auburn, Mass., (30:6:2), 68
Mercy, Shrewsbury, Mass., (56:2:3), 108
Mercy, Grafton, Mass., (56:9), 108
Mercy, Duxbury, Mass., (71:6), 127
Mercy, E. Bridgewater, Mass.,
(78:9), 133
Mercy, Ashfield, Mass., (81), 136
Mercy, W. Va., (82:5), 137
Mercy, Rowley, Mass., (92:1), 148
Mercy, Smithfield, R. I., (112:2), 171
Mercy, Woonsocket, R. I., (113:3), 172
Merril Danforth, Wayne, Ill.,
(64a:9), 114
Michael, (14:1:3:2), 36
Michael, Smithfield, R. I., (105), 167
Michael, (107:1), 167
Millard Fillmore, Greenfield, Mass.,
(35:3), 77
Minnie, Big Spring, Wis., (27:3:3), 62
Minnie E., Wayne, Ill., (64a:10), 115
Miriam, Boston, Mass., (10:3:3), 28
Miriam, Boston, Mass., (10:4), 28
Miriam, Boston, Mass., (13:5), 31
Miriam, Kittery, Me., (103:5), 163
Miriam M., Boston, Mass., (10:5:4), 29
Miriam W., Methuen, Mass.,
(13:6:5), 32
Molly, E. Bridgewater, Mass., (78:3), 133
Molly, Newfoundland, (91:3), 147
Morrill Allen, Hanson, Mass.,
(73:1:3), 128
Moses, Phillipsburg, N. Y., (14:1:7), 37
Moses, Phillipsburg, N. Y.,
(14:1:7:4), 38
Moses, Brookhaven, N. Y., 38
Moses, Rupert, Vt., (122:6), 180

17

Rhoda, Elmira, N. Y., (107:10), 168
Rhoda, Foster, R. I., (110:5), 169
Richard, Smithtown, N. Y., (14:5:3), 38
Richard, 135
Richard, Ashfield, Mass., 136
Richard, Lynn, Mass., (100:2), 160
Richard, (108), 168
Richard, Dublin, N. H., (115), 173
Richard, Dublin, N. H., (115:1), 173
Richard, Dublin, N. H., (116:1), 174
Richard, Va., (129:5), 184
Richard, [? Boston], Mass., (141), 189
Richard, Weymouth, Mass., (147), 190
Richard (Ear. Fam.), 188, 189, 191
Richard Lysander, Colo., (37:2), 79
Robert, (76:1:5), 132
Robert, Burrillville, R. I., (117:1), 175
Robert Chapin, Northmoreland, Pa.,
(32:4), 70
Robert C., Northmoreland, Pa.,
(32:4:3), 70
Robert E., Fulton, N. Y.,
(107:3:1:2), 168
Robert Howard, Chicago, Ill.,
(37:3:2), 79
Robert William, Sutton, Mass.,
(63:5), 113
Rose Adalaide, (59:3), 110
Rosina, Cassadaga, N. Y., (86:4), 140
Rosina, Buffalo, N. Y., (86:11), 142
Rosina A., Ashfield, Mass.,
(87:1:7:1), 143
Rosina Maria, Buckland, Mass.,
(83:9:1), 138
Ruby, Bradford, Mass., (98:2:4), 157
Rufus, Auburn, Mass., (30:6), 68
Rufus, Chester, [? Mass.], (98:1:2), 157
Rufus, Roxbury, N. H., (116:4), 174
Rufus, Silver City, Idaho,
(123:2:2:8), 181
Rufus Brigham, Fitzwilliam, N. H.,
(53:4), 103
Rufus Severance, Greenfield, Mass.,
(35), 76
Ruth, Salem, Mass., (3:5), 14
Ruth, Watertown, Mass., (15:3), 39
Ruth, Marblehead, Mass., (16:4), 40
Ruth, Weston, Mass., (19:2:5:1), 43
Ruth, Oxford, Mass., (20:5), 46
Ruth, Charlton, Mass., (22:1), 51
Ruth, Auburn, Mass., (30:1), 67
Ruth, Fitzwilliam, N. H., (52:8), 102
Ruth, Southboro, Mass., (55:1), 106
Ruth, Lynn, Mass., (100:3), 160
Ruth, (101:9), 160
Ruth, (123:2:2:6), 181
Ruth Ann, Charlton, Mass.,
(123:2:2:7), 181
Ruth Maria, Council Bluffs, Iowa,
(94:9:6), 150
R. M., (133:1:1), 186
Sabra O., Kittery, Me., (104:3:6:4), 164
Sallie, Ala., (129:1:1), 184
Sally, Norwalk, Conn., (14:5:7:3), 38
Sally, Medway, Mass., (48:7), 100
Sally, Chesterfield, N. H., (51:5), 102
Sally, Fitzwilliam, N. H., (52:2:2), 102
Sally, Pembroke, Mass., (72:4), 127
Sally, Ashfield, Mass., (88:1), 143

Sally, Smithfield, R. I., (112:9), 171
Sally, Gloucester, R. I., (117:4:3), 176
Sally, Mass., (135:4:3), 187
Sally (Ear. Fam.), 194
Salome, Me., (104:3:7), 164
Samantha, W. Va., (82:9), 137
Samantha, Marcellus, N. Y.,
(107:3:3), 168
Samuel, Rowley, Mass., (2), 12
Samuel, Salem, Mass., (3), 13
Samuel, Andover, Mass., (4), 14
Samuel, Andover, Mass., (5), 15
Samuel, Andover, Mass., (5:3), 18
Samuel, Andover, Mass., (7), 20, 92
Samuel, Andover, Mass., (7:2), 24
Samuel, Andover, Mass., (8:2), 24
Samuel, Salem, Mass., (8:2:1), 24
Samuel, Boston, Mass., (11:2), 29
Samuel, Boston, Mass., (13:1:2), 30
Samuel, Boston, Mass., (13:3), 31
Samuel, Smithtown, N. Y., (14:1:1), 36
Samuel, Phillipsburg, N. Y.,
(14:1:7:7), 38
Samuel, Brookhaven, N. Y., (14:2), 38
Samuel, Weston, Mass., (19:2), 42
Samuel, (19:2:2), 42
Samuel, Weston, Mass., (19:2:5:3), 43
Samuel, Oxford, Mass., (20:2:4), 46
Samuel, Athol, Mass., (47), 98
Samuel, Southboro, Mass., (47:1), 98
Samuel, Marshfield, Mass., (68:2), 124
Samuel, Norton, Mass., 125
Samuel, Duxbury, Mass., (70:4), 126
Samuel, Duxbury, Mass., (71:3), 127
Samuel, Searsmont, Me., (74), 128
Samuel, Searsmont, Me., (74:6), 129
Samuel, Dighton, Mass., 136
Samuel, Ashfield, Mass., (88), 143
Samuel, Bradford, Mass., (98:2), 157
Samuel, Bradford, Mass., (98:2:5), 157
Samuel, Norwich, Conn., (119:9), 177
Samuel, (125), 182
Samuel, Berkley, Mass., (126), 183
Samuel, Berkley, Mass., (126:1), 183
Samuel, Berkley, Mass., (126:2:5), 183
Samuel, Va., (129:2), 184
Samuel, Boston, Mass., (146), 190
Samuel (Ear. Fam.),
189, 190, 191, 192, 193, 194
Samuel W., Kittery, Me., (104:4:2), 164
Samuel W., Lynnfield, Mass.,
(124:1:3), 182
Sarah, Rowley, Mass., (2:2), 12
Sarah, Salem, Mass., (3:3), 14
Sarah, Boston, Mass., (9:4), 27
Sarah, Boston, Mass., (9:7), 27
Sarah, Boston, Mass., (11:4), 30
Sarah, Boston, Mass., (12:2), 30
Sarah, Smithtown, N. Y., (14:1:2), 36
Sarah, Phillipsburg, N. Y.,
(14:1:7:6), 38
Sarah, North Salem, N. Y., (14:5:8), 38
Sarah, Watertown, Mass., (15:1), 39
Sarah, Watertown, Mass., (15:4), 39
Sarah, Marblehead, Mass., (17:3), 40
Sarah, Amherst, Mass., (35:2), 77
Sarah, Southboro, Mass., (46:3:1), 98
Sarah, Southboro, Mass., (47:2), 99
Sarah, Medway, Mass., (49:3), 100

Thomas, Marshfield, Mass., (75), 131
Thomas, E. Bridgewater, Mass., (76), 131
Thomas, E. Bridgewater, Mass.,
(76 : 3), 132
Thomas, Natick, [? Mass.], (76 : 3 : 1), 132
Thomas, Ashfield, Mass., (80), 136
Thomas, Kittery, Me., (104 : 4), 164
Thomas, Va., (127), 183
Thomas, Va., (129), 184
Thomas, Providence, R. I., (131), 185
Thomas, Manchester, Eng., (131 : 1), 185
Thomas (Ear. Fam.), 191, 194
Thomas Davis, Cassadaga, N. Y.,
(86 : 2), 140
Thomas F., Kittery, Me., (104 : 4 : 1), 164
Thomas J., (129 : 1 : 3), 184
Thomas Walley, Boston, Mass.,
(13 : 1), 30, 204
Timothy, Bradford, Mass., (98 : 1), 157
Timothy, [? Charlestown], Mass.,
(143), 190
Timothy (Ear. Fam.), 189, 190
Turner, E. Bridgewater, Mass., (77), 132
Tyler, Shrewsbury, Mass., (56 : 2 : 7), 108
Tyler, (56 : 11), 108
Valentine, Foster, R. I., (110 : 6), 169
Wadsworth, (78 : 2 : 4), 133
Wadsworth, E. Bridgewater, Mass.,
(78 : 5), 133
Walstein, Me., (93 : 7 : 1), 149
Walter, West Thompson, Conn.,
(36 : 7 : 2), 78
Walter, Damariscotta, Me., (99), 159
Walter, Lynn, Mass., (100), 159
Walter, Lynn, Mass., (100 : 1), 160
Walter, Mass., (102), 160
Walter, (102 : 4 : 5), 161
Walter, (102 : 7), 161
Walter Brigham, Boston, Mass.,
(23 : 1 : 3), 54
Walter E. H., Holliston, Mass.,
(102 : 4 : 9 : 1 : 1), 161
Walter Hall. Barnston, Canada, 197
Walter Irving, Chicago, Ill.,
(64a : 1 : 3), 114
Walter Lyon, Providence, R. I.,
(65 : 4 : 1 : 5), 116
Walter Mason, Salem, Mass.,
(18 : 1 : 8), 42
Walter Polk, New York, N. Y., (67), 116
Warren, Ill., (74 : 5), 129
Wendell, Boston, Mass., (13 : 8), 32, 204
Wendell, Mass., (135 : 5 : 4), 187
Wilber, Portland, Or., (36 : 4 : 6), 78
Wilber Henry, Fitzwilliam, N. H.,
(53 : 10 : 3), 105
Willard, Boston, Mass.,
(76 : 4 : 1), 132, 204
Willard Jerome, Providence, R. I.,
(65 : 4 : 1), 116
Willard Peele, Salem, Mass.,
(18 : 1 : 2), 41
Willard Quincy, 204
William, Boston, Mass., (9), 26
William, Boston, Mass., (10), 27
William, Boston, Mass., (10 : 3 : 5), 28
William, Boston, Mass., (10 : 5 : 1), 28
William, Boston, Mass., (10 : 7), 29
William, Boston, Mass., (12), 30

18

William, Phillipsburg, N. Y.,
(14 : 1 : 7 : 5), 38
William, Smithtown, N. Y., (14 : 5), 38
William, Brookhaven, N. Y.,
(14 : 5 : 2), 38
William, (14 : 5 : 2 : 1), 38
William, Fredericksburg, Va., (17 : 6), 41
William, Big Spring, Wis., (27 : 3 : 1), 62
William, Boston, Mass., (52 : 2 : 1), 102
William, Easton, Mass., 125
William, Mass., 125
William, S. Adams, Mass., (89 : 5), 144
William, (104 : 3 : 3), 164
William, Kittery, Me., (104 : 6), 165
William, R. I., (113 : 4), 172
William, Dublin, N. H., (115 : 4 : 6), 173
William, (119 : 1), 177
William, (121 : 9), 180
William, Charlton, Mass., (123 : 2 : 2), 181
William, Candia, N. H., (124), 182
William, Brooklyn, N. Y., (130 : 7), 184
William, Boston, Mass., (134), 186
William, Boston, Mass., (134 : 1 : 3), 187
William, Lynn, Mass., (134 : 2), 187
William, Boston, Mass., (159), 193
William, Boston, Mass., (160), 194
William (Ear. Fam.), 194
William, 204
William, 205
William Abbott, Chicago, Ill.,
(29 : 3 : 3), 67
William Butterworth, Chicago, Ill.,
(29 : 3), 66
William Brown, 205
William C., Dedham, Mass.,
(130 : 7 : 1), 184
William Eaton, San Francisco, Cal.,
(123 : 2 : 2 : 4), 181
William Edwards, 205
William Ellery, (120 : 4), 179
William Harry, (38 : 3 : 1), 81
William H., Lanesboro, Mass.,
(89 : 1 : 1), 144
William H., New York, N. Y.,
(131 : 2), 185
William H. H., Wilbraham, Mass.,
(107 : 3 : 1 : 1), 167
William Irving, Chicago, Ill.,
(64a : 1), 113
William J., Jewett City, Conn.,
(119 : 10 : 5), 177
William Magruder, 204
William Mason, Reading, Mass.,
(124 : 1 : 2), 182
William Nelson, Albany, Or., (64a), 113
William O., Taunton, Mass.,
(126 : 2 : 3 : 3), 183
William Perry, Lake Mills, Wis.,
(28 : 8), 65
William P., Springfield, Mass.,
(33 : 4), 74
William R., Speonk, N. Y., 38
William R., 205
William Robert, Providence, R. I.,
(65 : 4 : 1 : 6), 116
William Stanwood, Reading, Mass.,
(124 : 1 : 2 : 5), 182
William Wilson, Boston, Mass.,
(10 : 1), 27

INDEX II.

19

John,	94	Rockwood,		Rose (m.),	73
Samuel,	95	Brainard (m.),	101	Sylvester,	149
Reade,		David,	101	—— (m.),	194
—— (m.),	161	Frank,	101	Scully,	
Reed,		Henry,	101	Elizabeth (m.),	75
Amelia (m.),	70	Josiah,	101	Seabury,	
Jared (m.),	133	Sabra,	101	Priscilla (m.),	125
Rebecca A.,	106	Waldo,	101	Seaver,	
Thomas,	94	Wallace,	101	Maria (m.),	73
Rees,		Roe,		Seaward,	
Sylvanus (m.),	186	David (m.),	202	Hannah (m.),	164
Reniff,		Rogers,		Sedgwick,	
Duverna Doloris (m.),		Betsey A. (m.),	38	John A. (m.),	114
	142	Ezekiel,	12	Seeber,	
Renne,		Jerusha (m.),	38	Claude Valentine,	65
J. H. (m.),	65	Roods,		Daniel A. (m.),	65
Reynolds,		Martha (m.),	108	Frank A.,	65
Adeline Ellen,	31	Rowe,		Fred. Austin,	65
Adeline Margaret,	31	—— (m.),	194	George Phillips,	65
Anne Foster,	31	Ruddock,		Mary Phillips,	65
Augusta Theresa,	31	Alvin (m.),	137	Robert Thomas,	65
Benjamin,	31	Rude,		Sarah Byrne,	65
Edward (m.),	31	Elizabeth (m.),	138	Sexton,	
John,	31	Fanny (m.),	137	Robert,	12
John Phillips,	31	Rundlet,		Rose,	12
Margaret Elizabeth,	31	Charles (m.),	200	Shaffer,	
Miriam Phillips,	31	Russell,		Jacob (m.),	175
Rice,		Abner (m.),	125	Sharp,	
Arthur William,	60	Arthur,	62	Sallie (m.),	142
Edwin Addison,	60	Edward (m.),	15	Sharpe,	
Ella Antoinette,	60	—— (m.),	62	Kasiah (m.),	46
Louis Phillips,	60	Sage,		Shattuck,	
Mary A.,	60	Dorothy (m.),	72	Chloe (m.),	174
Sarah (m.),	201	Oliver,	72	Samuel A. (m.),	105
William H. (m.),	60	Salisbury,		Shaw,	
Rich,		Edward Elbridge (m.),	28	Elias (m.),	148
Elizabeth (m.),	47	Mary (m.),	28	Elijah (m.),	138
Richards,		Rebecca (m.),	28	Elizabeth (m.),	201
Maria (m.),	177	Samuel,	28	Frederic E.,	148
Richardson,		Theophilus (m.),	177	John P.,	148
Adeline,	58	Salter,		Margaret,	148
Alpheus,	57	Hannah (m.),	191	Octavia J. P.,	148
Edward (m.),	57	Saltonstall,		Samuel (m.),	27
Edward Phillips,	58	Richard,	10	Shedd,	
Ellen Jones,	58	Sampson,		Robert G. (m.),	139
Hannah (m.),	100	Eunice.	93	Sheldon,	
Harriet,	58	E. C.,	31	George F. (m.),	170
Sidney Edwards,	57	Robert (m.),	127	Mary (m.),	76
Sidney Ernest,	58	Sanborn,		Warren J. (m.),	105
Rickard,		Rebecca (m.),	145	Shepard,	
Rebecca (m.),	177	Sanford,		Ira (m.),	107
Rider,		Bridget (m.),	194	Sherman,	
Abigail (m.),	202	Sargent,		David (m.),	43
Risley,		Eveline (m.),	68	Edwin F. (m.),	145
Sarah (m.),	171	Richard,	11	John,	131
Roberts,		Sawyer,		Mary (m.),	124, 125
Climena (m.),	77	Elizabeth,	139	Sarah Ann (m.),	170
Samuel (m.),	174	Sayer,		Seeley (m.),	180
Robinson,		Emma (m.),	114	William T., Gen.,	154
Charles H. (m.),	73	Scofield,		Shurtleff,	
Elescom,	139	Katie (m.),	75	William,	124
Elizabeth Pidge (m.),	92	Scott,		Sibley,	
Joel,	80	Benjamin (m.),	149	Jonathan (m.),	47
John (m.),	139	Benjamin, jr.,	149	John,	94
John,	202	Benjamin Sylvester,	149	Mary Charlotte (m.),	94
Lewis Taylor,	73	Lida A. (m.),	60	Solomon,	94
Mary A. (m.),	80	Lucretia (m.),	109	Stephen,	94
Nancy,	81	Lucy Eva,	149	Timothy,	94
William Shaw,	93	Rebecca (m.),	68	Sillsbee,	

www.ingramcontent.com/pod-product-compliance
Lightning Source LLC
Chambersburg PA
CBHW070807270326
41927CB00010B/2338